A CHRONICLE OF SMALL BEER:
THE MEMOIRS OF NAN GREEN

NAN GREEN

A CHRONICLE OF SMALL BEER:
THE MEMOIRS OF NAN GREEN
NAN GREEN

Edited by R.J. Ellis with an Introduction by Martin Green

TRENT EDITIONS

Published by Trent Editions 2004

Trent Editions
Department of English and Media Studies
The Nottingham Trent University
Clifton Lane.
Nottingham NG11 8NS

Printed in Great Britain by Goaters Limited, Nottingham

ISBN 1 84233 105 1

Contents

Introduction

It is not how a man dies that matters,' said Dr Johnson, 'But how he lives'. These memoirs of my mother, Nan Green, will tell you how one woman lived through the first seven decades of the twentieth century. Two qualifications are required for making the memoirs of anyone of interest to the general public at large: that the subject had an interesting life, and that he or she could write an account of it in a memorable way. I think that my mother fulfilled both these qualifications. Her memoirs are unfinished, but since a memoir is not a work of fiction nor a work of art, except in the hands of an artist, it cannot be rounded off in the sort of satisfactory manner that a novel can, with all the ends neatly tied up, leaving a sense of wholeness, of completeness. Not many lives are like that, save in very rare cases, cases where someone finishes his life's work, writes his will and dies. Shakespeare may be such an example. But Shakespeare was a genius whose life became his work, and there was no point in him hanging around after he'd finished writing *The Tempest* and said farewell.

My mother wrote these memoirs at my request, in the last two years of her life, mostly when she was on holiday staying with my sister on the Island of Mauritius. By the time I came to read them, and was raising various queries which I thought needed further explanation, she fell ill – or rather she gave up the idea of wanting to go on living further. She died in her eightieth year, in 1984. It was because there is a kind of dying fall at the end of the memoir, that I have felt it necessary to write this introduction.

The story of my mother's life is told as frankly and honestly as I think it is possible to have done in the following pages. To encapsulate briefly, she was born just after the turn of the century, in 1904, in Beeston, Nottingham, the third of five surviving children (one was 'snatched up to heaven' at about eighteen months). The family was fairly prosperous until the First World War, when the father's business and his health both collapsed at the same time, and the family moved to Birmingham. The mother never recovered from the effects of giving birth to the last child, became mentally disturbed and died in hospital. The father married again, his deceased wife's sister's daughter, who earned the undying enmity of her eldest step-daughter.

My mother's education was curtailed, as the family's now straitened circumstances meant she had to go out and earn her living and contribute to the household. She rebelled against the genteel, lower middle-class conformism of her parents, having lost her faith in God, in the same manner as Huckleberry Finn, when God failed to answer her prayers to alleviate the miseries of her younger sister, who suffered from asthma. Her interests led her to join the rambling association, then in the forefront of the socialist movement, where she met, fell in love with, and shortly afterwards married my father, George. He was a musician, a cellist from a musical family in Stockport. Times were hard for musicians, as for everyone else in the early 1930's; the Talkies had just come in, which meant that an itinerant musician without a job in an orchestra could no longer pick up work in cinemas, playing the Overture to 'William Tell' while cowboys chased each other round the ragged rocks. Shortly after they married, and after the arrival of my elder sister and myself, my mother and father moved to London, where he obtained a job playing in the orchestra at Lyon's Corner House in Coventry Street. They had both joined the Communist Party by this time, determined to try and do something about the inequalities of the world as they saw them, and it was at this time that the Spanish Civil War broke out. My father, with my mother's agreement, decided to go to Spain, to try and stem the rising tide of fascism in Europe. My mother joined him in Spain at the suggestion of Wogan Philipps, later Lord Milford and then married to Rosamund Lehmann, the man who had accompanied my father out to Spain, like him driving an ambulance for Spanish Medical Aid, before returning, wounded. The Republican hospitals were desperately short of administrative medical staff, and he persuaded my mother to follow my father. This was made possible by Wogan Philipp's generosity in paying for a boarding school (A.S. Neill's Summerhill) for myself and my sister Frances and by the devotion of our paternal grandfather. By the summer of 1938 my father was with the British Battalion of the International Brigade, counter-attacking the fascists and crossing the Ebro at Gandesa, near where my mother was working in a field hospital. It was agreed that the International Brigades, in common with all other foreign troops on both sides, be pulled out at the end of September (an agreement honoured by the Republic, but dishonoured by Franco, whose German and Italian supporters remained). My mother returned to London, but George was missing, and it was only months later that confirmation of his death came through. He had died the very day the British Battalion was pulled out, of wounds received on the last day of action, 23 September 1938.

My mother at once threw herself into the cause of Republican Spain, travelling to Mexico with a boatload of Spanish refugee children, then returning to England via a Greyhound coach across America to New York, where she embarked on the *Normandie*.

It was not long after her return that the war against Hitler broke out. For a while she became Invasion Defence Officer at Poplar Town Hall. Myself and my sister were evacuated along with the rest of Summerhill School to Llan Ffestiniog in North Wales, but my mother soldiered through the London Blitz, being bombed out twice. Later in the war, thinking that the children needed a father, she married again, to a fellow Communist who lived in the same house in Clapham, along with a group of Spanish refugees.

After the war ended, whilst keeping the interests of Republican Spain at heart (on a number of occasions visiting the country under her new name to give aid to striking Asturian miners, or to witness prison conditions for political prisoners), she threw herself into the peace movement, traduced by the Western press but of genuine concern to many others. In 1950 she organised the Second World Peace Conference at Sheffield. She greeted Pablo Picasso on his arrival (his motif of peace-doves were to become an icon of the peace movement). Picasso complimented her on her Spanish and embraced her on learning how she had acquired it. The Labour Government of Clement Attlee fell for the anti-peace propaganda and declared Picasso a persona non grata, along with a number of other distinguished foreign delegates, so the Conference was hastily uprooted and transferred to the more welcoming climate of Warsaw. She also went to the next peace conference, in Peking, where she worked as a Spanish-English translator, the Chinese being short on Spanish speakers. When she was invited to stay on, to work for the Foreign Languages Publishing house in Peking, she accepted, and her second husband agreed to join her out there, with the promise of some worthwhile work. She spent the next seven or eight years working in Peking, from shortly after Mao Tse-tung had come to power, until just before the 'Cultural Revolution', and in that time she made various visits to the remote regions, one with Rewi Alley, the legendary New Zealand sinologist. She also visited South Africa, via Mauritius, during the Mandela treason trials, much to the chagrin of the Government, who discovered after she left that there had been a dangerous Communist in their midst.

On her return to England in the late 1950's, she separated from her husband and took a job with the Communist Party publishers, Lawrence & Wishart. She also became the Secretary of the International Brigade Association, a post she held until she died.

Her last political energies went into organising and building up a living museum and archive of the British Battalion of the International Brigade, now lodged in the Marx Memorial Library at Clerkenwell Green.

Her faith in Communism, as a way towards a better and more equitable world, survived with her until the day she died, though she had to undergo the mental agonies of conscience over the exposure of Stalin's worst crimes, as well as the split between Russia and China, and she swallowed the line about 'historical necessity'. Though at the time of the Russian invasion of Czechoslovakia, she told the Secretary of the British Communist Party that she would tear up her party card unless the Party came out and condemned the invasion, it retained her membership. The last years of her life were devoted principally to her grandchildren by her daughter, Frances. Frances had married a Mauritian and his work as a silvi-culturalist led him to work for the World Health Organisation and then the World Bank. This meant that the family were never rooted in one place, so it was deemed best that the children receive their secondary education in England, supervised by their grandmother.

Her life was, as it were, willy-nilly caught up in the central issue that has dominated all our lives since the Russian Revolution. Claud Cockburn, another who was similarly caught up, encapsulated his involvement thus:

'People have asked me repeatedly – and the questions are natural in a period when the fact of Communism and everyone's relation to it are the central features of the world's political, social and intellectual life – how precisely I came to move into the Communist Party and how precisely I came out of it. Numbers of reviewers dealing with the first volume of this autobiography mildly complained that it did not answer the first part of the question. That surprised me, because I had supposed that the whole book, all the way from the nursery to the Spanish war, was, in fact, an answer'.

What my mother does not reveal about herself in these memoirs, is her warmth as a human being, one whose friendships were deep and much valued. This was in contrast to the persona she adopted for her political activities. Along with a lot of other Communists (Willie Gallagher began life on a temperance platform), the puritan ethic was deeply embedded in her. She was a highly moral person, her inherited faith in God transforming itself into a conviction about the possibility of mankind improving its lot by its own efforts: not so much a belief that heaven on earth was possible, but one that posited a belief there was no point in waiting for it to arrive unaided. In some ways her faith could be compared to that of an ordinary Catholic at the time of Torquemada, insofar as Communists today look back on the evils of Stalin with a repugnance equivalent to that brought by Catholics looking back on the Inquisition. That this faith sustained her until the end is something that I admired about my mother, though I myself shared the dilemma described by Jean Paul Sartre: 'If the Communists are right, I am the loneliest madman alive. If they are wrong, there is no hope for the world'. She did conscientiously wrestle with her belief, though she was totally bemused at the end of her days by the labyrinthine convolutions of the British Communist Party and the splits in it, which would mystify a nuclear physicist. It must have been astounding to her, not to say a source of despair (though she never did despair), that the leader of the Spanish Communist Party after the death of Franco, Santiago Carrillo, whose work she translated into English, came at the end of the day to represent no more than a handful of the Spanish electorate.

In her last years she was beyond that struggle and took heart mostly from her many grandchildren and the few friends who had endured, as she had, the buffetings of political change in the world following the end of the war against Hitler.

There has been very little reasoned debate in this country about the enduring influence of Communism, short-circuited as it has been by the adulation of such writers as Arthur Koestler, the hijacking of George Orwell (for example, *Animal Farm* and *1984*) and the burning insincerity of R.H. Crossman in his 'Introduction' to *The God That Failed*. Taking a look at some of the contributors to that last book again reveals in some the same deep faith that sustained my mother. Here is Ignazio Silon: 'My faith in socialism, to which I think I can say my entire life bears testimony, has remained more alive than ever in me'. The trick of discrediting whatever possible good might be achieved by the aims of most honest communists, meant that it was necessary to make the expressions 'Marxism', 'Communism' and 'Stalinism' interchangeable, and R.H. Crossman's triumph was to make this acceptable.

On a personal note, my mother was someone to whom I became closer as she grew older. The normal relationship a child has with its mother was broken, if you like, when she went to Spain and I went to boarding school at the age of five. When she returned to England, there was no home and no father. She had a series of shared, makeshift flats, up to the outbreak of the war against Hitler, and one that she acquired in the City, in Mitre Court, was bombed and totally destroyed when she had luckily decided to spend the night with friends she had been visiting earlier in the evening, after the siren had sounded. After leaving school, I had a couple of years in the flat she shared with my step-father (we didn't get on), and then I went out into the world to do my national service. In the course of this, she went off to work in China. So it was only in later life that I got to know her properly. She loved music, the arts, Shakespeare and *reading*. I could never understand her penchant for detective fiction, as it didn't seem right for a dedicated Marxist, but it remained with her till the end, like her faith.

The England that she returned to in the 1960s was a fairly bleak one for her socially, though I think her hankering for her native country had surmounted any blandishments her Chinese employers could offer. She had separated from my step-father, who had remained in China; half the circle of her friends who had been in the Party with her had left it as a consequence of the Russian invasion of Hungary. It was really only the cause that kept her going, and the work itself, and work to her was life itself. Translating the speeches of Fidel Castro (a lucrative business, since he was given to marathon speeches in those early days), working at her publishing office, looking after the affairs of the International Brigade Association, and finally building up the Brigade archive in Marx House.

She left the ceremony of her funeral in the hands of her comrades in the British Battalion, their banner draped over her coffin. In 1986 I took her ashes out to Spain, to scatter them on the soil which had been enriched by my father's body.

'You are history, you are legend; you will return,' said La Pasionaria when she addressed the departing International Brigades at the farewell parade in Barcelona in 1938.

A prophecy my mother fulfilled entirely.

Martin Green, March 1987

A Note on the Text

Nan Green's memoirs have not been previously published. This edition has been prepared from the typescript she herself prepared, with her holograph alterations inserted in the text and margin. An experienced touch typist and editor, Nan Green prepared a very clean typescript, but some silent emendations of spelling and grammar have needed to be made (to avoid the insertion of too many footnotes noting very minor adjustments). I have endeavoured always to edit with a light touch, however. On a very few occasions, relatively substantial sentence re-arrangements have been necessary. Where these occur, the changes are recorded in the footnotes.

Nan Green did not subdivide her memoirs in any way (there are no chapter divides at all) until very late on in her memoirs. To ease the reading process. some subsections have been inserted. These are numbered (and where no numbering appears, Nan Green herself inserted the subsection).

R.J. Ellis, January 2003

A CHRONICLE OF SMALL BEER:
THE MEMOIRS OF NAN GREEN

I

'Begin at the beginning', said the King of Hearts to Alice.[1] But what is the beginning? This is to be my Memoirs, not my autobiography, so it ought perhaps to begin with my first recollections, which are of a push-chair upholstered in pale bluey-green 'cut' velvet (moquette?) with wings, like an armchair, against which I could rub my cheek; and of going out for a walk with my very old grandfather, holding his hand and pushing my dolly-pram, and getting dog-dirt on my shoe and calling his attention to it (he took no notice and dragged me on to my immense and unforgotten disgust). I was probably between three and four years old. Or we could go back to the twinkle in my father's eye – though I don't suppose he twinkled much by that time as he already had three children and was anxiously 'moving up in the world'. I was told I was born in a great hurry. The delivery room had been made ready; the nurse (Nurse Marshall as I afterwards knew her) was in the house. But I wasn't expected that night and my mother, finding herself in labour, slipped out of bed to cross two landings with stairs between them, and I popped out before she got to the other bedroom. I never have had a great deal of patience, and have always been a very quick mover ('like quicksilver' said Mem) until age and arthritis slowed me down.

There used to be a huge Family Album, bound in squashy green leather, gold-tooled, with pages of board, gilt-edged, each with a sort of window in it into which photographs could be slipped. It was full of portraits of grandparents, aunts, uncles and cousins, but nearly all of them Kemps, not Farrows. Farrow was my father's name. He was the eldest of seven children. My mother was a Kemp, and the youngest of seven. Consequently our Kemp uncles and aunts were much older than our Farrow ones. Grandfather Kemp was, like the rest of his family, a very Worthy person. He had been, or so I was told, a bootboy in a wealthy family in Suffolk, and had shown such promise that his employer had given him some education (this would be around the 1820s), and he eventually became a policeman, rising in the course of time to Chief Warder in Wandsworth Prison and eventually Governor of H.M. Prison in Devizes, Wiltshire. His seven children were Emily, who died young of TB, Nancy after whom I was named, Charles, Richard, Alice and George, and then my mother, Maria, always known as Polly. Charles became a sea-captain, Richard and George joined the police (all of them, like their father, had the huge frames required by the Police in those days). Uncle Richard, like grandfather, became a prison Governor (at Filton, Bristol) and George was kicked to death while arresting a supposed criminal. Grandmother died young. Emily was already dying of TB. Aunt Nancy became the 'little mother' of the family at such an age that she never got around to learning to read and write more than very scrappily, though she had an excellent brain and played an extremely good game of Bridge.

Poll (my mother) at the age of sixteen, was 'bound apprentice' to the millinery department in Arding & Hobbs, at Clapham Junction.[2] This was while Grandfather was Chief Warder at Wandsworth. And 'bound' is not too sharp a word for it. She and her fellow-female apprentices were locked in their dormitories at night while the males were locked in theirs. She could go home for a weekend once a month. When the family moved to Devizes, she pined, and was eventually 'bought out' and lived at Devizes. She and Aunt Nancy used now and then to sneak out of Devizes on the Black Maria, descending a little bit short of Salisbury and going there on foot for a bit of shop-gazing or other entertainment, to await the return journey a little bit outside again. Aunt Nancy once told me that she, making the same trip alone, had returned with the Black Maria containing four prisoners, one of whom had gone maniacal on the journey. The warders in charge of the van had decided to take the maniac back first and had decanted the other three by the roadside, leaving Aunt Nancy, armed with a rifle, to guard them. This time her truancy had of necessity to reach the ears of Grandfather, with fell consequences.

It was at Devizes that Mother met Father.

Uncle Dick (Richard) being in some sort of training at Nottingham, had met and made friends with my father, and invited him to Devizes for a holiday, where he became enamoured of Polly.

I wonder how the Worthy Kemps regarded my father, who came of a totally different and much less Reputable family. Grandfather Farrow (whom I never knew, nor Grandmother Farrow either) was a maker of guitars and somewhat mixed up with the theatrical profession in Victorian London, when it was not particularly Respectable. I believe he drank (from hints dropped by Father who was a very temperate drinker indeed). He had seven children too: Edward (my father), Reginald, Julian, Edith, Florence, Herbert and a mentally retarded last one called Maggie. Edward, of whom I shall have more to say, became the Industrious Apprentice. They were all extremely musical. Reginald eventually taught music at a college in Hull. Julian got a lifetime job with a sewing machine company but sang at smoking Concerts and other entertainments, in a manly baritone. Edith was a professional singer, soprano. Florence married Uncle Fred – I shall have something to tell of her later. Herbert was our favourite uncle. He can't have been more than just out of his teens when we were little and was that delightful thing, a Funny Uncle, who used to entertain us with stories, poems, music-hall songs, doggerel verse, riddles and jokes, always making us laugh. Maggie, the retarded one, died young. I saw her once, I think. She had an old, wizened face but was dressed like a young girl. I recall the mere flicker of a sensation of strangeness and repulsion.

They all sang. Whenever they came to our house, there was singing. The uncles, even if one were humming a tune, would immediately and companionably join in with what Jane Austen called 'a slight but correct second'.[3] There were whole evenings while Aunt Edith would warble to the piano (her rendering of 'She is Far From the Band' used to fill me, listening in bed upstairs, with unbearable misery, so strong that I used to rush downstairs and beg her to stop). They sang glees, duets, and choruses according to the number of voices present. Herbert (Uncle Bert) taught us innumerable Victorian and Edwardian music-hall songs, many of which I can still remember. Such as:

Go, go, go for a ride in the car, car, car
For you know how cosy the tops of the tramcars are
The seats are so cosy, there's not much to pay
You sit close together and spoon all the way
There's many a Miss has been Mrs some day
Through riding on top of the car.

or,

My girl's promised to marry me when I've a hundred pounds
A hundred golden pounds, to buy a nice little house and grounds
And it won't be long before I call her mine
'Cos I've got a pound in the bank so I only want ninety nine.[4]

So there you have the mixture: the solid, worthy, respectable and rather humourless Kemps and the 'bohemian', singing, slightly seedy but jolly Farrows.

I incline to the Farrow side, both in temperament and sentiments.

By the time I was born, my father was, as I have said, anxiously going up in the world. Originally apprenticed to the lace trade in Nottingham, he had as quite a young man become a mechanic in a small bicycle workshop which eventually turned into the Raleigh Cycle Company. He was earning £3 a week when he married my mother, and this enabled them in those departed days to keep a servant from the beginning. The first of his three children were born in Nottingham: Elizabeth, Charles and Edward. He must have flourished financially because by 1903 he was able to move outside to the village of Beeston, into a house which he caused to be designed by a friend who was an architect. It was in fact two houses, semi-detached and the other was occupied by my grandfather (Kemp), his daughter (Aunt Nancy) and his granddaughter, the daughter of George (the one killed in the course of his duty as a policeman) whom he adopted, cousin Dolly. As our family grew and his shrank, Dolly suffered from epilepsy and died young and Grandfather died (aged ninety-four) when I was quite a small child. A hole was knocked in the wall that divided the two houses and we occupied some of the adjacent bedrooms. After me came Emily (my darling little sister Mem) and finally Richard, born prematurely and jaundiced, when I was seven years old – a tiny creature with squinting black eyes and a yellow skin – which did not fade for a good while. I was ashamed when strangers looked into his pram and exclaimed: 'Oh, look, a Chinese baby!'

We were proud of a bound volume of the monthly art magazine, *The Studio* to which my father subscribed, one issue of which contained a photograph of our house, mock-Tudor, entitled 'A Pair of Cottages at Beeston, Notts.'

Father cycled four miles to and from the Raleigh factory twice a day. At lunch it was my mother's habit to ask him: 'How many machines ordered today?' and I remember asking him 'How manysheens?' each lunch time, long before I knew what the words meant. He had become a chartered accountant, and was Company Secretary, and eventually General Manager. In the first years of the 20th century, Raleigh had become world famous ('the all steel bicycle') and it was seldom that the 'sheens' ordered were fewer than before. Great tension was apparent in the family once a year when he brought work home preparing the Balance Sheet. I never knew what it was, but knew that it was of immense importance. Mother, who caused the entire working of the household to circulate round my father's interest and comfort (I think she was a little afraid of him), disciplined, hushed and hustled us out of the way with special rigour when it was Balance Sheet time.

Mother, though she possessed a large and robust frame (like all the Kemps) was not strong; she may have been somewhat hypochondriac, always haunted by the fear of the TB which had killed her elder sister; these were the days, remember, when 'consumption' was an act of God for which there was little or no remedy. By the time I began to emerge from the intense subjectivity of the child (and I was slow to do so) and became conscious of her as a person rather than as a lap and a bosom she was already 'delicate' – though this was a sort of fashion among women and even young girls in those days; scarcely anyone admitted to robust health and I had more than one school friend whose mothers had taken to lying on sofas in early middle age though I never heard their reason for so doing identified ... 'Mother is delicate' was the explanation and it was thought rather a grand or at least interesting thing to be. Our mother was also fearful for us, particularly as she had lost her second child, the angelic Charles, from diphtheria when he was only four or five. She feared most to lose Edward, the next boy, whom she adored and spoiled, but even about the rest of us she was anxious. We were dosed every weekend with a loathsome medicine called Liquorice powder or another, equally loathsome, called Gregory powder – this was to 'clear our bowels' – which it did drastically every Saturday night or early Sunday morning. It is a wonder to me now that we did not all grow up heavily constipated from the absence of real exercise for our alimentary canals. I recall my father's scorn when the first of the doctors began to recommend wholemeal bread as a natural remedy for the English preoccupation with their bowels, though later he enthusiastically adopted Kruschen salts (enough to cover a sixpence every morning, taken in your first cup of tea [ugh!]). We were given iron pills, something called *Nux Vomica* (what was that for?), ipecacuanha, at the slightest sign of a cough and innumerable other medicaments, including Scott's emulsion (cod liver oil and malt) in sticky spoonfuls.

Not only were we overdosed, we were over-clothed. Vests, woollen 'combinations', known with loathing as 'combies', and consisting of a one-piece vest and knickers were covered successively with a Liberty Bodice, thick wool, taped to give strength to the figure, white cotton knickers, blue or brown woollen knickers, a flannel petticoat, a white cotton petticoat, black or brown wool stockings, hitched with tape to the bodice, a jersey and a kilt or dress were topped indoors with a white cotton pinafore and out of doors, in winter, with boots and an overcoat, scarf, gloves and hat. We had a change of clothes once a week, a 'Sunday best' outfit for church and back to the jersey and kilt on Mondays. The heavier items, such as the boys' Norfolk suits, the girls' kilts and dresses were not, as far as I know, ever washed – and there was no dry cleaning in those days. We can none of us have smelled very pleasant, but not as horribly as the children of the 'lower classes', many of whom were *sewn up in red flannel* for the winter.

Given the icy condition of the houses, one did, I suppose, have to 'wrap up well' but I am not sure if the constriction did not negate the effect of the wrappings. In one or two ways Mother deserves credit for being ahead of her time. She insisted, as long as we could afford it, on our wearing broad Daniel Neal shoes, even for dancing classes; and the Liberty Bodice was a huge improvement on the corset, into which quite little girls were often forced. Thanks to her I have never suffered from corns or bunions and still have nice straight toes and have never worn even what is now known as a 'firm control' pantie-girdle.

Despite all, or even perhaps because of it, we grew up healthy – all except Mem, who developed meningitis at the age of three and became 'the delicate one', suffering all her life from asthma, though even so she lived to the age of sixty-nine. Even Richard, the premature baby, though he remained bald until the age of four and stunted until his teens grew – or 'shot up' – into a man so tall and heavily built that like his elder brother, Edward, he was often taken for a policeman: neither of them, because of their appearance, could buy a packet of cigarettes 'after hours' at a time when it was forbidden for shopkeepers to sell them after eight o'clock in the evening.

Because this was a success story, attached, as he had the fortune to be, to a rapidly growing capitalist enterprise, my father never ceased to believe in the system, even though it went wrong for him, as I shall later relate. In my earlier childhood we were all meant to be 'rising in the world' with him and were sternly prevented from mixing with what were regarded as the lower classes. We were all sent to the one private school in the village, unbelievably snobbish in its exclusive ways. Of the forty or so pupils, none came even from a commercial background – except one, who – it was carefully explained to prospective parents – was the daughter of the village chemist but *did not live over the shop*. 'Behaving like a Board School child' was one of the worst things one could be accused of, and I was once the victim of a tremendous wigging (and, I now believe, the threat of expulsion) for having been caught in the Beeston main square, playing 'tickey' with some Board School boys round the Statue which stood there. Worse still, they were 'orphanage boys' who wore rough blue jerseys winter and summer and *no hats*. The boys of Miss Horner's (the school) wore caps winter and summer and we wore hats – 'No lady would be seen' without a hat and gloves, and dire was the punishment for failing to turn up to school without one or the other.

This upward mobility affected even our religious upbringing.

As he became more prosperous, my father became more and more High Anglican – eventually sending the two eldest of his children (Elizabeth and Edward, whom we always called Tod) to Anglo-Catholic public schools, where they developed a kind of religious snobbery and looked down on Low Church people and Protestants with immense scorn. Grandpa Kemp, next door, remained firmly Wesleyan Methodist. As a small child I often went to Chapel with Aunt Nancy and was rather less bored there than I was with Church of England services. It was noisier and less ritualised at Chapel and I remember the fiery preaching of the Minister, not for what he said but for the histrionic delivery of his sermons. The hymns were jollier too. At Church, there was the tedium of the long psalms and particularly the Litany. I grew into the habit of deliberate day-dreaming to pass the time while the Litany was being said. But I enjoyed the Benedicites – a shout of joy at the words of Neptune.[5] We began morning service at Church with the General Confession begging forgiveness for our miserable sins. 'We have erred and strayed from Thy ways like lost sheep ...' used to puzzle me, for the verb to err was not in one's everyday vocabulary and I didn't know its meaning. I puzzled it out until I came to the conclusion, which I held for a long time, that to err was to make a noise like a lost sheep – 'err-err-err'.

It was unthinkable that anyone should not be religious in those days. I never heard of or met a Freethinker in my childhood. One was either Church or Chapel and the Bible was the Word of God, every word true. There was at school one child and one child only who was not either Church nor Chapel and had to stay out of 'morning prayers' – nowadays called Assembly. He was a Roman Catholic and was a great friend of my brother Tod; neighbours once called on my mother to urge her not to encourage this friendship with a little Papist, lest Tod, I suppose, should be contaminated. To her credit my mother refused. Myself, I never at any stage 'got religion' – it was part of life and one said the prayers and went to Church (or Chapel) every Sunday without understanding. I remember asking my mother: 'Mother, I don't understand the Holy Trinity.' She replied: 'We are not meant to, my dear.' The seeds of doubt were sown. If God wanted me to believe in the Holy Trinity, I reasoned – vaguely and at long intervals – He would send me understanding of it. The idea of being a miserable sinner did not really affect me. When, in preparation for my first Communion (at the age of nine or ten), I began to go to Confession (in High Anglican style), I had to think hard to invent sins which would make the list spin out and sound holy enough. Elizabeth, who was and remained genuinely religious to the end of her days kept a list of sins which she used to consult before she went to Confession. I vividly remember an occasion when she was for some reason in charge of serving Tod and me our tea, and insisted that we say Grace. In one of the bound volumes of *Punch* which occupied our bookshelves[6] was a picture which amused us – a drunk who had been following a fire-engine of the old sort, with a fire on it and horses to draw it, which was still used in those days – collapsed in the gutter and yelling in his frustration: 'All right! You can keep your rotten old baked potatoes!' (the machine resembled those stoves from which hot potatoes were sold in the streets in cold weather). Tod started it and I followed. Each time we were told to say Grace, we put our hands together and said: 'All right! you can keep your rotten old baked potatoes'. Elizabeth was reduced to tears of anger and frustration – and I suppose the threat of hellfire for us both. We were not choked to death by our bread and jam. A further shoot in the seeds of doubt.

I am certain that my parents were good, conscientious and loving. But I can't honestly say I had a happy childhood; there was neither freedom nor freedom from care. Our friends were chosen for us: we must not play with anyone 'rough' or socially inferior. I didn't really like any of my school-mates or 'little playmates'. One in particular I hated was Patricia, a banker's daughter whose idea of fun – she was larger than I – was to drag me up and down stairs by the heels or pretend to push me out of high windows at her home. My so-called best friend was Kathy, a flaxen-haired, flaxen-eyelashed neighbour whose mother was one of the 'delicate' ones: I never saw her except when she was lying on a sofa. Perhaps for this reason Kathy was invited to accompany us on a seaside holiday and I didn't enjoy her company. She had two elder sisters, who filled her with lewd and poisonous sex-lore which she gleefully imparted to me, and which filled me with loathing, despite my utter ignorance of what it was all about. Practically the only enjoyment I had in Kathy's company was due to the presence in her house of bound volumes of the *Strand Magazine*,[7] which we devoured in silence for hours and hours, to the distress of her mother ('why don't you *entertain* your little guest?' she would complain). The Sherlock Holmes stories, much of Rider Haggard and other popular novels were serialised in these. At our home it was Arthur Mee's *Children's Encyclopaedia* – a combination of quite useful knowledge and rather nauseating religious instruction,[8] which one skipped. There were also bound volumes of *Illustrated London News*[9] and *Punch* from which I acquired a good deal of half-baked political information, particularly from the Tory cartoons of Bernard Partridge.[10] I read voraciously, being often chidden for 'spoiling my eyesight' and driven out to play (whereupon I would lock myself in the outside lavatory until discovered).

My real Best Friends in childhood were two imaginary girls called Big Bather and Little Bather, with whom I played for hours. We went to an imaginary school together, we held contests at skipping, bowling hoops and jumping from higher and higher obstacles. Mostly I won, but sometimes I magnanimously allowed one or the other to beat me.

Village life was filled with taboos and home was a place where the standards of a good child were impossible, for me at least, to attain. You must be Good, clean, tidy, devout, quiet, *incurious,* well-mannered and obedient, obedient; obedient to teachers, parents, and God. I don't blame them, but my parents truly believed that to spare the rod was to spoil the child. Physical punishment was always meted out by Father, behind the scullery door, and often the long wait 'until your father gets home' was worse than the short sharp beating on the bare bottom, though there were occasions when the beating was severe. As, for instance, what was known as my 'Georgie Brown tanning' – for having been caught riding my bicycle with a boy of that name on the main road to Nottingham, forbidden territory. Since I had not, on that occasion at least, deliberately flouted the rules but completely forgotten them in the enjoyment of the smoother surface of the main road in comparison with the rougher side roads on which I was permitted to ride, I smarted not only on my backside, but from a sense of injustice and humiliation. I recall, too, having been beaten for protesting violently that Tod was allowed to go out and play immediately after tea while I was expected to help with washing up the dishes. Seeds of feminism.

So many were the crimes, some committed deliberately and some in all innocence, for which one risked punishment, that it became part of my behaviour not to get found out. I became rather expert at deceit, though Mem, whom I often led into mischief, almost invariably got an attack of conscience and confessed. 'Mother said we weren't to do this,' she would remind me. 'I didn't hear her and you've forgotten,' I would reply. But, questioned as to why her socks were wet after paddling on the gravelly bank of the Trent (about a mile from home) she would break down, at once. She was never rebellious ... I was.

I yearned for approval, longed for a word of praise (which would send my self-conceit rocketting sky high). Conscious efforts to gain either, clumsy enough I dare say, were often met with *ridicule*, which hurt me more than beatings. I took to Walter Mittyish day-dreaming,[11] in which I did brave deeds and became a popular heroine (rescuing people from floods when the Trent overflowed its banks, for instance).

Though I feel sure they loved us, and did their best to bring us up in the paths of righteousness according to their lights, I cannot honestly say that I loved either of my parents. Neither did I love God, not even the Gentle Jesus to whom I prayed twice a day. God for me was the jealous God who visited the sins of the fathers, etc. And Father was mixed up with God the Father, a fierce old man with a beard who sat in the sky observing everything one did, and disapproving of nearly everything. I cannot describe the joy and relief with which I read, in my late teens, *The Way of All Flesh* and recognised in Theobald Pontifex and his wife the characters and principles – though far milder and less obnoxious – of my parents, which exonerated Ernest Pontifex and me too, from the guilt of not loving them.[12] I owe a great debt to Samuel Butler for enabling me to see the external forces that moved my parents to behave as they did, and thus to understand and forgive them. I do, though, find it hard to forgive the Christian Church for instilling the sense of SIN into its followers: miserable sinners, born in sin, Jesus Christ our saviour from sin (but we still went on sinning and hell-fire awaited us if we did not repent), the almighty and ever-living God who nevertheless visited the sins of the fathers on the children ... these contradictions were an insoluble puzzle. I shall here recount the event which played the greatest part in the destruction of my faith.

Mem suffered from asthma. In her childhood no remedies or alleviations had been discovered. I questioned the love of almighty God in permitting this helpless little girl to lie panting night after night, during an attack, fighting for breath. I slept with her in the same bed and agonised to hear her. What was God about, to permit it? Almighty God, I was told, permitted suffering as a trial, a test of goodness. But Mem *was* good! But if one asked, with sufficient faith, He would grant our requests. I decided to try. One night I got out of bed and went on my knees, begging and demanding of God, not to cure her – if he needed people to suffer, so be it. But at least, God, I asked, let me share it – Give her a night's rest while I had the suffering, half and half, I didn't mind sharing it. I prayed with all my might. There was no answer. My faith started to crumble, though I told no one and continued for a long time to take part in the religious life of the family. I hadn't the courage or the knowledge to challenge God openly, and furthermore the social life of the family went on centring round the Church. I was even confirmed, along with a lot of other little girls in white frocks and white veils, half hoping that the descent of the Bishop's heavy hand on my head might change my character. But nothing happened.

It later became the custom among historians to characterise the years before 1914 as 'halcyon days' but in reality they were not as halcyon as all that. Even I was aware of the rumblings of change – hearing of wicked strikers, upstart politicians (both parents being violently hostile to Lloyd George in 1911 for introducing the National Insurance Act) and those disgraces to their sex, the Suffragettes.[13] We even had one such creature in our village: a tall, rather fierce looking young woman who strode about during elections wearing a purple, green and white sash across her bosom. The first beginnings of the change that occurred in our family life preceded the declaration of war. Mother never really recovered from her last confinement, and gradually became a permanent invalid.

By this time the household had acquired another member — my mother's niece, whose history was briefly this: my mother's sister Alice had married George Rice, the owner of a livery stables in Richmond, Surrey. Alice did not live long and died shortly after the birth of a daughter, Marie. Marie had a sheltered and indulgent childhood, with her own pony, an expensive schooling and a doting father. In the course of time George Rice married the headmistress of the expensive school who turned into the Wicked Stepmother, violently jealous of Marie's affection and loving care for her own daughter, a cripple. The girl was taken from school and became a household drudge, a task she performed quite willingly because she was, and remained, what is called 'a born nurse', utterly self-sacrificing towards the sick child who adored her – to the mother's jealous rage. The death of the crippled child intensified its mother's hostility towards her stepdaughter, who at the age of sixteen ran away from home and took refuge with her godmother. She refused to return and, having no other resource, 'went into service' with a wealthy family in the Isle of Wight.

When our mother became ill, the aunts decided that Marie should enter our family as a sort of mother's help. Here she found ample material for her natural loving care – my ailing mother, the delicate Mem and the premature baby, Richard (Dicky), whose care she took over completely, to such an extent that he became almost her child and later cherished the belief that he really was her son, a belief strengthened by the fact that by some accident his birth was not registered until four or five years after it had occurred. When he told me of this we were both adults, and it caused me some hesitation before I told him that I had seen him the day after his birth, in my mother's arms in her own bed.

II

Violent change began with the declaration of war in 1914. We were on holiday at Mablethorpe on the East Coast, and I remember Father reading the news from his morning paper at the breakfast table. Battleships appeared on the horizon of what we had known as the German Ocean but thereafter called the North Sea. The holiday was curtailed and we all came back, to the beginnings of shortages, queues and the departure of young men from the families of our neighbours. I recall being sent with my brother Tod to stand in queues (not together but as if we were strangers) for a quarter of a pound of butter. Sugar, which had hitherto been given away with a pound of tea, became a precious commodity – sweets eventually disappeared from the confectioners' shops to be replaced by horrid, dry seeds called 'tiger nuts', which you chewed until a sweet taste emerged, after which you spat out the fibrous stuff. Cake became a rare luxury. There was at one stage a 'potato famine', during which we ate maize, turnips and swedes with such meat as could be bought.

Walking with Mother, pushing her wheelchair, we met a neighbour dressed from head to foot in black. Her two sons had been killed at the front, almost simultaneously. Mother uttered words of condolence. Weeping, the neighbour said: 'I have given my sons for the country.' I puzzled and puzzled. They were surely not hers to give? But I did not speak my doubts to anyone, lest I should be called 'unpatriotic', a term that for a while became the most abusive epithet to which one could be subjected. Cousin Fred (the son of Aunt Florence) lost his life aged nineteen. Most of the young men, my elder sister's contemporaries, failed to return after the war. This is probably why she did not marry until many years later. Seeds of pacifism.

Early in the war, we three younger ones were suddenly whisked away from home and sent to stay with elderly neighbours, friends of my parents. Nobody explained why, but a few days later a schoolmate took me on one side and said portentously, 'Your mother has had a stroke.' I did not know what this meant, but the fact that it was kept secret made it seem to me as if it were something shameful. We returned home, to find mother half paralysed, her face distorted and her speech slurred.

As if this were not enough, my father lost his job in 1916. He was an upright man and had refused the orders of the management to falsify the figures relevant to the payment of 'Excess Profits Tax'.[14] This sudden blow, to a man with a sick wife and five children to bring up, caused him to lose for a short time 'the balance of his mind' and he went to a mental nursing home, for what cannot have been a very long period, because by 1917 he was working in London, for the Ministry of Munitions and visiting us for occasional weekends.

Mother gradually recovered, at least partially, but her speech was slow, her mind was clouded and she was ill with anxiety. The household, now in 'reduced circumstances', was held together by Marie (by now known as Lela from the childish lips of Mem), a veritable tower of strength.

In the 1918 influenza epidemic it fell to my lot to fulfil my Walter Mittyish dreams and become a little heroine for a short time. My father was working in London. The rest of the family, along with most of the inhabitants of the village, caught the plague and each developed complications. One of the two village doctors died. The other worked heroically but could visit seldom. Mother, Nem and Lela developed pleurisy, Tod had abscesses in both ears, accompanied by agonising pain. There was no M & B, no penicillin, I don't even remember aspirin. I alone did not succumb to the germ, and had to nurse them all.[15] A kind neighbour came in each morning, lit the kitchen range for me and carried scuttles full of coal for the bedroom fires. There was no other help, except for occasional visits from the doctor who called at whatever hour he could manage. I made an ocean of barley water, changed beds, stoked fires and prepared 'invalid meals' which nobody wanted to eat.

At the height of this crisis I performed one of the bravest deeds of my fourteen years' life. In the middle of the night there was a tremendous crash downstairs, which roused most of my patients too. Ordering them sternly to stay in their beds, I took a cane and went downstairs to investigate, heart in mouth. I finally located the cause. A large iron kettle had fallen from the gas-ring in the scullery, bringing down some crockery with it ... Looking back I don't know how I managed to cope. But I learned *what you have to do, you can do.*

Despite what must have been my appalling nursing standards, they all recovered, which is remarkable. I remember taking to Lela, now able to sit up in bed, a dainty invalid tea with a boiled egg and some thin bread and butter. She sat with the tray in her lap and wept because she had neither the appetite nor the strength to eat it.

From here onwards, things seem to have darkened thick and fast. These, as I said, are memoirs, not an autobiography, or I would be compelled to do a lot of research into dates, because I am not sure of the order in which they happened. My father ceased working in the Ministry and set up a small workshop for assembling bicycles and repairing them. It failed, for the reason that raw materials in that end-of and post-war period could not be obtained. My mother had a second stroke and was sent to a nursing home, being quite helpless. My father obtained work with the BSA cycle company and we moved to Birmingham.[16] We were now in really reduced circumstances, and our first home there was above a shop in High Street, Kings Heath – what a come-down for a pupil of our exclusive private school! Soon after we got there my mother died, without my seeing her again. She cannot yet have been fifty years old. Lela, weeping when the news came, embraced us and said she would be a mother to us. I had little or no feeling of grief or bereavement: Mother had been ill and remote for so long that her loss did not affect me greatly, and as for Mem and Dicky, Lela had been their mother substitute for years.

Father had not yet got quite accustomed to his descent into the lower middle class. He sent me to another private school, a small one with quite unqualified teachers (but an ostentatious uniform) where there were just two pupils, of whom I was one, in the 6th Form and we seldom had any instruction because the few teachers were busy with the younger classes.[17] But his funds were just not sufficient to pay for the education of the younger ones. (Edward and Elizabeth were already 'out in the world', Edward as a bank clerk and Elizabeth as a teacher.) Swallowing his pride, he was forced to send Mem and Richard to a state school, where they developed in a far less snobbish atmosphere among working class kids. Both were bright. Mem won a scholarship to King Edward's Grammar School but was forced to give it up after two terms because of her health. During the year I was at the private school, I attended night classes in art – Pa having decided long before that I was 'the artistic one' – and from there I obtained a free place to the Birmingham City School of Art, having a slight facility in drawing and painting. My subject was book-illustration and I don't know how he imagined I would ever make a living at that. Be that as it may, he lost his job again and we moved to Manchester, just as I had won a further year at Art School with a bursary of £48 per annum. I was not permitted to stay in Birmingham (even though my Uncle Julian and his wife lived there and might have been persuaded to let me stay with them). I grew very bitter about this and refused to start again at night school in the new surroundings.

A lot of things happened to the family during this time, but I have selected this account because it shows how I turned eventually into the Black Sheep – different from my two elder siblings because I had not had their snobbish, High Anglican and exclusive schooling which coloured the rest of their lives, and different from the younger two who got a pretty good education in State schools and settled comfortably into middle class stability. Different also, I think, because I spent my adolescence, as it were, between mothers. The two elder siblings remembered our mother in active health and stable circumstances: my chief recollection is of an ailing, anxious near-helpless invalid who needed help in getting dressed, who was pushed around in an invalid chair and who liked to be read to (evening after evening by candlelight) from sentimental novels. The two younger ones remembered our mother hardly at all, and Lela, as I have said, became their mother-substitute, to whom all their affection was given. Me she left alone, mainly, I now suppose, from the fear of being regarded as a Wicked Stepmother such as she had experienced. I recall the enormous trepidation with which she broke the news to me of her impending marriage to Father – news which I accepted without surprise or resentment, unlike the attitude of Elizabeth and Tod. I was, I fear, far too concerned with the turmoils of adolescence to pay much attention to other people's emotional lives.

Our relationship was affectionate. I took her far too much for granted and she found me prickly and incomprehensible because I was by then striking out on my own in the bumpy process from childhood to maturity.

Dicky, who did satisfactorily at school, turned into an Industrious Apprentice like my father, got a job in an Insurance Company at the age of sixteen and *stayed with the firm for the rest of his life* until he retired at sixty-five, moving up into 'dead men's shoes' and becoming a man of property. Mem, battling against asthma in an absolutely heroic fashion, taught herself shorthand and eventually became a top stenographer whose flawless Pitman could easily be read by others and whose speed was such that she was in great demand for verbatim reports of company meetings and conferences. The brightest of us all, she was a gifted writer and could have gone far but for her health. She remained the 'daughter at home' unable to free herself from the care and affection of Lela; she had suitors and could have married; she had offers – notably of a job on the *News Chronicle*,[18] and could, I believe, have become a good journalist; but she lacked the courage to face an attack of asthma without the constant, devoted, intensely comforting care of Lela.

In between these two pairs of siblings, I spent my adolescent years in a period of family and social upheaval. Already a rebel, though not a very open one, I shut myself up inside my own head and took clerical jobs (my only qualification being good handwriting and an ability to concentrate) in place after place as my father moved about looking for employment. I made few friends and was regarded by my workmates as 'stuck-up'. Reading was almost my only joy; I haunted public libraries devouring such writers as H.G. Wells, T.E. Lawrence, Bernard Shaw, and the Fraser of *The Golden Bough* (all disapproved of by my father) and happening more by chance than choice on such enlighteners as Thomas Paine and Samuel Butler, who strengthened my unbelief and whose books I concealed from my father because they would have been anathema to him. I read a lot of rubbish too and haunted the periodic visits of Carl Ross, the British National Opera and Gilbert and Sullivan.[19]

When I was seventeen, father married again – Lela of course. She was already his humble slave as my mother had been; she loved his children and she loved him, and made him a perfect wife, caring for him with absolute devotion. As he grew older and his jobs became less and less important (and remunerating) she stepped in and started to let lodgings to boost the family fortunes, so that he should live as comfortably as he had done before. I approved of his re-marriage from the start, but Elizabeth, who had worshipped our mother fanatically and whose High Anglican precepts were against re-marriage, particularly with a deceased wife's sister's daughter who figured in the Prayer Book as someone a man 'may not marry', opposed it, even to consulting uncles and priests to try and prevent it. Lela never forgave her, though they became outwardly reconciled.

I may as well mention here that Lela nursed my father with enormous love and attention through his last illness many years later, but when he died Elizabeth, taking advantage of Lela's prostration, arranged for Father's burial in Nottingham alongside the body of my mother. I was away at the time and did not arrive until the day before the funeral, when I found Lela numb with grief and humbly outraged at this high-handedness. I offered to create a fuss and reorganise his funeral and burial, but she refused, fearing scandal. She would have loved to have his grave nearby, where she could go and lay flowers now and then, but the family home was then in Birmingham. She did not go to his burial.

Since Elizabeth no longer lived at home but was on her way to becoming a Headmistress, her disapproval was no longer felt in the family, which began to be more stable. I think, in dudgeon, she did not come near us for a long while. I now had a job (still clerical) in a big wholesale drapery warehouse in Manchester and here began to make friends, though still regarded by some workmates as stuck-up. Marie Brown, a senior in the office where I worked, befriended me. She was an enthusiast for the recently invented pursuit of Rambling (later to become Hiking and finally hitch-hiking, a form we would never have tolerated since we scorned to accept a lift anywhere). You got up early on Sunday mornings and donned your rucksack and boots and thick socks (later, to my father's immense dismay and disapproval, *shorts*) and took a train to some place on the outskirts which led to the Peak District; after walking for the whole day you took a train back to the city and Monday morning. It was pure joy. I started to live for Sundays and to neglect church altogether, defying parental horror and dismay with total callousness. Sometimes we were just two of us; besides teaching me map-reading, Marie, who was an ardent Irish patriot, told me about the troubles of Ireland and contributed to my political education.[20] Sometimes we joined groups – jolly groups of open-air worshippers who loved testing their strength against natural obstacles such as bog, mist, rocks and high hills, rolling home in the evening by 'ramblers' trains', almost drunk with fresh air and singing noisily with pure joie de vivre. Sometimes we got back in time to attend the Sunday Night Concerts of the Hallé Orchestra in the Free Trade Hall.[21] Bliss re-doubled.

I was consciously happy. Happy to possess a good pair of legs, a good pair of lungs to keep up with the fastest walkers, a good pair of eyes to revel in the ever-changing beauty of moors and mountains, a decent enough voice and a musical ear to join in all the songs; what must have been almost perfect health and the means of exercising and enjoying it. All that and music too.

Marie and I took a holiday with a rambling association (youth hostelling came later) at Eskdale in the Lake District. Long glorious days striding over the fells and up Scafell and other mountains, strung out behind a 'leader' who knew the ropes, and me always in the first five or ten; sandwich lunches and huge hearty meals in the evenings followed by do-it-yourself entertainment, dancing, amateur acting and sing-songs. We didn't sing pop music but formed little groups to do bits from oratorios (I remember taking part in a trio for women's voices singing 'Lift Thine Eyes unto the Mountains' from Mendelssohn's *Elijah*)[22] and some people brought their cellos, flutes and fiddles with them and performed solos. To be young really was Very Heaven then.

Alas, we moved back to Birmingham, in pursuit of my father's livelihood. I joined a local Rambling Club but it wasn't the same; a sort of Fabian earnestness prevailed – be-spectacled schoolmasters, elderly aficionados with long walking sticks, hearty schoolmistresses, studious clerks (I remember one whose delight was to be appointed leader of the next week's walk, who used to spread out the 6-inch to a mile map on his bedroom floor the night before and lead the whole walk from memory – down to the last stile, pond, footpath or bend – without once referring to the map).

It was in Birmingham that I turned decisively towards Socialism. I worked in a large Insurance office, and in the year when women obtained the vote at 21 (instead of 30 as previously)[23] was in charge of a desk where nine other young women worked out figures for workmen's compensation. The office manager sent for me. 'Miss Farrow,' he said portentously, 'most of the girls on your desk are twenty-one and will be voting for the first time. Now, I don't want to influence anyone – far from it – but I think you ought to realise that Labour Party policy is to nationalise insurance, and if you voted Labour you would be voting yourselves out of a job. *I don't wish to influence you in any way*, but if you could pass this on to the others it would be a very good thing ...'

That very lunch-time, taking one of my co-workers with me, I set out for the Labour party headquarters and put the case before an official. His answer: yes, of course we plan to nationalise insurance, but don't you see we shall need plenty of people to administer it ... You clerks, who do the main work, will be needed more than ever, while we shan't need those 'inspectors' who spend their lives at golf clubs, football clubs and hotel bars fraternising with possible customers to get them to change to your company. This rang a bell. I was friendly with a recently appointed 'inspector', who told me that, when asked, on application for the job, about his sporting proclivities, had replied that he played cricket in the summer and Rugby in the winter and considered he had got it on the basis of these.

We went back and reported this to our colleagues. I like to think that most of them voted Labour. I did. I began to call myself a Fabian and to read Fabian pamphlets,[24] which made sense. I didn't, however, join any party, but muttered about starting a trade union. This must have reached the ears of the management, for a meeting was held at which we were invited to vote for or against it. A very eloquent speech was made by a young woman who 'just happened' to be a niece of the boss, and the vote went in favour of the status quo. Trade unions were not for the likes of us; maybe they were needed by the cloth-capped working class but we were too respectable and too well-off to need one. I am almost certainly making myself too important, but immediately after this I was 'promoted' – to work in a separate room on statistics with a charming and lovable old Irishman. I could no longer exert influence on my colleagues, but his influence on me was tremendous and that of his fiery, rebellious little wife to whom he introduced me, even more so.

I had continued to correspond with Marie, and the next winter she invited me to come for a weekend that had been arranged by a group of the friends we had made. It was midwinter and there was snow on the hills. Lela protested. I had no boots. I couldn't go without boots. But I *must* go. Unwillingly I accepted her conditional offer to buy me a pair of felt *gaiters*, in which I would rather have been seen dead by my north-country friends. I set off wearing them, but stuffed them in my rucksack as soon as I was out of sight.

There was a group of about fifteen or twenty at the farmhouse where we were to spend Saturday night. Marie was there of course, and a man who was wooing her – a lowering, intense young man who now reminds me (though I didn't know it at the time) of Dickens' Bradley Headstone,[25] uncouth and passionate. (She didn't marry him but returned, not unwillingly, to the man to whom she was engaged, a silk-merchant who was temporarily in Lyons.) Of the others I remember very little except a Family: two sons, two daughters and their little, shy, energetic mother who was rather like a field-mouse. They were called Green. Their father, not present, was a professional cellist. The elder son was a pianist and the younger one, a cellist like his father, was only accidentally there, because he normally worked in the first-class orchestra on the *Aquitania*, which happened to be in dry dock. He was called George – a rather bear-like figure over six feet tall with a broad face and kind, gentle grey eyes behind steel-rimmed spectacles.

Some time during the evening I stepped out of the farmhouse to look at the frosty sky. Below, way down in the valley, was a village, lights twinkling in the houses. Above was a great arch of stars. George joined me. Look, I said, it's all upside down; the village is up there and the stars are below. George put his arm round my shoulder and rubbed his cheek against my hair. I think it was then that we fell in love.

Now there are ways and ways of falling in love, depending on who you are. I don't expect that I, young and healthy and tired with walking, stayed awake all night, but it felt as if I did. With joy, with delight. Those stars and that village kept swinging up and down. It wasn't romance that had come to me, it was *comfort.* I'd scampered around with young men before but had hated to be touched by them, and repelled their attempted kisses with a sort of loathing. But now here was a young man with whom I felt at home from the first moment, who hadn't tried to rush me but had gently shown his attraction and I knew it wasn't going to end there though I had no idea how it would go on, and didn't much care. We spent the next day striding mightily over the frozen hills with the group and didn't exchange a private word. I took the train back home in the evening in a trance of delight.

But George had not much time to spare. He would have to rejoin his ship in a week or two. He sent me a box of yellow tea-roses, and a love-letter saying that he had noticed a little speck on one of my eyelids (I have a mole) but could not remember which eye it was and wanted to find out. If he came to Birmingham the next weekend, would I meet him and go for a hill-walk so that he could verify? I met him at New Street Station (off a five-bob excursion train) and we set off for the Lickey

Hills.[26] It poured with rain all day without stopping once. Our first kiss was drenched with rain. Then he asked me to marry him and I said I would.

After seeing him off at the station again, I danced home, wet to the skin and floating with ecstasy. I didn't say a word to a soul about where I had been or what had happened.

I kept it entirely secret because I was *afraid of ridicule*. My father had a very heavy line of ridicule which he exercised whenever I showed signs of interest in any young man; he also produced a ponderous solicitude for my purity and welfare which eventually alienated those young men bold enough to come to the house and meet him. He was cordiality itself but the question 'What are your intentions?' underlay every word he uttered. I was determined that George should not be subjected, this early in our relationship, to this hostile parental scrutiny. I managed by getting up early and always seizing the post delivery as it fell through the letterbox, to conceal, more or less, the fact that we were corresponding. George did not long stay on the *Aquitania*, and took a job at one of Manchester's larger cinemas, where his brother, Ewie already played the piano. This was before, but only just before, the introduction of 'talking films', which threw hundreds of musicians out of work. I would go to Manchester for the weekend, spending Saturday evening in the cinema. When it closed about 11 o'clock, George, with one or two other enthusiasts, would make a tremendous dash for the railway station, stuffing boiled shirts into rucksacks (still in their evening clothes but with their rambling kit underneath) and catch the last train to Macclesfield, from whence we would set out by moonlight or starlight for a farm called Three Shires Head (on the borders of Cheshire, Lancashire and Derbyshire) where the farmer's wife would have a hot supper awaiting us, starting with a glass of hot milk with a dash of brandy, a drink of velvety smoothness. Cheshire cheeses stood in rows along the kitchen shelves. Early the next morning we would set out for a day on the hills, one of our favourite places being a rocky outcrop where one could learn and practice rock-climbing, a sport of which I now became a fanatical devotee.

We became closer and more in love with every occasion. But it was never feverish or 'romantic' – I just felt more *at home;* there was nothing we could not say to one another and our enormous joy in expending our full strength, striding like giants over moor and fell in all weathers was totally satisfying. It will surprise young people, accustomed in these 'permissive' days to jump into bed at first or second sight, that we did not sleep together and it will surprise Freudians, if there are any left, that I wasn't conscious of any wish to. George was by no means sexually inexperienced but he was possessed, in this as in other ways, of infinite patience and gentleness, and introduced me to sex very carefully and gradually and with a sort of whimsical matter-of-factness that made it seem perfectly natural. Ripeness is all, and I wasn't yet ripe. But I am sure that I was not 'repressed'.

III

We decided to become officially 'engaged' – and now the truth must out. He brought me an emerald ring and was to come and bestow it upon me on Christmas Day. I announced this to my father, whose reaction was one of *outrage*. Outrage because I had not confided in him; because he had had no opportunity to scrutinise George's 'prospects'; outrage at being denied the opportunity of being the Heavy Father; and, I think, *jealousy*. There was a brief, unpleasant 'scene'. He refused to speak to me for a day or so. Lela, burdened with his rage, urged me to 'make it up' with him. I refused. By the time George arrived with the ring, the matter had been smoothed over, though there were underground mutterings for my ears about 'tying myself to a wandering musician' and other scornful remarks that now remind me of Mrs Wilfer ('your daughter has bestowed herself on a Mendicant').[27] I remained entirely unaffected and – it seems to me – utterly callous towards Pa, who was only acting according to his Victorian lights; he was genuinely concerned for my welfare, though he was also jealous of any young man who took me away from him. He took to referring to me scathingly as 'a cello-player's fancy'.

The following summer, Marie Brown, who was now married to her silk-merchant, invited us both to stay with her in Lyons. We went mountaineering – real mountaineering with ice-axes, ropes, guides and all. To father's objection that I ought to be saving for my future home and not spending my money on holidays, I answered, how prophetically I did not then know, that one could lose furniture and bed-sheets but nobody would ever be able to take away my Matterhorn. The guide, a man called Chardin, set my self-conceit on its highest pinnacle by telling me that he had not felt obliged to slow down or take extra precautions on my behalf ... I must have been insufferable as I boasted about this to the family afterwards, and took to going to bed not by the stairs but up the outside of the house, from the back, from drain-pipe to window sill and moulding to gutter, into my third-floor bedroom window 'to keep in practice'. (It was really to show off.)

I was in my early twenties when Mem caught mumps. She lay in bed suffering distressfully with enormous swollen cheeks. Cocky as usual, I decided I was immune to it, as I had been to the influenza bug. Towards the end of the incubation period, I put the telephone to my ear one afternoon, to find that I could hear nothing. It seemed nothing but a spot of temporary bother, but when I got home my head began to spin and presently I could not stand upright, and I went to bed feeling seasick. The doctor was called. Evidently he had never heard of, or perhaps did not think of Mumps' Deafness (even though Mem was lying mumping in the next room). He diagnosed gastric influenza; advised me not to bother about the blocked ear ('we can syringe that out later') and went away leaving the mumps virus to devour the nerves of my inner ear and disorientate my sense of balance for a time. When the seasickness departed I went along to his surgery; he syringed. No result. Eventually he sent me to an Ear Specialist who blithely told me I should never hear again on the left side of my head, implying, if not actually declaring, that treatment might have been possible at the beginning but it was now too late.

Partial deafness is a handicap with which almost no one has any ready sympathy. While blindness or even partial blindness awakens pity and offers of help, deafness is regarded by almost everyone as stupidity, comical or irritating. Slowly and painfully I learned to live with it (to some extent lip-reading, manoeuvring myself in company on to the right side of as many people as possible, choosing acoustically suitable seats in concert halls and theatres – or sitting close to the stage so that I could read the lips of the actors). Other partially deaf people realise my disability, as I recognise theirs, but I have many friends who have never known. Some years later I got an infection in the other ear, which perforated. It became, and has remained, a considerable strain to hear conversation if there is other noise going on (the hum of cocktail parties; street noises; background music; dinner table talk – I have been compelled when dining with strangers to tell the person who sits on my left that if he wants to address me he should *touch* me first and not be surprised if I turn my whole head and shoulders round). I cannot tell the direction from which a sound is coming, and when someone calls my name I often have to turn 180 degrees to see where the call is coming from. Worst for me are the people who, on being asked to say something a second time, insist on *shouting*: this angers and flusters me and I give up.

Well, I have lived with, it, using my eyes to help my ears, particularly in traffic and at lectures or parties, occasionally making gaffes because on the basis of a few heard words I have guessed the rest and guessed wrong. But I have missed a lot of the richness of orchestral music and nowadays find a lot of pleasure in listening to symphonies on the gramophone with my *chin on the speaker.*

When my babies were little I never slept on my right side lest I should not hear them cry. But during World War II it was quite useful to put one's good ear down on the pillow and not hear the bombing until it got really near.

Up to now I have written only about the effect on me. Now I must tell about George, and this is not easy. The short ten years we spent together and his early death and the manner of it have quite naturally caused me to remember the good; he had plenty of faults, like the rest of us, but they were never such as to make me doubt our love. We grew closer all the time. I could honestly say, with Cathy Earnshaw ('Nellie, I AM Heathcliff!') that we became like one person.[28]

Great-grandfather William Green was a church organist, who had three sons: Ernest, Harry and William Alfred, George's father, all three professional musicians. Their mother having died young, the elder two successively married their father's housekeepers. William Alfred married Jessie and had four children – William Ewart after you-know-who,[29] who was always called Ewie; Jessie; George; and Winnie. Ewie learned the piano and after serving in the Army in World War I gained a demobilisation grant to study at the Manchester Royal College of Music; he became a professional pianist and orchestral conductor; he also played as an amateur the French horn and the trumpet. Jessie resembled her mother, both physically and in being non-musical, and married a school-teacher; George, whose father wanted him to become a bank clerk or something more secure and remunerative than a musician, studied the cello, ran away from home after leaving school and took a job in one of those trios who provided music in hotels and cafés; when he had saved enough money to pay the fees he went to the College of Music for a year, becoming a pupil of Karl Fuchs, a very eminent teacher. For a very short time, George attained the eighth desk in the Hallé Orchestra but as the musicians at that time were hired, and paid, only by the concert, and they didn't always need eight cellos, this was a matter more of professional prestige than financial gain. Even the leading players were at that time forced to take cinema jobs and, in the summer, jobs in seaside piers, where they used false names so as not to tarnish their reputations. Winnie played the violin, as an amateur, and eventually married Walter Penny, owner of a paper bag factory, who was an amateur viola-player. Their son, Stephen Penny reached fame as first violinist in the Hallé.

I don't know where this bit belongs, because I am writing now about George, but shortly after our engagement I took up the viola, first having lessons with Frank Venton (a pupil of Lionel

Tertis and first viola in the Birmingham City Orchestra) and later under George's tuition. I played very badly but got immense enjoyment from participating in the family concerts that took place in the Green home almost every weekend. Three or four years after our marriage, I chopped a piece off the little finger of my left hand, leaving an exposed nerve which made it impossible for me to touch the strings with that finger. I made clumsy efforts to go on playing, but eventually gave it up.

I can't describe George's character without starting with his father, William Alfred, who eventually became known as Grandpa Green not just to our family but to all our friends and a wide circle of acquaintances. At the time of our marriage, I had met him only once. He was living apart from his family. He had long provided for his wife and children by having two jobs: a clerical job in the daytime and a musical one in the evenings. They hardly saw him except on Sundays. His day-time job was with the Manchester Ship Canal Company, and he was transferred to London on that basis (the ship canal turned into Dean & Dawson the travel agents). He went into lodgings and spent the next few years trying to find suitable accommodation for his wife – unsuccessfully, because Granny Green had become so attached to the house where she had spent all her married life (the rent of which was only eight shillings a week) that she could not face the prospect of change and each time he brought her to London to look at some prospective new home, she went back to Stockport having rejected it. They became estranged, though he continued to send her the bulk of his earnings and to talk longingly of his retirement, when he intended to find a cottage in the country and persuade her to join him there.

I have only met a few people in my life whom I regard as solid gold all through. Grandpa Green was one of them. Flawlessly upright, wise, tolerant and astonishingly non-male-chauvinist (he instilled into his sons the absolute rule that no husband should allow his wife to wash a dirty nappy until the child was six weeks old and this is so much before his time that the time has not caught up with him yet), he was literally loved by all who knew him, and was possessed of an unfailing, marvellous dry Lancashire wit which made his conversation a delight. I can give only one instance here: describing an incident when the orchestra in which he was playing started to play 'God Save the King', he said that half of them had started in B and half in B-flat – which would, he said, 'have made even God think twice'.

Both Winnie and George inherited (or learned) this delightful wry sense of humour from Grandpa. George, too, had his gentleness, his wide tolerance and his love for and interest in people. George spoke always in a very quiet voice, which I scarcely ever heard him raise. Perhaps because of his large bulk – not only was he over six-feet tall, he had broad shoulders and very muscular limbs and his normal weight was around eleven stone – he never seemed to feel the need that smaller men have to be aggressive; I remember his using his fists only once, in an incident I shall describe later. He was not handsome, with a broad face, flyaway light brown hair, and a nose down which his glasses were always sliding. Only when he sat down with the cello did be lose his bear-like air of clumsiness: one instantly saw the reason for the broad, slightly stooping shoulders and the long arms with beautiful hands at the end of them. He was a good teacher, with infinite patience.

He had proceeded along the same leftward path as I – the path followed by many many young people of our generation and times – but had thought things out far more clearly than I had. He hated war, the arms race, unemployment and what was called 'overproduction' for their *wastefulness*. It was the period of two million unemployed: the Wall Street crash; the paying of US farmers NOT to breed pigs; the burning of coffee to keep the price up; the greasing of the slips for launching ships with bananas; poverty; the lack of education; the squandering of human potential; colonialism; and he longed fiercely and deeply, for working people to have access to culture and education – enjoy music and the arts, poetry and the plays of Shakespeare, sport and leisure. William Morris was his teacher (and later mine). He did not enjoy the trumpery boring music he had to repeat over and over again in the cinema, the cafés and dance-halls, where he was often employed and at one time, when he was incessantly playing sentimental tunes from popular 'musicals' in tea-shops and restaurants (*Desert Song, Student Prince*, etc), used to put his music upside down and read it from left to right in order to keep himself awake.

He thought things through, and he had the gift of explaining difficult problems in a clear and simple way: perhaps some of it was not as clear as it seemed in those days to us, the generation of young people to whom Labour Party socialism ('to secure for the workers by hand and brain', etc) seemed the answer to the ills of our world.[30] But *it made sense.*

He loved exercising his strength in all kinds of sport: swimming, diving, fell-walking, cycling and *speed*: he and his friend Leslie Sowerbutts bought motor-cycles and to this day it makes me shudder to recall the speed at which, with me on the pillion, we soared over the Peak District and elsewhere, whooping with joy as we took off over hump-backed bridges in Evil-Knievel leaps and bounds.[31] In the year before we married, George obtained a job playing in the pier orchestra at Colwyn Bay: I went to spend my summer holiday fortnight with him there. We ranged over Snowdonia day after day, tearing back so that he could join the orchestra in the evenings. Somewhere on Tryfan – long my favourite mountain – we became acquainted with a young woman called Evelyn Lowe. On the death of her parents she had inherited an estate near Betws-y-coed and had been forced to sell it, retaining only an acre of land and a small, solid stone-built cottage from which she used to go climbing alone. She spent most of her year abroad and offered us the use of the cottage whenever we cared to go there, an offer we accepted and used with immense joy.

The following November we were married. It was crazy, it was reckless, for the introduction of talking films had ruined the livelihood of literally hundreds of musicians whose main work had been in the cinema and the prospects of a man like George, who knew no other trade than the cello, were slim. My father had been right. He was 'a wandering musician'. On the very day of the wedding (in church, to please my parents) when everyone had left the house and my father and I were awaiting the taxi, he made his last effort to prevent what he saw as disaster. 'Now my dear,' he said, 'you know quite well that when poverty comes in at the door, love flies out of the window. It is not too late. You have only to say the word and I will go to church without you and tell them it is all off.' This went in at one ear and out at the other with the speed of light. He 'gave me away' with ostentatious gloom.

There was no wedding breakfast or reception. We hopped on a train and went to Macclesfield and thence to Three Shires Head where we spent our wedding night. Next day, after laughing in bed at the thought that because a few words had been said and a few signatures had been made, we could have been seen in bed together without surprise or scandal, whereas twenty four hours before we would have been outcasts from society, we strode off across the frosty hills for another day's joyful exertion.

IV

We went to live in lodgings, and later in an unfurnished flat, in Manchester, where George still had a job (in the largest cinema, which provided intervals of 'live' music between the films). As my contribution to our livelihood, we opened a small business – the service of lunch-time sandwiches to offices in the centre of the city. We had a small room with a large sink, a telephone, and a cooker; a stock of tinned meat and fish; reams of grease-proof paper; and hundreds of labels printed with the words SQUARE MEAL SANDWICH SERVICE. We issued circulars, with a price list and the telephone number, and pushed them through office doorways for two weeks. We had three bicycles, two of them ridden by errand boys and one by George. George did the marketing and shared in the delivery. I prepared sandwiches all morning and answered the telephone with the orders (two ham, one crab and one corned beef and pickle) and saw to the despatch. The hours between eleven and two o'clock were a nightmare of flurry and chaos. George then went to work. I cleared up and made ready for the next day. Our evening meals consisted almost entirely of left-over scraps, stale bread and wilted salad-stuff.

We never made a vast profit, but it kept us going and we did not get into debt. At the end of thirteen months, two factors put an end to the venture. The first was the trade slump in Manchester. From supplying cheap lunches to ill-paid typists and clerks, we began to receive orders from managers and supervisors, while our former customers brought bread and dripping from home, if they still had jobs. We fired one of the messengers; the other one began to peculate. Unwilling to behave like 'capitalist bosses' we did not fire him but earnestly lectured him until he promised to mend his ways. He went on peculating. The other and decisive factor was that I had become pregnant, to our immense joy. 'To think of all those months,' sighed George contentedly, 'when I worried whether we were going to have children at all!' (It was actually less than six.) To pay the wage of someone to do the work I had done would have been disaster. We closed the business. It had served its turn. The only piece of 'capitalist enterprise' we ever undertook.

Things got difficult. We could not pay the rent. Having applied for a council house in Stockport we were put on a waiting list and went to stay temporarily with Granny Green and Winnie (the only child left at home). At my first visit to the antenatal clinic in Stockport, I was discovered to have alarmingly high blood pressure and was ordered to follow a horrid, tasteless diet (no salt, no meat etc.) and take no exercise whatever. Granny Green was immensely kind, preparing my special food and bringing it to me on the sofa where I lay unwillingly and crossly, reading and listening to the gramophone. In three weeks I went back to the clinic. The blood pressure was just the same. They accused me of not sticking to the diet, etc. and bought me into the maternity home to make sure. At the end of three weeks the blood pressure had not diminished at all. Resignedly they let me go home, with awesome warnings about headaches, swollen ankles and eclampsia, warning that I *must* have a GP present as well as the midwife when my time came. I went back to normal activity, cycling, swimming and walking, ate what I fancied and had a supremely normal pregnancy which George did his utmost to share. He read medical books to find out all about the process, and oiled my tummy night after night. One night after he had returned from work, he invited me to go for a walk. I was feeling lazy, near my time, and grumbled, how would he have liked to walk everywhere with an extra seven or eight pounds in his tummy? He went into the kitchen, got a 7lb bag of potatoes, buttoned it into his macintosh and led me out. He also, though he did not let many people see it, *knitted* tiny garments for the baby.

Two days before Frances was born, George developed toothache. His face swelled so much that his glasses were pushed out of shape. Twenty-four hours after she was born, the swelling went down. *Couvade.* He underwent the ridicule of his fellow-musicians blithely.

The maternity home operated on the spartan Truby King plan (a New Zealand doctor who invented what was then a revolutionary regime for rearing babies). Healthy children who weighed over 7 lbs (Frances weighed 8) were fed strictly at four-hourly intervals from 6 a.m. to 10 p.m. and not during the night at two o'clock. By the time the mother left the maternity home, the baby had got into the routine (at least mine had) and slept between 10 p.m. and 6 a.m. without a murmur. Babies were also put out into the open air three days after birth, snug in their prams of course, but *not wearing bonnets*, and stayed there during the hours of light, except for feeds. They were bathed every day in warm water, but a jug of cold water was poured over them just before taking them out of the tub into a nice warm towel. An inexperienced mother, I operated this scheme inflexibly. Frances *throve.*

George doted on her. In true Grandpa Green tradition, he washed her nappies for the first six weeks, and even afterwards if needed. He nursed her, talked to her, sang to her, played the cello by her cot. He bathed her and always cut her finger- and toe-nails, showing infinite patience and gentleness.

Women have written often enough about childbirth and I don't need to describe it, except to say that I got through it with éclat, falling fast asleep in between pains, almost to the end of labour (about eleven hours), needing no anaesthetic and glad, glad, glad to the end of my days that I experienced that last agonising climax and heard my Frances draw her first breath and shout out 'I'm here, I'm alive!' The GP arrived an hour after it was all over. The clinic doctor, who had warned me about eclampsia, looked in the next day (she was also the medical officer of the maternity home) and stared at me, saying, 'Well, you are the biggest fraud in Stockport!'

A month later I went to the post-natal clinic. My blood pressure was exactly as before, and exactly as it continued for years afterwards, with no ill-effects. I don't regard myself as a medical freak: I just think the clinic was too rigid about the rules and perhaps by now there is enough medical experience for a condition like mine to cause no astonishment or concern.

The council house was ready just after I came out of hospital. It was the rule then to keep a woman in hospital two weeks, allowing her to walk about in the last three days, and letting her bath the baby the day before leaving.

We joined the Independent Labour Party. It had become necessary to *do* something about our beliefs. I think someone recruited us, though I was edged in by a colourful poster showing a long ladder resting in water. On the ladder were arranged four figures, the topmost being the figure that was always used in those days of a 'capitalist boss' (top hat and morning suit) and at the bottom the worker had his mouth just above the water level, and the capitalist at the top was leaning over his shoulder and saying: 'For the sake of the country, chaps, we must all go down one rung'.[32] The kind ILP group local began to arrange its meetings in our house so that I should not be prevented from attending by having to care for Frances. We read the *New Leader* and began to digest scraps of Marxism and to attribute the chaotic state of society to the existence of the system.[33] It was the year of the 'National Government'[34] ... I was pushing the pram down the main street one morning when an Irish friend, who managed to combine the job of principal tenor in the choir of the Catholic Cathedral with an outspoken and unshakable atheism, jumped from his bicycle, which he threw down on the tramlines, and came towards me shouting: 'And now what do you think of your Ramsay Bloody Judas Iscariot Macdonald!!!'

We lived from hand to mouth, in the barely furnished council house, which had, fortunately, a largish garden in which we grew plentiful vegetables. On Mondays I would buy four pennyworth of bacon bones, to which throughout the week I would add root vegetables, tinned tomatoes, lentils and beans. On Fridays I took Frances to the baby clinic and afterwards had lunch with Granny Green (a real meal). Saturday night was fish and chips or stewed tripe, and around nine o'clock in the evening, a visit to the market where the butchers' stalls (in those days of no refrigerators) would be selling off lumps of beef or mutton at knockdown prices: if you waited until the right moment, you could get quite a substantial portion for one or two shillings. It must have formed a fairly adequate diet because I continued to breast-feed my baby for more than nine months and she grew into a firm, but never fat, rosy, active, bonny little girl, walking at ten months, uttering her first words in a deep baritone voice and friendly and responsive to everyone she saw.

George's cinema job disappeared. For a while he played, with furious distaste, the banjo in Jack Hilton's dance band.[35] Later he was offered another café job – on the guitar. He could not play the guitar, but borrowed one, sat up for a whole night teaching himself to play it (it is not, like the banjo, strung the same way as the cello), went for the audition next morning and *got the job*. But that ended too. I believe at that time, apart from the Hallé orchestra, there was only one job for a cellist in all Manchester – at the Opera House, and this was held by Douglas Morris, a friend of ours. George got a 'gig' – a week's job in a musical show at some seaside town, I forget where. This was the first time he was 'unfaithful' to me, but he told me about it immediately on his return and it didn't seem to make any difference. (It never did, for there were subsequent occasions, but since he always kept me informed, sometimes in advance, there was never any deceit; it is *deceit* which poisons a relationship and I was so absolutely confident in his love that the mere fact of his having gone to bed with someone else had no effect on me at all). I said I would deal with his faults as well as his good qualities ...

The last warning from the post-natal clinic, still worried about my blood-pressure, had been that I should not attempt to have another child for at least three years. They did not offer any advice on how to prevent this (contraception was still a dirty word in those days) but even if they had done so I would not have listened. Just under seventeen months after Frances was born, Martin came into the world.

There seemed no hope of work in Manchester or Stockport. We had £30 between us and starvation, and I had paid the advance fee of £4 to the maternity home where I was booked to have my second child. About a month before the birth was due, George gave me £20 and took £10 and set off for London. There he shared the dingy lodgings of his father, and looked around for work, living on one shilling a day. He met an old friend, a pianist, Arthur Olerenshaw, who introduced him to the agent who hired musicians for Lyon's Corner Houses,[36] and, just a week before Martin's birth, started with the orchestra in the Corner House at Tottenham Court Road, at a weekly salary we hadn't seen for over a year.

We had given up the council house. For the last two or three weeks of my pregnancy I had sent Frances to my father's home, where the ever-loving Lela had revelled in caring for her. I spent the time waiting with George's sister, Jessie and her husband Harry Grisebrook, who made no secret whatever of his reluctance to have me in his home. He would come home from work each evening and greet me with 'What! Still here?' Whether my regret at being a burden to him worked as a counter to the onset of labour or whether, because he was a very large child, Martin was post-mature, he weighed nearly 9lbs, causing a longer labour then before, and tore his way out so that I had to be stitched.

All new babies are beautiful to their mothers, but even I had to laugh when I saw my squashed-faced little boy, who so resembled a caricature of his father that it was almost uncanny. He seemed perfectly healthy and I was on top of the world, having my 'pigeon hair'. But trouble began before he was fourteen days old. Don, the three-year-old little boy of Jessie in whose house I had been staying, developed whooping cough after I had left for the maternity home. I must have caught it from him, and the poor little baby from me. I think this must be unusual, as the newly born are said to have immunity from various infections. At all events, I and he had begun to cough a day or two before my fortnight's stay in the hospital was up – if it can be called coughing, for he didn't know how to cough, and was racked to pieces and choking.

Even worse, he was only five days old when there was an incident which I have always regarded as 'the occasion when I died'. It was the habit in the nursing home to give all the mothers a senna mixture daily to keep their bowels in motion. This was thought to be so important that Matron, on her daily rounds, used to ask every mother: 'How-are-you-today-have-you-had-your-bowels-moved-today?' in one breath, like that. One morning the night nurse, having given us our breakfast trays – there were just two of us in the ward – suddenly remembered we hadn't had our senna and said hastily: 'Don't start your breakfast for a minute, I'll fetch your medicine.' She went to the medicine room and picked up the bottle, which was almost empty. Seeing another bottle with a similar dark mixture, she hastily emptied some into the senna bottle and brought it to us. I got the top dose, which was *neat belladonna*; the girl in the next bed got hers slightly diluted with senna mixture. I gulped mine down. My mouth instantly turned so dry that I seized my teacup – but found I could not lift it. At the same moment the whole world turned bright orange, as my pupils dilated.

'Your eyes look funny,' mumbled the girl in the next bed, looking at me.

Fortunately for me, or I would not be writing these lines, the night nurse instantly recognised what she had done and told Sister. (She then walked straight out of the hospital, mounted her bicycle and set out for the river, to drown herself. But she met the day nurses coming up the drive, who stopped her and brought her back).

Sister came bustling into the room with two enormous jugs of water.

'Listen, girls,' she said loudly and clearly and with immense wisdom, 'you've been given something in your medicine which *won't be good for your babies.* I want you to throw it up' — and proceeded to pour jugs of the salty water down our throats. I have always found it difficult to vomit and the first jugful had no effect on me. Now began a time of confusion, of which I remember only some details. It dawned on me that I had been poisoned. The only thought that remained dimly with me was my baby, my baby, my baby, I mustn't die. Doctors, hastily summoned, appeared, moving, it seemed to me, as slowly as battleships coming into dock. I believe I was stomach-pumped but don't remember it. I wanted to sleep, to be allowed to lie down. At either side of me, at the head of the bed, stood a nurse, two lovely white bosoms on which I kept trying to rest my head, only to be slapped in the face, and told, 'Wake up, Mrs Green, wake up.' In the ordinary way I suppose they would have walked me up and down, but having so recently given birth it was thought inadvisable. At one moment I dimly heard one of the doctors say, of the girl in the other bed: 'It's all up there, you can let her lie down' (he meant that she had thrown up sufficiently but it had quite another meaning for me). 'I mustn't die, my baby, my baby, my baby' was the only coherent thought in my mind. I *repudiated* death with all my might and then lost consciousness, except for swallowing nasty cups of black coffee, and the cry of 'Wake up

Mrs Green!' Eventually, I don't know how much later, I was allowed to sleep. I returned to consciousness at eight in the evening, to a world still bright orange, to the hazy sight of the night nurse, leaning against the door post and saying:

'I have prayed today as I have never in my life before.'

My eyesight did not recover for several days, and I was not allowed to breast feed my poor little Martin until it was considered that the poison had gone from my system. To develop whooping cough on top of this was a bad start for him.

At that time there was no immunisation nor remedy for whooping cough, which had to be allowed to 'run its course'.

My brother Tod, one of the few kind things he did for me, fetched me by car straight from the nursing home to Birmingham, where I collected Frances, and then drove me to London. George had obtained a furnished flat in Hampstead and our scanty furniture was 'in store'.

The next weeks were pretty grim. In unfamiliar surroundings, not recovered from childbirth and the belladonna trauma, with no friends nearby and two sick children – for eighteen-month-old Frances naturally developed whooping cough, too – with George sawing away on his cello at the Corner House from noon till midnight, with intervals so brief that he could barely make the journey home and back; with a hostile landlady whose mentally defective son had the habit of wandering in and out of our rooms, mopping and mowing, and who objected to the tyre marks made by the pram on the glossy lino of her entrance passage (so that I had to haul the pram upstairs and then dash down to wipe away the marks), with a single gas ring on which to boil two sets of nappies and the sicked-upon bedclothes – no detergents, remember, and no disposables – coughing myself and soothing the coughing Frances, I coped, I don't know how. *What you have to do, you can do* ... But this was nearly automatic, irrelevant beside the battle for my baby boy. Even today, with the benefits of modern medicine, whooping cough is a killer. Well below his birth-weight, not knowing how to cough, racked to pieces and choking, he had to be fed again each time he vomited (no Truby King regime for him) with expressed milk and three drops of brandy in it (havoc with my lactation), I wrought night and day to save his health; I never admitted that I might lose him – hadn't I repudiated death for his sake? A baby's first real smile is a glorious event for any parent and we had shared our delight at Frances's. But when Martin first responded, silver trumpets played heavenly fanfares in the air. He began to gain weight, to cough less, to lift his head, to sleep for an hour or two at a time. My bonny boy.

I am taking too much credit for myself. George fully shared the anxious days and sleepless nights and – insofar as his somewhat scanty leisure permitted – the nappy washing and other chores, while Grandpa Green was a tower of strength. George had had, at the beginning, an additional preoccupation in the shape of a girlfriend he had acquired during our few weeks' separation, who refused to be as temporary as he had from the start explained (as he invariably did). This was one time (and there were other occasions, though not many) that I experienced pangs of jealousy, but I found the emotion so humiliating that I trod it down after a short struggle.

(What is it about orchestral fiddle players – chiefly violinists and cellists but rarely basses – which attracts the romantic yearnings of young woman? I believe it happens even to this day, in spite of the superior pull of pop-singers and punk-rockers. For a fourpenny cup of coffee, a succession of young women would come night after night to sit in the Corner House and gaze soulfully at their heroes. They knitted ties, baked cakes, offered to darn socks, wrote love-letters and hung around outside the bandroom ... mostly young girls from the provinces or Ireland, living in lodgings or hostels and far from home; poor lasses, they put a bit of romance into their lonely and impoverished lives. George had a succession of them, some of whom he failed to convince that he was a happily married and quite unromantic figure until he invited them to tea at our house, which never failed to show them the hopelessness of their dream. One or two became friends of the family. I believe this seldom or never happens to trumpeters, percussionists, or other wind players, with the possible exception of flautists.)

The coughing died away. The kids began to thrive again. Our life became normal.

Largely at the instigation of George, who saw that I was rather dismal and no wonder ('too much wife-ing and mothering and not enough other pursuits,' he said), I rejoined the Independent Labour Party in Hampstead. It was not at all like the Stockport group, consisting mostly of middle-class students whom I found patronising. We met, in evenings, under the leadership of one Jon Kimche, a know-all who laid down the lore in a god-like fashion, discussing esoteric Marxist texts and confusing (to me) economic theories. One evening, in a contrary mood, I asked him what he meant by '*our* theory'. 'I mean the London School of Economics,' he replied. I stood up. 'I didn't come here to learn London School of Economics' economics,' I said, enjoying my dramatic moment, 'I came here to learn Marxist economics!' And swept out. We were back in political limbo though we continued to read the ILP paper *New Leader* and to puzzle over such bits of Marx, Engels and Lenin as came our way.[37]

I haven't dropped any names so far (except Karl Fuchs, George's teacher) but now I begin. Waiting for an Underground train one night, I got into conversation with Geoffrey Grigson, who was then editing the book page in the *News Chronicle*.[38] He must have decided I was at least literate, if not intelligent, because he offered to send me books to review; trashy novels they were and ten lines for each was what he wanted. I hired a typewriter and set about it. I *earned money* for the first time since Frances' birth, and my self-conceit was immense. Actually the money was less than what I received for flogging the books to one of those dealers who buy up review copies for fifty-per-cent of the published price, so long as they are in 'mint' condition.

There are advantages and disadvantages in every situation, say the Chinese. The situation of a professional musician's family has both. The musician is working when everyone else is at leisure, and his leisure time is when everyone else is at work. Advantage number one: the father is at home in the mornings when the children are awake and has thus more time to spend with them than a father who arrives home from his work only to see them put to bed. It is no real disadvantage to his wife that she has to start her housework in the evenings, except that when she has prepared her husband's evening meal, eaten around midnight, he isn't ready quite to go straight to bed but, in the course of natural rhythm, needs to spend some time relaxing and digesting it. We would go to bed about 2 a.m. But of course the little ones would be joyously awake around six or seven. I learned to manage with five or six hours sleep. Another disadvantage for the musician is that the friends with whom he spends his leisure are almost exclusively other entertainers, of whom I found two sorts: those who loved music, and those whose fathers 'put them to the trumpet', or the flute or the trombone, as another father would apprentice his son to a printer or mechanic. In the heyday of professional music before the talkies, this was as good as any other apprenticeship, but in the big debacle of cinema orchestras many of these latter ones got out for good and became chiropodists or chicken farmers. Our friends were those in the first group and our leisure activity was making music together – trios, quartets, quintets, duets, according to who turned up. I was sometimes allowed to play the viola ...

I was also enrolled in two or three of Grandpa Green's orchestras. He was in considerable demand as a conductor with the amateur orchestras of big concerns like insurance companies and building societies. Most amateur musicians don't like to study the viola, which isn't a solo instrument and for which very little has been written. So in dark green velvet evening dress, my fiddle case under my arm, I would sail off to the Abbey Road Building Society or the Pearl Assurance, to try and hold my own (or that of two or three others) against a plethora of fiddlers, cellists or flautists ...

But to return to advantages and disadvantages. A great deprivation for a musician is that he cannot go to concerts or the opera and hear the music he loves – at least without considerable fuss and disarrangement. On the all-too-rare occasions when I went with George to the Old Vic (Shakespeare) or Sadler's Wells (opera) we paid *one shilling* for our seats; but George must pay a deputy to do his turn at the Corner House (£2) so the evening cost us quite a slice of his weekly salary. There is a moment in *The Marriage of Figaro* where I once looked at George and saw him in tears – tears of exaltation at the heavenly music and tears of sadness that too few people were given the opportunity and the education to share it. (I can never restrain my tears to this day when the moment comes.)

Cycling to work one day through Camden Town, George encountered a small café which had, surprisingly, a small lending library attached. For two pence one could borrow a book – and they were all Marxist works, or near Marxist. He borrowed *The Coming Struggle for Power* by John Strachey.[39] He read it in the daytimes, I in the evenings. We reached, jointly, the same conclusion. Both of us decided to join the Communist Party.

I have not dealt with the *overriding* disadvantage experienced by the musician and his family in the late 20's and early 30's. Insecurity. Corner House orchestras were hired not by Lyons but by an agent who could, and did, hand out jobs as he chose, for a month at a time. For reasons which I shall explain a bit further on, George was shifted from place to place and from band to band. What we knew as 'shirt bands' were for a time the fashion: in a blue satin shirt and red cummerbund, George for a time was a member of 'Michael Garrity and his Hungarian Gypsies', the only difference from last week being that instead of having to get up boiled shirts and wing collars, I now only had to wash the blue satin shirt, a rest relief. But sometimes there was a month when he didn't have a job at all. And there was no unemployment pay, for at that time unemployment pay was not granted to those who earned more than a certain weekly sum, and while he *was* employed, the musicians' pay exceeded this sum by a few shillings. We got into financial difficulty, got behind with the rent, and had the Bailiffs. The bailiff's man was good-hearted. 'I can't take your beds and the tools of your trade,' he said to me kindly, 'and I must have a few forks and spoons as a token. But I shan't look under the eiderdown, or in the oven ...' (I kept my Matterhorn!).

In the long sunny summer of 1933 we lived in a tent down in Surrey while George cycled to and fro (he was in work again) every day. My lovely children ran about naked and grew as brown as berries; we bought milk, butter and home-made bread from the wife of the farmer on whose land we were settled. I had three books and three books only to read during that three months: the *Collected Works of William Shakespeare, Anti-Dühring* by Frederick Engels and – I don't remember why – Joseph Conrad's *Victory*. Might have done worse. Engels was so enlightening I felt I knew the answer to all the problems of dialectical materialism.[40]

V

In September, we found a flat in Bloomsbury, near the Free Hospital. It was a converted bakery, with one huge room, an enormous fireplace, a kitchen and a bathroom. But I had to find work, things were too precarious for us to rely on George's intermittent earnings. At that time there was a strong trend (I don't believe it became law but had almost the force of law) that married women should not be employed by anyone. Posing as single, I got a job in the advertising department of a wholesale chemists, and the kids began to attend the day-nursery on top of Kingsway Hall, run by Baptists. I rose early, pushed the pram to Kingsway and went thence to Snow Hill; there I did a day's work and fetched them at 5.30 (looking anxiously around as I pushed them back home in case any colleague should see me).

Our life as members of the Party took different shapes. I was enrolled in the local group (we called them 'cells') and George in a group of musicians, who had found an urgent and very necessary communist mission to revitalise the Musicians' Union. The two children liked it at the day nursery. I was rather dismayed at first, being still hostile to Christian teaching and Christians, to find them singing hymns, learning Bible stories and so forth. But the Baptists, those at least, seemed to be not only tolerant people but joyful Christians and it seemed to me that the Bible stories did no harm, having been so mixed up with fairy stories and popular 'comics', like Mickey Mouse, that all were regarded as agreeable fiction. Indeed, Frances once produced a drawing, mostly scribble, and explained that it depicted an incident at a party, where Donald Duck would not behave himself so they put him in the dustbin: there's the dustbin, Mammy, and that's Jesus and Mickey Mouse sitting on the lid to keep him in. The nursery had a good kindergarten teacher who didn't believe in smacking. Both children sailed through mumps and chicken pox without the slightest harm. Our sectarian attempts at counter-indoctrination had much the same effect as my parents' attempt to make me into a little Christian (*vide* the General Confession, etc.) had on me. Martin joyfully carolled Four Widgey Workers (forward ye workers) while Frances, surveying the plinth in Trafalgar Square on the occasion of a demonstration, asked earnestly, 'Mummy, which is Comrade Come-rally?'[41]

To digress: throughout my life controversy has raged, and still rages, about day nurseries, and the 'need' of the child to be with its mother for the first three, five or what-have-you years of its life. Psychiatrists, social workers, doctors and clergy, mostly men, have all hammered away at this, telling mothers what to do and totally forgetting that there are thousands of women who *must* 'go out' to work, that there are thousands who *like* to pursue a career or engage in work that gives them an interest outside the home; that there are thousands who prefer domestic chores and that all would like to be *able to choose*, if there were enough day nurseries to go round. None of them, as far as I know, ever stopped to consider that model of domestic virtue, the Royal Family, all of whose children were put in the care of nurses, governesses and public schools, and were separated from both parents for long periods (royal tours, etc.) without being regarded as 'deprived' or potential delinquents. The only time I recall when these arguments and theories, varied as they were, died down or were actually reversed, was the period of the Second World War when women were *needed* in industry, the forces, etc. Then new theories appeared, showing that the Good mothers were those who tied up their hair in headscarves, put their children in nurseries or left them with grannies, and sang while they worked in Royal Ordnance Factories.

Little children need mother love. Of course they do. But it doesn't always or all the time have to be mother who gives it. Fathers can – George did. Since he never worked on Saturday mornings and I did, I used to arrive home at lunch time to find the lunch prepared and all three of them, having had a whale of a time doing 'housework', sitting together in the bath playing at whales and getting nice and clean after their toil. Good loving nursery nurses can give it; grannies can give it, as I shall tell, and so can grandpas, as Grandpa Green so magnificently demonstrated.

Frances and Martin spent from eight to five daily at the nursery on top of Kingsway Hall. When I got there at ten past five they were dressed in their outdoor clothes and came running along the corridor to greet me, as joyful to see me as I was to see them. How many such moments would there have been if we had spent all day in each others' company, with me performing exasperating chores and they getting under my feet? I pay my grateful tribute to the Baptists of Kingsway Hall day nursery.

Besides our over-enthusiastic and almost totally ineffective efforts to bring up good little communists (I shall have a lot to say about this presently) George and I did do our best to give them a decent moral upbringing, without fear or superstition. We answered all their questions as truthfully as we knew how: George, who possessed immense patience, spent hours answering such questions as, 'What makes the sky blue?' in terms they could understand at least partially. (Both of us were foxed by Frances' query: 'How do poisonous snakes poison other poisonous snakes?'). In particular we wanted to give them the facts of life *and* death, as soon as, and no sooner than, they questioned them. (The idea that Grandpa Kemp had 'gone to live in the sky with Jesus' not only terrified me as a child, since I had seen his dead body, but it had also sowed an enormous doubt as to the truth of what the grown ups told me.) We buried every dead bird we found, explaining gently that they would 'rot into flowers and fruit, with Adam and all mankind', like ourselves. Frances asked, at about the age of five, where we had got Martin from. We had been planting mustard and cress on flannel, which made it easy. Daddy got a little seed and put it in my tummy and it grew into a baby. Where did Daddy get the seed from? followed. Answer, pause for thought. Then I suppose he put it in your mouth? asked the logical child.

Thus the business of procreation was made clear without difficulty or embarrassment. (Frances must have passed this on painlessly to Martin, for he never asked ...) We regarded ourselves as progressive parents, but in reality we were merely part of a multitude – I can't recount the number of friends who were subsequently discovered to have gone through the same experience, gradual decline of Christian belief, disgust with Victorian morality, revelation of Freud, A.S. Neill, iconoclasm of Shaw, Wells and Co., and above all the Russian Revolution, dawn of a new day for us all.[42] (Only a few weeks ago Ken Campbell[43] told me how at the age of sixteen he stood in a field, looked up at the sky and shouted: 'You're not there!' The Wrath of God didn't fall. Freedom!)

We concerned ourselves with the children's moral and social education. Grandpa Green took charge of their musical education. Before she was six years old, Frances (and sometimes Martin) had been with him to Sadler's Wells matinees and heard *Hansel and Gretel* and the *Snow Maiden* more than once, and seen some ballet. We sang – how we sang: Hymns learned at Kingsway, folk songs, nursery songs and jingles, bits of opera, tunes from Gilbert and Sullivan. Frances once took our breath away by rendering 'Nymphs and Shepherds' word and note perfect quite casually while helping me to lay the table for Sunday lunch. Martin, endeavouring to keep up, told me one day about a new hymn at Kingsway. 'And did you sing it too?' I asked. 'No, but I stood up and wagged my teggies!' he replied. Dear Lilian Baylis![44] You could get into the gallery at Sadler's Wells for sixpence.

George's party life, as I have said, was spent at that time with a group of Communist and near-communist musicians. The advent of talking pictures had played havoc with the membership and funds of the Musicians' Union, which was deep in the doldrums. The Communist Group decided to try and revitalise it. There was plenty of scope (and need) for the effort, for there was a growing number of dance bands, members of which often had other, daytime jobs and worked for peanuts and the love of jazz, undermining the wages of the professionals. The Union was not known to them. Moreover, the entrance fee for the Union was *two guineas*, which few felt able to afford. Our group carried a resolution in the Union to reduce the entrance fee to ten shillings for a limited period, and started a recruiting drive. They began to publish a rank-and-file journal entitled *Crescendo*, which they sold principally in Archer Street, Soho – a sort of 'slave market' where unemployed musicians stood around each noon and agents, looking for 'gig' players (one night stands) paraded up and down selecting the instrumentalists they wanted. (It was rather like the 'Call-on' in the dockland areas those days. Word would somehow get round that a man down there wanted a saxophone player or a drummer, and the saxophone players and drummers would all rush to the spot.)

Crescendo was a four or six-page duplicated paper in a yellow cover. I cut the stencils. And ran them off on a hand-operated rotary duplicating machine in our Bloomsbury flat. Others stapled them together. I am (humourously) regretful now to say that sometimes I enrolled Frances or Martin to turn the handle, reciting: 'I am driving. A nail. In the coffin. Of capitalism.' – an incantation which must have had as much meaning for them as 'We have erred and strayed like Thy lost sheep' had for me in the past. (One or two of those members of the early 'Ginger Group' are still alive. For them I am still a sort of Honorary Member of the M.U.) The Union got back to stability and gradually progressed to the power and influence it has today. Someone will doubtless

write a history of the Musicians' Union one day. This episode will
not loom large, I am sure. But I like to think that, up to my
elbows in filthy duplicating ink, I had a small part in its story and
that, but for George and his communist friends, it might have
been quite different.

As for my own Party involvement, it was in a 'cell'. I had better
explain right away, because it is relevant, that in our whole-
hearted enthusiasm for the Soviet Revolution we adopted and
embraced organisational and political methods, including their
names, as laid down by Lenin in quite different circumstances. A
group was a cell. We engaged in Agit-Prop (agitation and
propaganda). The Central Committee was the Politbureau. Shortly
after we joined, we went into the streets and we sold a pamphlet
called 'For a Soviet Britain'.[45] It made us feel good to converse
with one another in such jargon. It is in the nature of
revolutionaries, especially young ones, impatient for change, to
think that by imitating the most recent successful revolution, one
can bring it about. Hence the Maoists; hence the Castroites and
the worshippers of Che Guevara; hence those young ones who
went on demonstrations shouting Ho-Ho-Ho, Ho Chi Minh.[46]

We were young, impatient for change, and human. And we
thought we had the answer to everything. Follow the Soviet
Union, the world's first socialist state, and all would be well. And
to some extent we were right. Right at all events to defend the
Soviet Union because it was the world's first socialist state, the
hope of mankind, surrounded by hostile states and hated viciously
by our enemy and theirs – capitalism and imperialism and their
menacing threat: Fascism and war. Hitler in Germany, Mussolini
in Italy, the rape of Abyssinia, Japan (aided by Chiang Kai-shek)
slaughtering millions in China; wherever one looked – France,
Spain, even Moseley and his Blackshirts in England, fascism was
in the ascendent.[47] It was a matter of extreme urgency: democracy
and peace, or fascism and war. And the Soviet Union was our
bulwark.

And there was so much to be done. We supported the Hunger Marchers, risked arrest by getting on soap boxes to address signers-on at Labour Exchanges (unemployment figures had reached almost three million), chalked VOTE LABOUR on whitewashed slogans on walls, marched to Trafalgar Square shouting SANCTIONS MEAN PEACE, CLOSE THE SUEZ CANAL![48] (The first time I got on a soap box I shouted my voice away in the first five minutes and had to be rescued by the Chairman; the second time I got so agitated that I stepped off the box and fell into the gutter – this drew a rather larger crowd than usual because several people stayed to see if I would do it again). We sold the *Daily Worker* in the early morning outside factory gates and in the late evening outside Underground stations;[49] we gave away leaflets, sold pamphlets in the streets. Not far from our Heathcote Street flat was the Pindar of Wakefield, where the League Against Imperialism held regular Saturday night hops, attended by Africans, West Indians, Indians, Chinese and many other nationalities. I was there every Saturday night, and recall the dignified, remarkably 'English-gentleman' figure of the Secretary and Master of Ceremonies, Reginald Bridgman.[50] Even nearer was Britannia Street School, home for some years of Unity Theatre, which gave progressive plays like *Waiting for Lefty* and annual political pantomimes;[51] I nipped over from home every night to man a 'literature stall' in the interval of the performance.

'Marxists,' wrote a contributor to *The Times* in 1949, 'draw an enhancement of life, a passionate faith and an all-out devotion from the sense that they are servants and instruments of the immanent process of history. Historical necessity is on their side.' This is how we felt in the early 1930's. Our lives, social and political and cultural, were made over to the Party. My own introduction to Party life was not actually fortunate, and it says much for the basic truths of Marxism that I survived the first few months. Our 'cell' (soon to be incorporated in a proper Branch) was led by a man whose chief interest was in hair-splitting discussions of Marxist texts and who was defeatist about political action. 'The Party is weak, comrades,' he used to intone at nearly every meeting. His remedy was that we ought to disband and enter the Labour Party en masse. We were a group of ten or a dozen people, only one of whom was a manual worker: a Welsh building-labourer to whom we all looked up as our only 'proletarian'. His main contribution to our education was to growl at us, and particularly at the cell leader, whom he called Comrade Gravel (his name was Greville), as 'armchair socialists' ... It took me a little time to realise that he himself never took part in any activity and spent most of his evenings in the pub. I went to try and recruit his wife. 'No, Mrs Green,' she said. 'I reckon communism begins at home, and when he begins to stay at home with the kids and give me a night out now and then, I'll think about joining.' The poor woman really thought that his evenings had been spent, as he told her, in 'party work'. I tackled him about this in the group. He growled surly male-chauvinist abuse at us and stopped coming to meetings altogether.

Nevertheless our 'cell' was a happy group. The sharing of difficult tasks for a common ideal brings people very close together and it was 'glad, confident morning' for us. Mainly students, with a handful of clerical workers like me, two jolly sisters, daughters of an Italian restaurateur, a sign writer, a billiard marker and a cartographer, we lived a Bohemian life, all hard up and financially insecure, helping one another out of holes and endlessly discussing not only Marxism but life in all its aspects. But *basic* Marxism we got. In our rejection of everything we characterised as 'bourgeois', babies were thrown out with the bathwater with reckless abandon. Marriage was an outdated institution; children should be taken from their parents at birth and brought up by the State; property was theft ... I remember a young woman sniffing a bunch of violets on my table and saying guiltily: 'It may be bourgeois, but I do like flowers!' There was much changing of partners, in the name of sexual freedom.

But strangely enough it was to George and me, the only firmly and 'conventionally' married members of the group, that many of them came for help and advice or shoulders to cry on. Because, as George once said wisely, precisely because we were happily married with a stable relationship and two lovely children. We were the free ones, really.

The children having attained school age, they began to attend the local elementary school, only a few yards from our house. Frances was mightily pleased. She had been pestering a long time to go to 'a proper ABC school' but I didn't want to separate the two of them, so we waited until Martin was almost five before changing over. I managed to continue working for a time, because there was a group of social workers who ran a midday meal service for such mothers as I at Coram's Fields,[53] and when they finished school at four o'clock we had a charlady who gave them their tea and waited until I arrived from the office.

But what to do in school holidays? Chance provided the answer. The LCC[54] had just then passed a bye-law prohibiting shopkeepers from cluttering the pavement outside their shops with goods. We had an acquaintance who sold second-hand books. About half his stock was displayed outside on the pavement and was brought in at night, filling the shop completely. He offered, quite casually, to give us this surplus if we would cart it away. Our flat, the former bakery I have described, had one enormous room. We lined one entire wall with shelves and brought the books there on a coster-monger's barrow. We hired a pitch, including two trestles and some boards, at Caledonian Market, which used to open Tuesdays and Fridays. Each Tuesday and Friday we pushed a barrow load of books up Pentonville Road (George pushed and I pulled) and in the afternoons, George having gone to work, I pushed back the stock we had not sold (or rather allowed it to pull me downhill). Incredibly, provided we did not have two rainy days in succession, we made more in these efforts than I had been earning weekly in my office job! Our stock was replenished in the following way: I visited specialist second-hand booksellers all round Bloomsbury, especially near the British Museum, offering to buy books they did not want. These specialists sought their books at country sales, where they often bought lots of 100 or so book to obtain perhaps four or five they wanted, and were quite willing to sell their surplus to me at ten bob a barrow load. I learned quite a lot about the second-hand book trade from this experience.

Pleased with this success, we decided to set up another stall for the sale of Party literature, next to the first one. This did not make money but any loss was offset by the secular sales. The market authorities did not approve of this stall, and tried to prohibit it, on the grounds that it might cause 'disturbance'. It would not be we, we argued, that caused the disturbance, we were doing something perfectly legal. Now, whether the authorities encouraged or initiated this, a notice appeared one Tuesday on a site opposite ours, saying that the Fascist party was going to hold a meeting there on the Friday. This might well have brought about a nasty scene. We left the children with friends that day and set up our stall as usual. The stall-holders around us, with all of whom we had made friends, rallied round in a magnificent way, particularly two chaps who sold secondhand motor parts and tyres; these two from the moment the market was opened up in the morning began, without saying a word to us, to stroll up and down in front of our stall casually *swinging huge spanners* and they were soon joined by others ... We had done nothing at all to instigate this, a gesture of pure spontaneous solidarity. The Fascist meeting did not take place.

In the summer of 1935 we spent a fortnight at a Party Summer school, where we hammered out the lessons of the 7th World Congress and the new line of Dimitrov – the united front against Fascism.[55] From scornful hostility towards social democracy, which some, at the behest of the Communist International, called 'social fascism' (with fatal effect in Germany for instance), we set about building unity with the Labour Party. I am not writing a history of this phase in the Communist Party of Great Britain nor of the Communist International, both of which are still (1979) being pieced together by those whose rose-coloured spectacles have been replaced by clear glass, or by those younger ones who never had them. I am just telling how the events of those days affected me and other rank and filers. The degree of unity we achieved at grass-roots level – in the teeth of the implacable hatred of the Labour leadership – now almost surprises me.

The 'cell' by now having been amalgamated with others into a Branch (of which, I honestly don't know why, I was made Secretary) I went to the Labour Party candidate in the election at the time to offer our help. He accepted, on condition that we did only the background work – addressing envelopes, folding and filling election addresses, flyposting and even chalking VOTE LABOUR, but not canvassing nor speaking at meetings. We worked so hard that he paid grateful tribute to us, but we ruined it all by issuing our own independent leaflet saying (in effect), 'Communists say vote Labour', which caused him to accuse us furiously of having lost him votes.

Meanwhile George, having achieved 100 per cent orchestra trade unionism in the Tottenham Court Road Corner House, set about recruiting the waitresses into the Transport and General Workers Union. (At that time these girls were paid ten shillings a week from which, beside their insurance contributions, a shilling a week was deduced to pay for their uniforms, and were expected to gain the bulk of their livelihood from tips and commission). He was moved to the Strand and soon the orchestra there was fully organised. He was moved to Coventry Street, with the same effect. *Crescendo* was crescendo!

How we rejoiced in the next few months when William Gallacher was elected to Parliament. How we cheered the victories of the Front Populaire in France. How strong we felt when we stopped Moseley's Blackshirts from marching through Stepney.[56]

Along with hundreds of others, I had held in my pockets a batch of tiny little leaflets which we were to release, if our demonstration had been successful (as it was), calling for a march to Victoria Park. I shall never forget the triumph I felt when, having thrown the leaflets into the air and seen them fluttering down, I presently felt a movement in the immense crowd as it formed into a procession and started down the road. We were on the winning side ...

And all the while we were enthusiastically doing 'party work'. The two young daughters of the Italian restaurateur joined our group and they and I took it in turns to sell the *Daily Worker* in the evenings outside Russell Square tube station. The *Daily Worker* was not recognised by the Newspaper Proprietors Association and did not enjoy the facilities of the newspaper trains, etc. Consequently, to be sold at breakfast time, it has to come off the press early in the evening of the day before publication (and even so, in places further north, it was out a day late: and hundreds of devoted communists met early trains and cycled miles, in all weathers, to bring bundles of the paper to newsagents or even to deliver to private houses. I do not feel at all sure that such self-sacrificing zeal could be found in today's party in so consistent a way, though I know many who continue to carry on boring, humdrum, day to day activity with no reward but a sense of duty done). Anyway, the girls and I stood outside Russell Square tube station, having collected our quire or two from Britannia Street around 8.30 p.m. and shouting 'Read tomorrow's news today!' It wasn't always easy. People sneered. Soft-hearted gents with an eye to something else began by saying, 'I hate to see a nice girl like you reduced to this: let me buy up the lot and then come with me and ...' People spat, and said, 'GO back to Moscow.' But there were rewarding incidents – for example, the coster who had a barrow opposite the station selling fruit, and in the winter hot chestnuts, established himself my protector and used to cross the pavement if he saw me being harassed and square up all his five foot nothing, growling, 'You leave the young lady alone, see!' Or the rather elderly prostitute whose 'beat' included Russell Square and environs, who bought the paper regularly and one night confidentially said, 'Listen, love, if you have to go away at any time, tell your husband to get in touch with me. I'll see he gets a nice clean girl.' In return for the costermonger's help and friendship, I used to warn him if a cop approached – he was allowed to ply his trade only if he kept moving, and had to push the barrow a few yards to right or left whenever one went past. But there was *one* cop (who turned into a friend and eventually joined the party) for whom I kept a folded-up copy of the paper and stuffed under his cape as he strolled past by sleight of hand.

But the clouds of war were darkening fast and Fascism was gaining ground all over Europe.

VI

It was early in 1937 that George and I were shopping in Leather Lane, London. He said: 'I've got to go to Spain.' I said 'Yes.' I can't recollect that we discussed the matter any further at that moment. Later he told me that he was confident that I could and would 'hold the fort' at home; I agreed that I could, and would. Because by now the British Government had invoked the obsolescent Foreign Enlistment Act, we decided to tell no one of his departure.[57] By chance, the Spanish Medical Aid needed someone to drive a truck out to Spain (in convoy with a couple of ambulances). George drove the truck. The day he left we told Grandpa Green he was going, so that he could come to the offices in Oxford Street and say goodbye. When I spoke to him on the telephone, he simply said: 'Aye, if I were ten years younger, I'd go myself,' and sped to the farewell.

After he had left I went to the conductor of the orchestra he was then working for, to tell him George wouldn't be playing for him any more. He was completely flabbergasted. 'But what about the job?' he kept asking, as if no musician could for any reason give up a job in those days of insecurity.

This was early in February 1937. My sister Mem, on being told the news, wrote to me: 'How history does knock one about ...' to which I replied: 'This is where we start knocking history about.' Harry Grisebrook, my brother-in-law, sent a letter full of heartfelt abuse to George for 'deserting' his wife and family. 'Listen,' I wrote back full of outraged pride, 'George and I are thinking of more than our own children, we are thinking of the children of Europe, in danger of being killed in the coming war if we don't stop the Fascists in Spain.'

'Holding the fort' was not easy, but was not nearly as difficult as it might have been if I had not had support from the Party and other anti-fascists. Our (Jewish) landlord instantly reduced the rent we paid for our flat by one third. I got a job in a nearby office from whence I could come home by four o'clock to meet the children from school. Grandpa Green was, as ever, the tower of strength. The children, who missed their father, were nevertheless proud of him. A canvasser for the Conservatives in some local election called at the house, asking for Mr Green. Frances stoutly told him: 'My Daddy has gone to Spain to fight the Fascists.' With Grandpa Green devotedly baby-sitting, I continued to serve as Branch Secretary, cycling round to visit every one of our sixty-three members at least once a month.

Early in July 1937, Wogan Philipps came to see me.[58] He had left England driving one of the ambulances in the convoy that George had driven in. He brought a proposition. It seemed they needed someone like me (an organiser) to assist the Medical Aid Units from Britain, which had plenty of nurses, doctors, ambulance drivers and stretcher bearers but not enough administrative personnel. He had brought a request that I should go out to Spain; he himself had been wounded and did not intend to go back. The son of a peer, he was not without resources. He proposed to free me to go to Spain by paying for my children to go to *any boarding school of my choice.* (His wife, Rosamund Lehmann later wrote that Wogan had undergone 'a Pauline conversion to Communism', and after George's death Wogan wrote, 'knowing George changed the whole course of my life.')

I walked up and down for a *whole night* of turmoil, trying to decide what was best. I talked it over with Grandpa Green the following day. What was best for the children? If it had not been for the existence of A.B. Neill's Summerhill School I could never have contemplated sending them to boarding school. But I believed in Summerhill and knew that they would be in an atmosphere in which their father's action in going to Spain would meet with full sympathy and approval. They would be in the country, have fresh and healthy food, learning in freedom – and Grandpa Green would see them every week. But ought I to leave them? Hadn't I promised George to 'hold the fort'? Would the separation (however temporary) from both parents make them unhappy? Was I rationalising a desire to escape from the heavy responsibility I was burdened with?

I don't know. To this day I don't know whether I did right to go. But anyway I went, intending to return in no more than six months, and staying, in the event, for almost a year. Without Wogan's marvellous generosity and Grandpa's flawless love and devotion it would not have been possible. My dear friend, Winifred (then married to Ralph Bates), who was in charge of British medical personnel in Spain, told me years later that she opposed, when it was suggested that I should be sent for, my leaving London because the Party Branch, of which we were both members, would 'fall to pieces' without me as Secretary. It didn't, of course. No one is irreplaceable.

Our good, kind landlord, out of anti-fascist sympathy and the kindness of his heart, not only refused the last fortnight's rent but purchased the whole wall-full of books (remnants of our Caledonian Market venture), which added a decorative touch to the flat, though as books they were nearly worthless. Ed Ostrey, a Canadian medical student and member of our Branch, agreed to accommodate a huge theatrical 'skip', containing such of our household goods as I deemed worth retaining. What incredible kindness I have met with during my life!

The children were fitted out for school and both left happily, hardly finding time to say goodbye when, in a railway carriage full of future friends, the train pulled out. (Martin was already concentrating on a train set carried by a boy of his own age – with whom he remains friends to this day). Wogan stood me a slap-up farewell lunch at the now-defunct Holborn Restaurant, saying, 'You'd better eat as much as you can because you won't get anything like this in Spain,' and that evening I caught the train for Paris, with two heavy suitcases containing a few clothes and a vast quantity of medical supplies.

Paris was the scene of the International Exposition, where, before catching the night train to the Spanish border, I stood spellbound at Picasso's *Guernica*, noted the competitive vulgarity of the German and Soviet pavilions, and snorted in disdain at the British contribution – mostly tweeds, pipes, walking sticks and sports gear, I seem to remember. Then to the station, to catch the train to Puigcerda, on which I encountered Wilfred Roberts, the Liberal M.P., who was one of the leading figures in the National Joint Committee for Spanish Relief – a very broad organisation ('united front') of which Medical Aid was an associate, though separate.[59]

By the afternoon of the following day I was in Barcelona, with the address of my destination on a piece of paper, two heavy suitcases, next to no money and few words of Spanish. There were no trams and no buses – there was a temporary power cut on and it was Sunday in any case. Failing to get through on the telephone I set off, dragging the suitcases and, by showing people the paper at every crossroads and following where they pointed, eventually reached Calle Balmes, the reception centre for Medical Aid people.

The wild enthusiasm which had characterised Barcelona twelve months before was no longer so much in evidence, the Anarchist '*incontrolados*' having been brought to some extent under control, and hardship was by then beginning to leave its mark on the scene.[60]

People looked tired, drawn and often shabby – but gallant and not downhearted. Buildings were pitted with the pockmarks of machine-gun fire. Dust and rubble gave off that acrid smell which afterwards became so familiar to me in embattled London three and four years later. Yet an incredibly battered tramcar was proceeding slowly through the street; it had served as an armoured car, with which, during the first days of the Fascist rebellion, a group of workers had successfully stormed one of the public buildings; now decorated with slogans and banners, it was accompanied by a group of gay young people collecting for the Red Cross. I was told this happened every Sunday. And carnations were being sold in the flower stalls on the Ramblas!

My perceptions are quicker through the eyes than through the ears, and both are quicker than my *uptake*. I take a long time to draw conclusions, and thoughts and impressions tumbled around in my head as I set about reconciling my imagination with reality. I found myself wishing I could swallow some sort of mixture which would make me (in terms of a then new kind of process which gave much greater depth to black and white films) *panchromatic*. It was all too new, and things happened so fast that I had no time to consider what they meant.

My destination was already arranged. Next morning I was given a *salvo conducto*, a sheet of paper entitling me to travel to it. Travel, how? At all exits to Barcelona there were guard posts which stopped every vehicle leaving the city and loaded them with passengers to wherever they were going – a kind of military hitch-hiking. After an hour or so of waiting, I was shoved on to an open lorry with about twenty others and we set off. After spending the night at the convalescent hospital in Benicassim, where I met Angela Guest,[61] I went through the same process next morning and later in the same day found myself at Huete, in what was called 'the English hospital'. To my profound astonishment, I found George there.

Now, George had left for Spain with the firm intention of joining the International Brigade as soon as he had delivered his lorry, and I had only a vague idea that he was still retained in the medical service. (Letters were censored, and one sent the replies to a code address which did not indicate where the writer was). He had sent me some carefully guarded accounts of battles in

which he had participated, of the death of Julian Bell and that of
Izzy Kupchik and others we knew,[62] and a vivid though typically
understated account of his first experience of aerial bombardment
('strafing') in which he described how he lay in a ditch and
'experienced a sudden fondness' for his *hands* – the hands, don't
forget, of a cellist.

A little while before my arrival he had burned the skin of one
arm by getting under his ambulance to examine a choked feed
of petrol on a mountain road, and freezing petrol had run down
his arm, taking off an area of skin. He had been sent to Huete
for treatment and was almost recovered. Meanwhile he was
appointed Political Commissar of the Hospital.

It was pure chance and good fortune that brought us together
now. I had not had the ridiculous idea that I was going to Spain
'to join my husband' and, though I had a deep-down hope that
we would meet, I had no expectation of this incredible bonus.
It was sheer unadulterated joy.

George was a good Commissar. I shall later recount a couple
of typical incidents to illustrate his qualities. Part of his job was
to promote the welfare of patients and staff, and on this day he
had arranged a concert for such patients as could walk or be
carried to the large 'recreation hall' – formerly, perhaps, a chapel
in what had been a monastery. He had bought himself a cello;
a Bavarian lad with an injured leg played the violin (by ear), the
village plumber was an excellent guitarist, though equally illiterate
musically, and a Catalan patient, also with a leg injury, played
the *bandurrión* (a sort of mandolin). George taught them tunes,
and they already had quite a credible repertoire. A departing
patient had left behind an accordion. Early in the afternoon
George showed me this, and said that I should play it with his
orchestra that evening. 'But I can't play the accordion!' I protested.
'You will, by tonight,' he replied firmly. The keyboard side was
of course easy, since I had had piano lessons as a child. I learned
a dozen or so chords during the afternoon and dutifully took my

place in the orchestra that evening (it must have sounded dreadful).

Next day I was introduced to my job: Assistant Secretary. The Chief Administrator was British, as were the surgeon in charge, theatre sisters, ward sisters (who included three New Zealand nurses) and one or two ambulance drivers. Somewhat to my disillusionment, I found that there were wheels within political wheels, colouring the relations and actions of this collection of people. The anti-Communism of the Conservatives and the Labour leadership had its reflection here, and I came to suspect (though never to prove) that the Foreign Office had its long finger in this and other pies.

Nevertheless, tremendously devoted work was done and the Spanish people (patients – mostly peasants, staff and the villagers of Huete) were a glorious example and lesson to all. The training of village girls as nurses and wardmaids was speeded by their eagerness to learn and their devotion to the work, far out-running the expectations of our nurses. Like Cromwell's men, they knew what they were fighting for, and loved what they knew.

I have never forgotten an old grandmother to whose cave-house (half of Huete's houses consisted of caves hollowed out of the hillside in the village) I went, trying to recruit women for the hospital laundry and linen room. Her daughter, for whom I was searching, was out and she was surrounded by several grandchildren, one or two of whom were of school age. On the whitewashed wall of the cave were stuck some children's drawings, done in coloured crayons. 'Look,' she said pointing proudly to them, 'before the Republic there wasn't a pencil in this village, and now all the children go to school. YES, my daughter will come and help! Those wounded men are fighting so that our children can learn.'

My principal workmate was Pere Barat, a gaunt, frail-looking Catalan about thirty years old who had TB. Like many Catalans he spoke French and Castilian as well as his mother tongue, which is to some extent a mixture of the other two. In the scanty intervals of our work of keeping the hospital records, he patiently taught me Castilian (using French, which at that time I knew better). For my first lessons in what later became almost a second language to me and contributed to my subsequent history, I thank Pere (Pedro) for the kind, patient, persistent, thorough grounding he gave me, supplemented by study of a huge *Jesperson* Grammar.[63]

I don't want to exaggerate the political undercurrents. The British nurses were absolute models of efficiency and devotion and most of them entirely 'non-political', caring only for their healing mission. I shall never forget, as a single example, Dorothy Lowe,[64] a sister who had served most of her nursing career in the British Army, who received in her ward three injured men who, because of negligence in another hospital, were near to death. Through sheer *nursing* she brought all three back to life and health, cleaning up their disgraceful bedsores, tending their wounds, supervising their diet and scarcely leaving them day or night. And all this, remember, before antibiotics had been heard of, before M & B had emerged from the laboratories, in a chronic shortage of medical supplies of all kinds, when soap and water was often the only antiseptic available and even the supply of soap was terribly short. A history of the achievements of the British medical units in Spain is long overdue. I hope someone will write it.

This is a chronicle of small beer. I can only tell what I saw and experienced. Here is the tale of some of the day to day problems which George, as Political Commissar, had to cope with. Our patients, reflecting the composition of the Spanish People's Army, were mainly peasants. Their experience of hospitals had, in the main, been limited to such hospitals as were run by the Catholic Church, manned (or womaned) by nuns, who in the main (and in the old days) were more concerned with saving souls than with saving bodies. Rightly or wrongly, a good number of our patients were *afraid* of nuns. Now, some of the British nurses cherished, as was natural, their status, which was often indicated by details of their uniform (as it is today in such institutions as St Thomas's Hospital where the difference between a blue belt and a white one is a step in an upward direction). These nurses, having been Sisters at home, were proud to wear headgear consisting of a white square, folded into a triangle with the point hanging down their backs. This head-dress terrified some of the patients, resembling as it did that of some nursing orders. It fell to George to persuade these British Sisters to forego their status symbols. It was difficult, but he succeeded. I watched him one day trying to shift an enormous cupboard with the aid of two very young stretcher-bearers, Spaniards. They pushed, pulled and heaved without making any difference.

'It is impossible, George,' said one of the lads.

'To Communists nothing is impossible,' George replied. One more heave, and the cupboard moved ...

One night, someone came running for George. The hospital guard, an Irishman, had managed to get drunk and was behaving violently. I ran, with George, to the guard post. George looked on for a few moments and then said in his quiet voice: 'Well, sorry Paddy, old man!' and with one well-calculated punch to the jaw, laid him out and carried him carefully away.

A fiesta was planned, I think it was to commemorate the October Revolution, in which the hospital invited the entire village to participate. In preparation for this, a bar was set up in what had been the crypt of the monastery and was now the garage for ambulances. To make an inspection pit, some flagstones had been removed, uncovering some human bones. An American artist, one of our patients, devised a banner to hang at the back of the bar, depicting caricatures of Franco, Hitler and Mussolini and, to point the lesson, had hung some of the bones beneath the banner. The point was raised, might this not antagonise the villagers, to whose ancestors maybe the bones belonged? In the aftermath of my personal repudiation of the Christian religion, I was vehemently in favour of leaving the bones there. 'I don't like finding myself on the opposite side to my wife,' said George, and proceeded to remind us of the meaning of the Popular Front.[65] The bones were taken down and re-interred, and I swallowed my lesson without too much difficulty.

During that month (November 1937) George experienced a musical triumph. An invitation came to bring his 'orchestra' to Madrid and broadcast some music for England, as accompaniment to an appeal for medical supplies. George was to make the appeal. We rehearsed and rehearsed, and set off for Madrid in a truck belonging to the hospital. The old *fontanero*, the village plumber/guitarist, who had been there once before in his life, croaked sadly and repeatedly as we drove through the darkened streets: 'Madrid is not Madrid without lights!' In an extremely Heath Robinson sort of studio we played our tunes, gritting our teeth lest Bavarian Willi, as was his ineradicable habit, introduced an extra beat into his bar to the confusion of the rest. All went well to our enormous gratification, and we were visited early next morning by two chaps from the Radio, proposing that we should stay another night and make a *world* broadcast. Alas, our truck had to get back to Huete and we had to go with it.

VII

In December, George at last attained his desire and was discharged to go to the front and join the British battalion. At almost the same time, I was appointed Administrator of a hospital for convalescents at Valdeganga, which had in the past been a hydropathic hotel, being located by some hot springs of chemically-impregnated water which emerged from under the ground nearly boiling. It had been a health resort for rich people; there were marble bathtubs with silver-plated taps in the shape of swans' heads.

My job at Valdeganga was not an easy one. The accounts and records were in a state of confusion. The hospital was paid so much per head of patients – consequently if the number of patients fell we got less money per month to run it and to remain solvent we sometimes had to layoff staff, mainly girls from the nearby village, which was an anarchist stronghold. Angry deputations on behalf of the temporarily unemployed followed. Rightly or wrongly we suspected Huete, which was supposed to send us *its* convalescents, of hanging on to them unnecessarily for the sake of its solvency. At intervals, when a battle raised the number of injured, they would send us a new batch of patients and then we could bring the staff up to full strength again. The village girls, mostly wardmaids and kitchen hands, slept together in two dormitories and as it was winter, and a mountainous situation (snow fell that Christmas, very unusually) they often shared beds for warmth; *scabies* broke out among them. It became necessary to decontaminate them, their clothing and their bedclothes simultaneously. The majority of the girls possessed only one pair of corsets, which they refused to give up ... the Austrian Medical Officer bullied them, I was for persuasion; Frank Ayres, the Political Commissar, explained and explained and explained; and we eventually won the battle.

I am sorry to say that the Medical Officer had become a drug addict, and was appropriating the hospital's supply of morphia; to obtain more, he had to obtain my signature for a requisition. When I began to suspect him, he invented an unknown addict among the patients and protested that, 'these people were so cunning that it was impossible to trace them.' He also made passes at me, not I am sure for my beaux yeux but to neutralise my hostility.

I believe that due to the altitude we were all infected with a touch of 'mountain sickness' and lived in a permanent state of mild excitement. The physiotherapist (an excellent one), a refugee from Austria who had done all her training in England and had joined the Communist Party there, possessed a Teutonic political rigidity and started a whispering vendetta against Frank the Commissar because he flatly refused to remove some Anarchist literature from the patients' library ... This was at the height of the Soviet-inspired hatred of 'Trotskyism', which spilled over into the Communist movement everywhere and made heresy-hunting a righteous crusade for many members.[66]

Wise old Frank Ayres, whose experience in the movement was longer than that of all the rest (a Yorkshire railwayman, he had joined the Communist Party in its earliest days and had worked politically in several countries), ignored the vendetta. The Medical Officer now did something which turned us into open enmity. Frank was summoned to make a short visit to England, to report to the Spanish Medical Aid Committee on the needs of the hospital service. He had been keeping a little book of memoranda on the behaviour and characters of the medical personnel with whom he had been in contact. He considered whether to leave this with me to keep in my office safe, but decided that it would be asking

too much to expect me not to read it. I don't know whether I
would have done so or not, but at all events it would be a great
temptation. Consequently he gave it to Anita, with whom he had
started to fall in love. His confidential reports would be quite safe
with her, since she didn't know a word of English. Anita was the
assistant housekeeper at the hospital, a former film star whose
personal beauty was matched by her nature, and who had
volunteered for the medical service from the outbreak of war. She
was assistant to an elderly, sly and sycophantic woman called
Felisa, who, wanting to stand well with the Medical Officer and
to curry favour with him, reported that Anita had a book hidden
under her mattress. Frank had been gone only a few days when
this wretched man reported her to the civil police as a spy who
had stolen Frank's book to give to the enemy. Police came in the
middle of the night and whisked her away to prison in the town
of Cuenca, some miles away.

I charged off to Cuenca next morning and after several tortuous
days of interviews, depositions, counter-depositions, enquiries and
table-thumpings, succeeded in obtaining her release (returning in
triumph with her to the hospital from which she was promptly
fired by the MC and went to Valencia, her home town. He now
turned on me, first inventing an accusation of embezzlement,
against me on the flimsy ground that I did the book-keeping in
an account book which had, when I first took it over, nothing in
it except a figure, on the first line of the first page of 1000 pesetas.
As this meant nothing, I had simply turned the page and started
my accounts on the second page, ignoring the first. He called a
meeting of staff and patients and, having filched, or caused to be
filched, the account book from my office, began a heavy diatribe
against me. 'What has happened to the thousand pesetas?' He
failed to make the accusation stick – it was too silly, but mud
had been slung and sides were taken. The atmosphere
deteriorated. Eventually he drove me to the Medical HQ in
Albacete, where he made God knows what allegations about me

to the authorities (some of which followed me round to my later jobs though I did not know it until much later). Unable or unwilling to verify or prove these charges, the authority (I can't remember who) interviewed me with the pretext that for a Medical Officer and his Administrator to be at Loggerheads was bad for the hospital, and I was therefore ordered to resign.

(Among the allegations I *did* hear of in a sort of preliminary gruelling by two Austrian officials, was that I was an imposter; not Nan Green at all but actually the wife of Egon Erwin Kisch, the Czech writer.[67] Indignantly I produced my passport, which was confiscated: I only go it back after vehement protests and lying denials.)

Angry and apparently friendless I went back to the hospital, collected my things and found myself again in Albacete with nothing to do. I went to the Commissar of the International Brigades; it wasn't his affair but he agreed to send me to the medical HQ in Barcelona, where I could be re-employed. I got on a crowded troop-train, but before it had gone far it stopped and remained on the lines for 24 hours (though we did not know it, the road to the north had been cut by the Fascist breakthrough to the coast). At which point, to my tremendous relief, Frank appeared like a god out of a machine and whisked me off to the villa at Valencia where medical aid personnel had their second reception centre, like the one in Barcelona – Frank, having been charged in London with the care of Spanish Medical Aid personnel, and having heard that I was on a train leaving for Barcelona.

I cannot leave this episode without going back to say something about the hospital at Valdeganga, where some splendid work was done and where I had many happy times. All round the hospital, on the mountainsides, lavender grew wild. When you walked, brushing against the stunted plants, you released their lovely perfume. The villagers were, except when agitated about the wardmaids, immensely friendly. We gave a children's party for

New Year 1938. Parents came and happily watched their offspring feasting (how we managed it I don't remember, but we gave them each *one chocolate*, something most of them had never seen, to end their meal). In the remote village of Valdeganga there had been a great deal of intermarriage – it seemed as if all the children introduced each other as 'my cousin', and a number of them had the common feature of the two middle fingers of each hand being joined together. At the end of the feast, one child started singing in rhyming couplets a well-known tune and this was taken up by one after another, each providing a new verse. It began 'Long Live the English Hospital, Long Live all the Wounded!' and I remember no more words but do remember my astonishment and emotion at the succession of verses and the childish voices joining in.

The village had a very small power station, the manager of which used to come to the hospital on Saturday nights with his wife for our weekly dance. He played the fiddle and she the piano. Half or more of our patients were sufficiently mobile to dance, but there was great difficulty about partners for them. Village girls in those days could not be *touched* before marriage by any man but their fathers or brothers, and to have danced with a stranger was likely to ruin the chance of a husband. I prepared, and recited each Saturday night, an earnest speech pleading with the girls to regard these wounded men as their brothers, but only a few of the bolder ones responded; the rest danced with other girls, while our poor patients danced with one another.

The fiddle player was called up, and his wife left the village to go to her parents. Out came the old accordion, and for two or three hours on Saturday nights I sat on the bar at one end of the recreation room, sawing away at foxtrots, paso dobles and the everlasting 'Over the Wave', only about ten tunes in all. The kind bartender (a patient) used to keep filled at the side of my stool a tin mug full of very rough, sweet vermouth. It was my weekly trial of strength-in-the-head to pack up my instrument at the end, sling it over my shoulder and walk in a dead straight line to the door and across to the hospital.

The Austrian physiotherapist, notwithstanding, and quite superseding her mischief-making, did wonders in devising equipment for the exercising and re-training of injured limbs. We had two ping-pong tables which were a grand inducement to the use of stiff or wasted arms and legs.

An elderly Canadian called Arthur Tazzaman, who was ill with gastritis and suspected the cooks of poisoning him – to such an extent that I formed a rota of people to sit with him at meal-times and exchange plates as soon as we were served, conquered his pain and disability to the extent of rescuing three wrecks of motor vehicles that lay about the roadsides on the way to the hospital and, with the help of everyone who could hold a spanner or recognise the parts of an engine, built the three wrecks into one complete new truck. He almost wept with anxiety each time he saw it being driven out of the hospital by our slap-happy Spanish drivers, and almost wept with relief each time it came back unharmed.

Frank had returned from England to wind-up the English section of the hospital at Uclés – newly adopted by the Spanish Medical Aid Committee. I don't know how Uclés came to be chosen, but the reason for the adoption reflected the dichotomy in the 'broad' movement in England, which had very real problems. The 'Aid Spain' movement had to contend with that proportion of public opinion swayed by the intense campaign of the Conservatives (and their mouthpieces in the press), which sought to present the Republican side as REDS, regardless of the fact that at the outset of the war the Popular Front was broadly socialist and the Communist Party at no time had more than two Ministers in the Republican Government. Franco, to them, was a gallant Christian Gentleman conducting a sacred crusade against the wicked Reds, stooges of Moscow, etc. This picture of the struggle did not much affect the vast majority of workers in Britain, but the Aid Spain movement needed and wanted support from wealthy supporters whose humanitarian sentiments were not always strong enough to overcome their fear of being characterised as 'fellow travellers' or worse. The British Medical units had started from Britain as a purely humanitarian mission, but had naturally become involved in the anti-fascist struggle as a whole, which involved association with Spanish communists and the International Brigades, as well as with Spanish socialists, Republicans, and other parties from left to right. What were known back home as 'English' hospitals, of necessity came under the control of the Republican Government; British medical staff were attached to units of the Republican Army and their admiration for the-Spanish people's magnificent struggle naturally affected their political thinking. In London, there was a kind of ceaseless effort to keep or present the medical missions as politically 'pure', in the effort not to alienate the committee members or fracture the broad front of the movement.

Uclás, as I see it, was just one more effort from the London committee to establish a new and totally *uninvolved* charity venture. A fresh batch of British nurses, hand-picked for their non-Left character and background, had been sent to this new venue and a lot of money was poured in to assist the hospital with equipment and other things it lacked. There was to be a 'Leah Manning Ward',[68] a new operating theatre, and the beginning had been made to improve the sanitation (which was deplorable). In fact, so 'uninvolved' were the Spanish staff and management that they leaned heavily to the Right. (When Franco troops arrived in 1939 after the Republic's defeat, some of the doctors got out their fascist blue shirts from their suitcases, and went out to greet them.)

Old Frank had been sent from London to wind-up this venture. He took me and Anita with him. We found: a line of concrete pipes leading down hill from the hospital (an ex-monastery, far larger than the one at Huete) to what was intended to be a new septic tank; money had been sent from England to complete the job but some of it had been temporarily 'diverted' to pay the hospital staff. A dry moat round the whole building, into which they had been throwing soiled dressings, and bits of amputated limbs, was now the home of a large rat colony; an empty ward with a notice over its door to say it was to be the Leah Manning Ward and a general state of. hostility towards us. There was no job for me. Anita took charge of a barely furnished little house which had been given over for a British Nurses' Home. I undertook, to the best of my ability, while I waited for the official call that Frank had demanded from Barcelona for me, to do what I could to raise the morale of those poor British girls who had been thrown into this shambles: one of my daily jobs was to delouse them when they came off the wards. They were not permitted to go on night duty. I remember one of them weeping – she had a patient who was paraplegic, and one night a rat had got into his bed and gnawed his leg, which of course had no sensation in it. She had procured four big tins, filled them with disinfectant and set the legs of the bed in them. The night nurses had removed the tins because they 'looked untidy' ... I also manufactured a shower bath out of a biscuit tin (into which holes were punctured) which was set on the wall in a corner of the garden; standing on a chair I used to pour jugs of water while the girls washed themselves below.

I can't have stayed there more than three or four weeks, waiting for the official call Frank had demanded for me to go to Barcelona. But I remember May Day 1938, because I broke down for the first time. There was no one in the house. I had had no letters for nearly a month. I didn't know where George was. I started thinking of previous May Days, the gay flags and slogans, of pushing my darling children in their double push-chair from the Embankment to Hyde Park, and began an overwhelming weep. I went into the kitchen, put my head into the roller towel on the back of the door and the floodgates opened. Frank and Anita came in and found me. Dear Anita came quickly, put her arms round me and wept with me. Presently she said: '*What are we crying about, Nan?*' Gruff, practical old Frank brought cups of strong tea and aspirins. Many years later he told me that up to that moment he had regarded me as admirably efficient and stony-hearted, but then my tears had warmed his feelings into affection.

The only other useful job I did during my short stay at Uclés was to assist Frank's wooing of Anita. His Spanish at that time was rather more limited than mine and I was on hand as an interpreter. '*Que dice*, Nan?' (what does he say) was Anita's constant question. Mind you, they could, I am sure, have managed very well without me. But those two dear friends, on their silver wedding anniversary in London twenty-five years later, drank a special toast to me as their 'go-between' ...

Soon the official call came for me to go north. How to get there? The road was cut. The Spanish authorities refused, quite rightly, to give me any sort of safe-conduct papers. I can't remember how, but Frank managed to arrange for me to travel to Marseilles on a British battleship (the *Sussex*), as ostensible escort to one of the English nurses who was being invalided home. The excruciating gallantry with which the officers of the *Sussex* provided for our comfort (starting with cups of tea in delicate china and thin white bread and butter with raspberry jam for our first meal on board, not to mention the stationing of a seaman outside our cabin, ready to escort us up the companionway to the deck, carrying anything such as a book we might have in our hands) made the three-day voyage dreamlike in contrast to the rough, sparse rations and conditions we had been used to. Three times we were asked: 'Has anyone shown you where the BATHROOM is?' At Marseilles I saw Penny on to her train, purchased a long list of medical supplies with which I had been charged to obtain by Frank, and went to the British Consul for a permit to return to Spain. He severely accused me of 'using the British Navy as a taxi-service to get about the

Mediterranean', which was of course precisely what I had done. However, after some persuasion he gave me the required document. I flew back to Barcelona; it was the first time in my life that I had ever been on an aeroplane.

There was a job ready and waiting for me. I was to go to the front, as secretary to the Chief Medical Officer of the 35th Division.

It would have been wise, at this stage, to fight my way through the sinister series of events that had led to my dismissal from Valdeganga, and demand vindication. I did not do it. First, I was so glad to have a job again. Secondly, I convinced myself that, since everyone in Barcelona believed in me sufficiently to send me to a responsible job, and since it was a critical stage in the war, I would be wasting everyone's time just to put myself in the right again. Winifred, it is true, tried to warn me, saying that word was going round that I was an 'adventuress'. I did not heed her, partly because I was trying to suppress a stain on my conscience. In the last turbulent days of Valdeganga I had fallen victim to an ephemeral affair with a patient, a man much younger than myself, which in that over-charged atmosphere (I have spoken of the mountain-sickness) had exploded – and gone out like a rocket. The Medical Officer must have known about it, and probably a lot of others. I was feeling deeply guilty and wanted to put it behind me.

It was not wise because the MC had filed a scurrilous report on me, which had reached not perhaps the medical service but a much higher and more powerful authority, charged with the scrutiny of Communists from all countries. One has only to read a work like Artur London's *Confession*[69] – showing how the mere fact of having served in Spain was enough, in Eastern Europe in the late 1940's and early 1950's, to bring one under suspicion of having been an agent of the Gestapo or the United States, with all the horrible consequences that befell International Brigaders in Czechoslovakia, Rumania, Poland, Hungary and elsewhere. But this is hindsight. It could not have been foreseen at the time, and as matters turned out I did not reap then or later the consequences of my folly (and cowardice).

Barcelona was showing the signs of siege. People's faces were drawn and pale. The civilian rations were more exiguous even than the meagre allowance we received as military. Everyone carried a little cotton bag, containing their daily ration of dark, unpalatable bread, which was no longer served in restaurants – and Spaniards love to eat plenty of bread with all their meals. The port was bombed daily. The children, or a goodly number of them, had been evacuated to places further up the coast, to those heroic 'children's colonies', which continued to educate them, care for them and give them all that love which the Spanish people lavish on their children. A visitor, out from England on behalf of one of the British committees whose main object was to help the children, recounted how she was surprised to find all the tables in the dining room of one of these colonies spread with white table-cloths, with flowers set on them. When she asked if this were not a rather unnecessary expense, she was told: 'But we bring them up to be cultured.' But war-weariness was becoming apparent.

I set off for the front. The front at that time seemed to be the absolute keystone of the fight against Fascism and war. Hitler must be stopped. Even my small contribution might be of help. I was charged with escorting a one-woman deputation from Australia, a railwayman's wife who had been sent by her organisation (of railwayman's wives) which had raised the large sum necessary for her journey, to visit Australians who were serving in Spain and to report on the entire situation of the struggle against Franco. She was a great soul, sturdily determined to undergo any risk or hardship to carry out her mission and to justify the confidence shown in her by her fellow-countrywomen.

Though we did not know it, preparations were beginning for that last great campaign of the Spanish People's Army, the crossing of the Ebro. Leaving Alice at her destination, I reported to the

HQ of the 35th Division Medical Corps and was introduced to Dr Len Crome, the Chief Medical Officer. My job was to type his despatches in formal Spanish; to keep the divisional medical records and turn them into usable statistical information and to stamp every official document which left the HQ with an official rubber stamp that was hung round my neck and stayed there until I left the front four months later. I also acquired a sack of tea, a Primus stove and a small quantity of sugar.

I have sometimes thought that the serving of tea at all hours of the day and night, which made me a sort of welfare officer for our unit (the HQ staff, doctors, ambulance drivers, mechanics, cooks, etc.), was perhaps my main contribution to the battle of the Ebro – apart from the statistics, which *would* have been extremely informative and useful had the battle ended as we were determined it should.

There is a lot of waiting about in an army in wartime; when the battle is raging, morale is high and everyone is busy. It is the waiting about, sometimes not knowing what one is waiting *for,* that brings out the grumbles, boredom, the doubts and discomforts, the homesickness and anxieties that have a bad effect on morale. We were a mixed lot – Spaniards, British, Americans, Canadians, united in purpose but diverse in language, background and culture. It was not my aim to give political pep talks: that was the job of the Commissar. My aim was to try and keep people cheerful. Oddly enough, I found that one of the best antidotes to gloom was to start a conversation about *food.* 'What are hot dogs?' I would ask, and four or five North Americans would instantly and excitedly start to describe their version. We were living on a sufficient but extremely dull diet, consisting mainly of beans, which were affectionately called 'Dr Negrin's Pills' – Negrin having given us the slogan, *'Resistir es Vencer'.*[70] 'What are we eating today?' someone would ask. 'Resistance!' would be the answer. One might have thought that this dwelling on food, the nostalgic descriptions of Sunday ice-cream, Mother's apple-pie, a really good *paella* rich with saffron and garlic, sundaes with chocolate sauce, treacle-tart and custard, would have made people gloomy, but it didn't. It cheered them up.

The HQ of the 35th Division Medical Corps, when I joined it, was located in a decrepit farmhouse. As I sat typing one day in a small dusty 'office' upstairs, a tall, bushy-bearded, bespectacled figure walked in. It was George. A totally unexpected encounter for us both. We embraced, hurriedly exchanged news, read the letters we had each received from dear faithful Grandpa Green and talked of the children ... Then he had to leave. But I had seen him. He was *alive*!

We moved very soon after that to the neighbourhood of a remarkable 'first emergency' hospital, which had been set up in a cave, a natural wonder with a huge rocky overhang, set in the side of a steep hill. Because of the deplorable state of the roads, the People's Army medical services had developed the custom of bringing its most seriously wounded men to improvised hospitals as near to the front line as possible, to avoid the jolting and sometimes lethal transport to the Base. It was here that I saw Leah Manning, a Labour MP, and a member of the Spanish Aid Committee, on a visit to Spain, sit up all night holding the hand of a dying man, one of her constituents. She was brave, was Leah, and had already earned the gratitude of the Spanish people by her tremendous work for the removal of some thousands of Basque children to England in the early stages of the bombardment of the Basque country. My dear friend Patience Darton was nursing at the care hospital, caring for the wounded night and day and often going without sleep for twenty-four hours or more. We were under canvas in a valley below. My office was now the open air and my quarters a mattress, on which, if the weather was good, I slept out of doors (otherwise in a bell tent along with several men).

But we were on the move, nearer again to the river we were soon to cross.

Now we were in a little mountain village called Bisbal de Falset, almost overlooking the Ebro. Not far from us, though we did not see them, the units of the 35th Division were preparing for the crossing. In the first days of July, for the sake of morale, and to celebrate the 14th,[71] it was decided to hold a fiesta for the village folk. There were to be speeches, a children's day and a sports day. I was given the task of organising the village women, whom I met every day at the only fountain, exchanging news and gossiping while our jugs filled from the slow trickle of water. I began by calling on the Mayor (*Alcalde*) who was not at all forthcoming. 'This is not a job for women,' he told me. 'Women haven't anything to do with politics, we shan't have a woman speaker.' 'But what about Pasionaria?' I asked.[72] 'Ah, *she's different.*' Fortunately I found a small group of local mothers. They baked cakes and dainties as far as their meagre supplies, eked out by contributions from our rations, allowed. They hung colourful shawls and bedspreads from their balconies. There was a procession of singing children through the main street watched by weepy mothers (and weepy me). There was a picnic, games, singing and dancing. Next day we had the sports. The sports day was remarkable. There was only one flat surface in the whole village, the main road which passed at the end of the main street. This became the race-track, the athletic ground and the football field. Our lot (the medical people) played a group from the fortifications unit who were stationed there too. The whole event was intermittently interrupted by convoys of huge lorries coming down the main road towards the river, laden with arms and ammunition. Everyone knew where they were going, and what for, but nobody said a word. (The crossing of the Ebro, a day or two later, took the enemy completely by surprise.[73] There were no Quislings in Bisbal.)

We crossed the river by night, one night after the first of the troops. With Crome and his Adjutant, we drove down steep hairpin bends through the dusty dark, but all along the route we could hear and sometimes see the local peasants laying down swathes of branches to fill up the potholes and hacking away at the rocky sides to make the corners more manoeuvrable for heavy vehicles. We just made it by dawn.

It was a scene of desolation, with still unburied bodies lying by the roadside, shattered dwellings and huge piles of jettisoned material, papers, suitcases, bedding, even rifles, showing the haste with which the enemy had made his get away. We set up our first HQ at (I think) Flix, in the buildings of a power station where the (German) technicians had left us some well-built slit trenches in which to take refuge when the bombardment began, which it soon did. We were too near a pontoon bridge, and all the bridges were bombed throughout the hours of daylight; we could not get enough work done in the circumstances and moved away from the river bank to a relatively undamaged farmhouse where, in addition to our HQ, we had a 'first emergency' operating theatre, supplied with electricity by a small, temperamental generator nursed with immense skill and care by Kozar.

Now my job grew intensive. Each day the doctors in charge of four front line dressing stations sent in their lists of the day's casualties; my job was to type these out, classify them into various categories (head wounds, leg wounds, amputations and so on; the base hospitals to which they were sent, the weapons which had caused their injuries – mortars, shells, bullets and others) and to turn these figures periodically into graphic form, with the aid of a box of water-colours and some drawing instruments. The casualty lists were sent off every day at four o'clock to the higher command, where they would be co-ordinated with those from other divisions and matched to reports from base hospitals, which revealed how long, for instance, it took for a man with a compound fracture of the tibia to work through his treatment and get back into action, or the urgent need for more tin helmets (of which there were shockingly few). There were a lot of casualties; an avalanche of work descended with which we could barely cope (though I still went on making tea) and for an agonising few moments every day I scrutinised for George's name.

We had daily air raids and were sometimes under shell fire. An illustration of the terrible handicap under which the whole army was fighting (due to the criminal policy of 'Non-Intervention') is that when planes came over we had no need to identify them as the enemy or 'ours'. A glance at the sky was enough. If it was one of ours, the sky was full of bursts of anti-aircraft fire, while if it was one or more of theirs – and they often came in formation – an occasional puff of smoke was all that could be seen.

The peasant family to whom the farm belonged had moved to a village further in the rear. Two or three times a week the farmer and one or two daughters used to risk their lives by trudging several miles, making their way over a road-crossing that was constantly being shelled, to keep their irrigation ditches clear and thus save their vegetable harvest. One day, for some reason, we received an issue of *shoes*, among which there was a pair of woman's shoes, leather, which were too small for me. I gave them to the farmer's daughter. The next time they were due to visit us, the whole family came, including their small, dignified granny, who was carrying in her apron four new laid eggs for me. They had all come under fire to satisfy Spanish obligation by making a return gift.

There were almost forty of us – doctors, orderlies, stretcher bearers, drivers and office staff. I begged some flour from the cookhouse and a small frying pan from Kozar: there was no milk but with flour, water and four eggs, I made thirty-eight pancakes (a sort of miracle of the Feeding of the Five Thousand), each with a tiny sprinkling of sugar, on which we feasted.

The bridges across which all our supplies reached us were under incessant bomb attack. Sometimes all of them were damaged and could not be repaired for hours or as much as two days, though the fortification units slaved heroically. One of the most urgent requirements was blood for the transfusion service (then in its infancy). Being fortunate to be a Universal Donor and a sedentary worker, I was recruited to give some of my blood by direct transfusion, an unforgettable experience. Lying down beside a seriously wounded man, on the point of death, I watched as the colour came back into his lips, his breathing improved and he turned back towards life. Nowadays the transfer of blood is a far more scientific business and the simple grouping used at that time has become immensely more complex (I wasn't given even a Schick Test, there wasn't time).[74] During those early days of the Ebro campaign I actually gave 200cc of my blood three times in little over two weeks. I felt no ill-effects, except that my legs seemed rather heavy for a day or two afterwards. On each occasion I received (by regulation) a *vale* – a piece of paper entitling me to a tin of condensed milk and an egg. Neither was available. But on the third occasion Kozar, sitting by his generator, had seen someone running to fetch me to the operating theatre and by the time I emerged he had managed to snare a rabbit and was cooking it in his little frying pan. It was so fresh that the heart, lying in a saucer beside him, was *still beating*. Dear Kozar, yet another of the quite undeserved benefactors who have adorned my life.

Its first onslaught over, the 15th Brigade got a few days' rest. I visited the British Battalion, a raggle-taggle bunch of weary men, scattered over an arid hillside. George was there, unharmed. We spent two evenings together and one whole night, on a louse-infested sofa. I was taken to see Sam Wild, the Commander of the Battalion.[75] Dear, gruff old Sam's first greeting was 'Ave you etten?' (pure Lancashire hospitality). He told me that George had been 'mentioned in despatches'.

They went back into the lines, where the British won the name of the 'Shock Battalion' for its part in the near successful attack on 'Hill 481' outside Gandesa.

But the long, slow, desperate and heroic retreat of the Spanish People's Army, battling against the overpowering superiority of the Fascists, aided by German and Italian troops and war material in growing force, had begun. We lost ground. There were a few hours when our hospital and HQ were actually between our own and the enemy lines. We had to retire quickly, back towards the river where we set up in yet another derelict farmhouse, not far from a railway tunnel, which had been converted into a hospital for safety from the air.

Crome was replaced by a medical Chief from the crack 5th Regiment (the Communist regiment which had throughout covered itself with glory and was a byword for courage and military efficiency). Enrique Bassadone[76] was a contrast to the easygoing but nevertheless highly efficient Crome, who had a devastating irreverence for bureaucracy and liked to surround himself with eccentrics and oddballs. Highly professional, with a batman to keep his spotless uniform in order and wait on him at table, Enrique didn't approve of women and always addressed me in the third person – to which I naughtily replied in the second person, the universal habit in Republican Spain.[77]

At this time we received the news that the Republican Government had decided, in view of the endless shilly-shallying in the League of Nations about foreign troops 'on both sides' – equating with the utmost cynicism the comparatively few *volunteers* who had come to Spain to risk their lives in the fight against Fascism with the armies of conscripted men from Germany, Italy and Portugal, not to mention the aeroplanes, etc. which they brought with them – to call this bluff by withdrawing *all* the members of the International Brigades, sending them home and proposing a proportional withdrawal. This disregarded the fact that a great many of the volunteers had no home to go to, having come from fascist countries, to return to which would be to court imprisonment and death.

VIII

We were to be sent home. George had sustained a slight head-wound, which was soon stitched up and healed, but the hospital to which he had been sent wanted to keep him for treatment of the suppurating sores on his legs (we all suffered from them in various degrees). Learning of the coming withdrawal George had insisted on returning to the Battalion to take part in the final action with his British fellow-soldiers. He came through our HQ with a note stating that he had been discharged from hospital *at his own request.* We spent an hour or two together, eagerly discussing which of us would reach England first, and how it would come about; who would see the children first – and we agreed that George should not shave off his beard until they had seen it, because Grandpa Green had told us they were fascinated by the idea of a bearded Daddy. The 22 September had been fixed for the withdrawal of the British Battalion; our little group in the Divisional HQ (mostly drivers, mechanics, American and Canadian) was to engage in training their Spanish successors and we had no date fixed for our departure. George was convinced that the British and French governments, seeing what was at stake in their own interests after Munich,[78] must now take steps to release the vast stores of military supplies, which were being held up at the French frontier in the name of 'Non-Intervention'. He was joyous at going back into the lines for his final swipe at the fascist enemy, and sent me a note on his return to the Battalion, repeating the conviction that the desperately-wanted war supplies must 'even now' be pouring in.

The 22 September came and went. Though I was still at the

front, I sighed with relief that George was not on the casualty lists I had studied daily with dread.

On the night of the 23rd, two chaps came and wakened me. 'George is missing,' they said.

Due to an unexpectedly severe enemy attack, the British had been asked to spend one more day in helping to repulse it in the Sierra de Pandols. In spite of desperate resistance, they had been forced to retire and when the time came to call the roll, George did not answer.

I didn't say anything. I pulled up the sheets round my suddenly icy-cold shoulders and lay down, trying to grasp the thunderbolt. It must not, it could not be true. 'Missing' meant 'He might be alive, he might be dead' – and this thought began to repeat itself in my mind as if a needle had been dropped on a gramophone and had stuck in the groove. My dear colleagues next morning made a pact among themselves not to leave me alone for a second and established a sort of rota for the purpose. It was *too kind*. I would have liked to be on my own and try to come to terms with the situation. I *must not* weep. I *must* cherish hope. He-might-be-alive-he-might-be-dead repeated itself with bewildering monotony in my waking thoughts for the rest of my stay in Spain and for the following months, gradually changing to despair. We left the front, we handful of internationals, a couple of weeks later, having handed over our jobs to our Spanish successors. We drove back across the river in an open *camion* and I recall the sudden surprise and delight I felt as we drove through our first village, on the far side, to see women in the streets! I hadn't seen another woman for weeks, and wished I could get down and embrace them – There you are, my sisters, my dear ones, weep with me! We stopped in Asco, where I began to telephone all the hospitals to which casualties might have been sent, spending hours shouting down crackling, buzzing, intermittently silent lines. Eventually I had an answer that raised a faint hope. At some hospital they said they had a George Grey, not too seriously wounded, a Frenchman. Could it be a mistake? I must go and find out!

I do not remember how I got to Barcelona. But there I received the tenderest sympathy and most practical help from Peter Kerrigan, at that time the correspondent of the *Daily Worker*.[79] Dear Peter facilitated my journeys to five hospitals – the one I'd hoped for denied all knowledge of any George Grey at all … There was nothing to do but to go home.

The Catalan chauffeur who drove us (me and one of the English nurses – Margaret Findlay or Dorothy Rutter?) to the border was preoccupied with worry about his little son, who was sick. At the French guard-post I begged and pleaded to be allowed to enter France, buy some condensed milk and cross back to the Spanish end – about 20 yards – to give it to him; it was surely harmless to introduce sealed tins of condensed milk into Spain? Please let me! He refused. We made our way to a café for a meal. I ate two bits of a white roll and some fresh butter (neither of which we had tested for months) and then was absolutely unable to get another morsel down … In Toulon I bought a pair of shoes, my *alpargatas* being almost worn out.[80] Then took the train – I don't even remember whether for Calais or Le Havre.

How was I going to tell Grandpa Green? How – and *what* – was I going to tell the children? 'He is missing,' I told Grandpa, and the sharing of the burden with him seemed to make it heavier rather than lighter. But it was comforting to be with him. We went to Summerhill the next day (a Sunday). Neill was at the station – he usually went there to meet parents on Sundays. I told him, and then hastened to the school to find my darlings. 'Daddy isn't coming just yet, we don't quite know where he is,' was the best I could do. But some child had overheard me speaking to Neill, and half an hour later Frances came to me and said: 'Sally says Daddy is *missing*. I don't want him to be missing!' I must give them hope but I mustn't give them too much hope … one doesn't tell lies to one's children but what is the truth here? He-might-be-alive-he-might-be-dead ...

That afternoon there was a tea-party, someone's birthday I think. I sat and watched my two eat their jelly, sandwiches and cake. In between every spoonful or mouthful Martin looked across at me with such blazing love in his bright brown eyes – so like the look in his father's grey ones when he used to sit beaming at me in the early days of our marriage, saying 'I'm doting on you!' – that I could hardly bear it. Frances refused to admit to herself that her father might not come back. She buried it inside herself where it began to canker. She experienced an *adult* grief but had no outlet for it.

Summerhill had been good for them and good *to* them. And when the time came for me to tell Neill that I by myself could not pay their fees and must take them away, there came another stupendous kindness. He offered to keep the two of them for the fees of one. Yet another of those fantastic acts of generosity that I have received all my life. My debt to Neill is unrepayable.

I went right on working for Spain – 'merely changing the front and the weapons', as the International Brigaders put it. The war was not yet lost. The fight was still going on. Food, medical supplies, everything was needed more than ever, and the political struggle – 'Save Spain – Save Peace' – more urgent still. My day-time job was the National Joint Committee for Spanish Relief. I shared a small basement flat in Bloomsbury with Winifred Bates and together we formed a voluntary group: 'British Medical Units from Spain', in which we organised all the nurses, doctors and others who had returned, to speak at meetings, to hold meetings, to raise funds and write to the press, local and national. A deputation of nurses set off to visit Mrs Chamberlain,[81] to ask her intervention on behalf of Spanish women and children. She was not at Downing Street, so they took taxis and went to Chequers, where they found *barricades* at the entrance to the drive. They had informed the press, which made headlines of the story. Angela Guest, always original and daring, by herself upset a tin of red paint on the steps of No. 10, to represent the blood of the Spanish people, and also made press headlines. The struggle became more and more desperate and now doubt began to creep in as to its outcome ...

Doubt meanwhile was stealthily coming over my spirit. As the days wore on and there was no news I began to know in my heart that if George had been alive he would somehow by now have managed to communicate with me, though I invented all sorts of fantasies to keep alive the fragile flame of hope. (Could he be a prisoner, seriously ill or blinded and unable to write ...?) I was an embarrassment to my friends, who did not know whether to console me or offer hope. In my youthful intolerance I had declared that funerals were superstitious nonsense, but now I knew, and have since realised even more strongly, that a funeral is a necessity for those left behind, enabling them to give vent to their grief and to *draw a line* under a stage of life after which one must get on with it in a new way, come what may. But I had nothing to come to terms with. Was I a widow or a wife? When must I begin to tackle life without my other half?

The long nightmare came to an end. Early in March, when the end was drawing near in Spain and the exodus from Catalonia was about to begin, I got an official letter from the Republican Government telling me that George had died on 23rd September. Winifred, who watched me open it, told me afterwards that she knew what it contained because my face went grey. What I built up in the next few hours was the determination not to show that I was shattered; for the sake of the children, who must discover that I could now cope with being both father and mother to them, and for the sake of George, upon whom no blame must fall. Pride, pride in his having given his life for the cause we all held dear must be the keynote.

Letters of condolence arrived, few but precious. Wogan wrote that 'knowing George had altered the whole course of his life'. The Musicians' Union presented me with a cheque for £60 and a despatch case inscribed, on a little metal label, with recognition of the work he had done for the Union. Paddy O'Daire gripped my hand and said 'He was a great guy'. These and others were of immense comfort.

Now I could tell the children. Frances, poor sweet, could not accept the news. She continued to tell her schoolmates fantasies about the cake she was going to bake for her Daddy when he came back ... She became actually ill, ran a mysterious high temperature, and Neill sent for me. The very day I got there, Neill, with characteristic wisdom, had sent a girl to play with her in bed who was an orphan. Conversation turned to fathers. 'I haven't got a father,' said Sally. 'That's funny, neither have I,' said Frances ... I had brought her something she wanted – a 'grass skirt' in which to dance like a Caribbean girl. She looked at it and wept. 'What is the matter,' I said. 'Don't you want it after all?' She burst into tears and flung herself into my arms, saying 'I only want Daddy.' Now we were able to cry together.

Martin, I think, with the resilience of a younger child who had not grasped what it meant, actually took longer to work the loss out of his system (if he ever did). Two years later I found him in bed, one night, staring at the ceiling. 'What's up, can't you get to sleep,' I asked. 'I am *trying to remember Daddy*,' he replied. 'Ah,' I said. 'I don't have to try because you are so like him that whenever I look at you, I can remember him very well.'

IX

Back to March 1939. One morning the *Evening Standard* put
out placards saying 'ON TO BARCELONA'. Blazing with anger
I rang up the editor and accused him of fascist bias. The placards
disappeared with the next edition. That day, or the next, I had
lunch with Dr Audrey Russell, a member of the National Joint
Committee. As we waited to be served, she looked at my hands,
which were clenched into fists (trying, I suppose, to hold back
the fascist advance). 'Unloose your hands,' she told me. I did so,
and unloosed a flood of tears. I thought till then that I'd cried all
my tears.

The Chamberlain Government recognised Franco and the
exodus from Catalonia had left thousands of refugees in
deplorable camps on the beaches of southern France. The
National Joint Committee quickly set to work to send relief, and
in particular to collect the money for the chartering of an entire
ship to send refugees to Mexico, whose government had
generously offered asylum. I was enrolled to collect donations at
meetings, and discovered an ability to wrest money from the
pockets of the audience – not by any means with the force, the
charm, the magnificent oratory and ability to send an audience
home with nothing in their pockets but the bus-fare of Isabel
Brown (described by Hannen Swaffer as Britain's top woman

orator, with Lady Violet Bonham Carter as a near second) but sufficiently eloquent to be teamed with Sir Peter Chalmers Mitchell, whose first-hand experience of Spanish fascism had been published in his book, *My House in Malaga*, and the Earl of Listowel, a 'broad front' figure of great drawing power.[82] Together we stumped southern England, speaking at meetings and collecting funds for the ship.

A French vessel was chartered, the *SS Sinaia*, whose usual run was to take pilgrims to Mecca. It could hold about 2000 passengers. A group left for the camps, to draw up the passenger list with great care – to make sure that whole families were enrolled and to try and ensure that the list reflected the *political* composition of the Republican side, without bias towards any particular group.

Now a relatively small problem came up. The ship held only a limited number of people. Observers must go with it, but every observer would occupy a place which might have been used by yet another refugee. Sir Richard Rees and William Brebner, a Quaker, were to go from the National Joint Committee,[83] but if anyone else went, it ought to be someone who could be useful on board and who could come back and campaign for more money – for yet another ship was the intention. I could speak Spanish; I could be useful on board, and could return with first-hand information to tour the country appealing for more funds. Leah Manning, bless her, suggested me, and the Committee agreed.

(Winifred had left for the USA and the flat was now shared with Ena Vassie, another of the Spain nurses.)

Hastily borrowing a number of white coats, to make me look a bit professional on board ship, I packed up and set off for southern France where the ship lay ready. A covey of British VIPs were there to see her off. Two snags delayed the departure; first, the port originally settled upon was found to have a draught insufficient for the ship to enter and it had to move round to Sete and all the refugees (not yet embarked) with it. Secondly, when we got there, it was found that the list had been drawn up by someone who did not know that Spaniards invariably use their patronymic *and* the name of their mothers – or in the case of married women, the name of their husband followed by their patronymic (thus Francisco Fernandez Sanz is not Mr Sanz but Mr Fernandez, and his wife is likely to be called Carmen Fernandez Uribe, and is not Mrs Fernandez) and had allocated cabins for husbands and wives with what were supposed to be the same surname – a huge confusion which was settled by an all-night assembly of the whole 2000 persons on the quayside and the calling out of names by a loud-hailer. It got settled eventually and with everyone safely on board and matched with the right partners and parents, farewell speeches were made by the Duchess of Atholl, Wilfred Roberts MP, the Mexican Ambassador who was going with us on the ship accompanied by his wife, and others whose names I don't remember.

The voyage took twenty-three days. My job, I discovered, was to see to the feeding of the very young children for whom no arrangement existed in the ship's facilities. On the first day, a group of (refugee) doctors interviewed all the infants and children under two years of age and allocated them to one of five or six diets. Supplies of various kinds of infant food had been brought on board. I coordinated the diets into quantities, and every three hours descended to the galley where I stirred, with the aid of two hardworking Spanish girls, great saucepans full of milk and different paps, distributing them in a made-over barber saloon to the mothers, either in bowls or in feeding bottles which had to be sterilised between feeds. I hardly ever got up on deck.

There were two interesting breaks in the voyage. The first was at Madeira, where the ship stopped to take on water, and the Captain asked some of us who possessed passports to go ashore and buy him some wine. Sir Richard, William Brebner and I, together with Georges Soria, a French journalist who was to write

up the voyage for the French press, went off into the hills to
some cellars, furnished with tables, and chairs made from barrels
and 'tested' glass after tiny glass of Madeira. Having made our
purchases (I have absolutely no 'palate' and could not tell one
from another, but someone must have been proficient) we
returned a bit tipsily through Funchal, where we were held up
by a procession of Fascist Youth, armed in black shirts and
jackboots. Soria, with whom I had up to that point spoken only
in French, suddenly leaned over my shoulder and said, in
excellent English: 'Fuck them all!' – to my great delight.

Our second stop was Puerto Rico. Here, the island's supporters
of Republican Spain had arranged an absolutely magnificent
reception and treat for the refugees, with a huge banquet and a
fleet of charabancs in which they proposed to take everyone for
a tour of the island.

Alas, the American authorities refused permission for them to
land. There was a lot of altercation, in which the Mexican
Ambassador took part, but to no avail. Only those four of the
passengers who had gone ashore at Madeira were permitted, and
even then the Yanks tried to stop me on the grounds that they
had not got a *woman* officer to search me; I stepped defiantly
before the Marine officer and *dared* him to go ahead.
Shamefacedly and grumpily he let me pass. We walked with the
'Spanish Aid Committee' which had organised the reception. They
took us to see the scene of the banquet which had been prepared,
and for a brief run by car to show the beauties of the countryside.
Meanwhile, a portable platform had been brought to the quayside,
where local worthies made speeches of solidarity and affection.
When we got back to the ship, we were stunned to see that the
mountain had come to Mahomed!

The whole side of the ship was festooned with ropes and
lengths of string, on which a whole crowd of Puerto Ricans were
fastening sausages, roast chickens, joints of meat, loaves of bread,
baskets of fruit, cakes and biscuits, every imaginable kind of food,

which was being hauled aboard by their Spanish friends lining the rail above, while speaker after speaker on a platform below addressed them through a megaphone. It was a scene of sheer love, and difficult to describe whether those on the ship or those on the shore were more moved. I caught sight of a very small ragged boy, probably a bootblack, tying a sandwich – probably his lunch – on to a string and smiling angelically to see it hauled above. The scene continued all day and the crowd stayed until we sailed in the evening. I did not witness the farewell because one of the gifts they had brought us was a number of churns of *fresh milk*, and Maruja, Antonia and I had to get it sterilised and distributed to our babies before it went sour. (A very gifted Catalan cartoonist, at the end of the voyage, presented me with a sketch of myself, white-clad, sweeping about with a preoccupied air, holding several babies' feeding bottles. It was lost when I was 'bombed-out' in London two years later.) Dripping with sweat and exhausted with emotion I went to bed.

Shipboard is one of the classical sites for *rumours*. As we neared Veracruz and people began to express their uncertainty as to what would happen when we reached shore, the strong rumour went round that all the women were to be put in convents and all the men in barracks. The Mexican Ambassador and his wife, who were not themselves sure of exactly what was planned, went round with reassuring words which did something to allay the mischief.

What happened when we finally docked I did not see, as I was below in the galley preparing the last baby-foods so that the children should leave the ship with contented tummies. But I found, when it was all over, that after a number of Mexican government figures – and Dr Negrin, who had come to welcome his fellow-countrymen – had made brief speeches, the refugees simply walked ashore, being handed as they reached the bottom of the gangway a printed, addressed card saying 'This is where you will eat. This is where you will sleep'. They could then step into freedom! Two luxury liners which were lying in Veracruz Harbour had been made ready for children, a big warehouse had been cleared and fitted up with beds and showers, linen etc. for men. Someone handed me a note from Dr Negrin saying he couldn't stay to see me but thanked me for my help. I went ashore and wherever I walked, fellow-passengers rushed to embrace me, exclaiming: 'Look! We are free!'

My helper, Antonia, who had come from Spain as the eldest sister of an orphaned family (three brothers and two sisters), met me next morning to say that she and two brothers had already *found jobs* in a restaurant kitchen and were staying right there. I mention this because, later that year, when war broke out, she wrote to me inviting me to bring my children to safety, promising that she and her family would care for us until we were settled! The overwhelming generosity of it made me weep.

After a day or two in Vera Cruz (where for the first and only time in my life I had *more than enough oysters* to eat) we three British went on to Mexico City. The sudden change of altitude from sea level to over 5000 metres made us feel breathless and a little crazy; we panted when climbing stairs, and spoke to one another with wrong words tumbling out. A further example of the extremely practical planning of the Mexicans was that the Government had invited each of the states that make up the federation of Mexico to say which trades or professions they could best use, endeavouring to select according to need: peasants, farm workers and mechanics for agricultural areas, factory workers where there was industry, and so forth. People with *skills* were in great demand. Spanish Republicans were assured of sympathy. Even manufacturers and landowners, part of that Mexican bourgeoisie which had throughout the war had their own movement of support for Franco's side in contrast to the official government attitude, wanted skilled people and (I was told by a Mexican friend) felt a sneaking sort of pride in the valiant fight of the people on the Republican side.

It was necessary for me to gather as much information as possible in the shortest possible time as ammunition for the fund-raising speaking-tour planned for my return. I made rapid visits to fairly nearby places where the refugees were being settled. Here is one of my early findings. Mexico just then had a remarkably progressive government that had introduced land reform in the shape of the *ejido* system, a sort of cooperative farming. I visited an *ejido* where some Spanish farm workers had arrived. There was a tractor, the gift of the government, but it was standing idle, having broken down and there being no one with the ability to repair it. Just one day after the Spaniards got there they had done the repairs, to the admiration and joy of the villagers ... with incidents such as this filling my notebook I went back to Mexico City, where there was some difficulty in settling certain types of professional people, such as lawyers, poets and *catedracticos*.[84] Doctors were in immense demand, but some (though not all) of them were very unwilling to go to the areas where they were most needed – the countryside. ('But how am I to get my daughters married?' queried one of them, 'if we are stuck out here among these peasants?') Let me add that this involved only a minority – I found lawyers who had become chauffeurs and poets who were washing windows for a livelihood, as well as surgeons who had cheerfully packed up the sets of instruments with which they had been provided by the National Joint Committee for Spanish Relief and set off for remote areas with unselfish resolve.

I must get back to England. Anxious to use as little money as possible in travelling, I booked a ticket for the Greyhound Bus which left Mexico City daily for New York, a journey of three days and two nights, not at all comfortable, trying to sleep sitting up and in a heatwave. In New York I stayed with a warm-hearted Jewish family whose son, a brilliant student, had been killed in Spain. His father, mother and sister had all joined the Communist Party of America because, said the mother, 'it will take three of us to make up for him.' Mac Kraus, a member of the Abraham Lincoln battalion who had returned to his former trade of taxi driver, took me for a lightning tour of New York and I gave a press interview for the American counterpart of the National Joint Committee before sailing for England on what must have been one of the last peacetime crossings of the *Normandie*.

War was looming closer and closer. We were thrown into dire confusion (at least I was) by the Soviet pact with Hitler, which in our blind faith we found it difficult to justify, though we could see and feel ashamed of the criminal shilly-shallying of the British Government who sent a third-rate Foreign Office chap to Moscow to discuss the support of Poland ... We had watched the betrayal of Czechoslovakia, but did even this explain the pact with Hitler? I tried. At first I put my faith in an 'escape clause' which I was sure the Soviet Union must have written into the Pact. And reasons were put forth by the party: to gain time, breathing space, whether correctly used or not (as it turned out) to prepare for the inevitable onslaught in 1941.[85]

I began a process which I subsequently described (and still do) as 'I can't help thinking ...' Today I have, in the words of Nazim Hikmet, 'unlearned blind faith',[86] but blind faith takes some shifting and it was merely a small slide into the avalanche which took hold of me now ('Can't help thinking that the Soviet Union had reasons which are unknown to us' is not really comforting) and I have comrades still who can't help thinking that the events of 1968 in Czechoslovakia or the invasion of Afghanistan can be explicated in this manner. It reminds me of the fifty or more years it took for Darwin's discovery to undermine the blind faith of those whose lives were guided by the idea of the absolute truth of every word of the Bible. Anyway it happened.

The Committee had begun to organise a nation-wide speaking tour for me. I addressed a few meetings in the Home Counties, but the entire scheme fell to the ground on the declaration of war. No more refugee ships would be able to leave. Moreover, for the first few weeks all public meetings were banned, and theatres, cinemas etc. closed. My journey had turned out to be almost useless.

Top: Nancy Drucilla farrow (Nan Green, centre) with sister Emily (Mem) and brother Richard (Dick)
Bottom left: Nan, in mountaineering gear
Bottom right: Nan Green and husband George on holiday in the Peak District

Top left: Nan and children in London before leaving for Spain
Top right: Nan with Grandpa Green, a friend, Frances and Martin, 1936
Bottom: Nan on board *The Normandie*, after escorting refugee children to Mexico

Top: George Green, second from right, with Wogan Philipps, second left, and poets
Ewart Milne, left, and Stephen Spender
Bottom: Impromptu concert at a hospital at Huerte, south-east of Madrid, during the
Spanish Civil War. Seated playing the cello is George Green; his wife, Nan, stands
behind him, instructed to play the accordian for the first time. A Bavarian violinist and
two Spanish guitarists make up the remainder of the ensemble.

Top left: Nan Green giving a cup of tea to Leah Manning MP in Spanish hospital
Top right: Nan Green with second husband, Ted Brake, in China
Bottom: Nan Green, mid-1970s

X

It has fallen my lot to be *somewhere else* at certain historic moments. For example, to be at the Ebro front when the Munich events took place – and the newspapers reached us with difficulty, being snatched up before they could get to us. I was somewhere else when war was declared on 3rd September 1939. I had taken Frances and Martin back to school, being driven by a friend who had a car, and while we were somewhere between London and Leiston the declaration of war became public and the farcical blowing of sirens took place. We got to Summerhill and met serious faces. Don't go back to London, they said to us. Stay here a few days and wait. What for? Haven't you heard? We went back to London and in the first village we passed I saw groups of school-age children carrying little cardboard boxes strung round their necks. 'Look,' I said, 'a school picnic!' Joe, not understanding me at all, made no comment. In the next village the same sight. 'Another Sunday school picnic!' I said wonderingly. At this point it dawned on Joe that I had *never seen gas masks* (and hardly heard of them).

Exactly as we had prophesied, the war in Spain had been Hitler's rehearsal for now. For those of us who had been there, it was a simple continuation of our fight – an anti-fascist war. It was so, too, for many Communists, including our General Secretary, Harry Pollitt, who wrote and published an anti-fascist pamphlet entitled *How to Win the War*.[87] But after weeks we were thrown into a period of confusion. The Executive Committee of our Party had decided (we are now told, whether correctly or not, by a decision of the Communist International, which has never to this day published its deliberations) that it was an *imperialist* war and thus not deserving of support by Communists, whose aim should be to go over the heads of governments and appeal to the workers of every country to unite against their exploiters. Harry Pollitt, persisting in *his* belief, left the Executive Committee and went back to the trade which he had not practised for years, that of a boilermaker.

I had the misfortune (or the good fortune), at this stage to be confined to hospital, with a suspected gastric ulcer, the result I suppose of the miserable diet we had endured in Spain. I thus missed most of the heated discussion which went on in our ranks, and emerged from St George's[88] entirely unconvinced as to the correctness of 'the Party line' but lacking the moral courage to defy it openly (just as I had earlier suppressed my loss of Christian faith before the family); disregarding 'dusty answers' and devoting myself wholly to the unfinished task of aid to Spain, avoiding the painful process of thinking things through. Up to that moment my life in the Communist Party had been 'a glad, confident morning'. There was black and white, good and evil, the world was at the crossroads, democracy and peace, or fascism and war. 'Faults on both sides there may have been but the Spanish Republican cause was right, legal, totally justified. Franco was a perjured rebel, assisted by those enemies of democracy, Hitler and Mussolini, who were hurtling Europe towards war. What a fortunate group we were, those who went to Spain, with a clear, uncomplicated cause that has remained untarnished to this day! I was now sharing the Bloomsbury flat with Ena. We agreed that with our joint earnings we could just about manage to support a Spanish refugee, and having deposited £50 and signed a declaration that we would not allow our guest to 'become a charge on the public funds' we awaited his or her arrival. By an absolutely incredible coincidence, it turned out to be none other than my Commanding Officer from the 35th Division, Enrique Bassadone, who had disapproved of women at the front, treated me with icy formality and never addressed me except in the third person. It must have been a fearful blow to him; to find himself dependent on two independent young women, not at all disposed or indeed able to behave like a batman or a devoted household slave, cheerily expecting him to cook his own lunch, make his bed and perform the only chore he ever enjoyed – 'doing the blackout' – a complicated business, since in our semi-basement we had horizontal skylight windows at street level which had to be filled each evening with black-out cloth mounted on frames. We addressed him as 'tu' from the first moment, and he replied in the same person.

Early one morning, four days before 3rd September, Ena spied two figures walking slowly past the window, as if in search of something. 'Surely we know those two?' she asked. They were Frank and Anita. Frank had refused to leave Spain when the Medical Aid came home because he was determined to marry Anita with such legally water-tight formalities as would enable him to bring her to England without hindrance from the Franco authorities. He had become a civilian, worked in a garage, and paid visit after visit, filled up form after form and untangled yards of red tape in the confusion of defeated Valencia, with new officials muddling up and obstructing everything they could.

Ena rushed into the street and dragged them in, my dear dear friends! How we talked, embraced, laughed and wept for joy and sorrow. I had heard nothing of them for months and had been full of fears as to their fate. How Frank had come to know the name of the street was that he had Grandpa Green's address nearby and went there. He was out at work but his landlady knew the street name but not the number and he had been walking slowly up and down, whistling a Republican tune for some time before we spotted him. With a bit of contriving and furniture shifting we managed to squeeze them into the flat, where angelic Anita without a moment's delay began to do as much housework as we would allow her (there was one occasion when she actually darned a hole in one of my handkerchiefs!), while Frank set out to look for work and accommodation. It did not take him a very long time to find both. They moved into a neighbouring street, and eventually Enrique went to stay with them – though not for long because he discovered quite by accident that he had been born in Rio Tinto, which somehow entitled him to British nationality and he could thus go to Oxford and study (or re-study) medicine so as to be able to practice here. Then Ena married her Harry and left.

The work to be done for Spain diminished. I went from the National Joint Committee for Spanish Relief to the Parliamentary Committee (set up by Wilfred Roberts) and finally to the British Committee for Refugees from Spain, whose task was to find jobs and provide for the livelihood of those Spaniards who had managed to reach England (and a few International Brigaders from Fascist countries). British organisations and individual families undertook to give hospitality to these refugees, far less numerous of course than the ones in Mexico, and the committee raised and provided enough money to give each a small allowance of 'pocket money'. But like those in Mexico, the majority found work of some kind, preferring to be independent, and we were gradually left with a somewhat similar group of unenterprising intellectuals who could not follow their professions and didn't choose to wash windows or drive cars. I felt it was time to do something more worthwhile.

My first idea was to get a job somewhere away from London, in the country somewhere, where I could have the children to live with me. I spent two weeks applying for jobs in Somerset and Wiltshire: I found plenty of jobs – but no accommodation for anyone with children. Landladies could well afford to be choosy as so many firms had evacuated to neighbouring towns. Summerhill had moved from the Suffolk coast to North Wales, where the kids were virtually safe from air attack or invasion, if that should happen. So I left them there for the time being and went back to London and took a job in Poplar Town Hall, where I eventually became, astonishingly, Invasion Defence Officer.

Astonishingly, because, as I remember it, a leading question had been put in Parliament not long before as to the advisability of employing members of the Communist Party in the war effort; the guarded reply was that while there was no objection to the employment of communists, it was not advisable to put them in positions of great responsibility (or words to that effect). Now, at that time I had been appointed by the Party, along with some others whose names I am not going to mention even now, to make some preliminary arrangements *in case* of the Party being made illegal (as it had been in France) or *in case* of a German invasion, either of which seemed possible, though remotely so. I was recommended to keep quiet about my political affiliations and beliefs – not at first an easy task for one who had, like an early Christian, been 'testifying in season and out of season' for years.[89]

I smugly thought I was successful, particularly when after a while I was appointed Invasion Defence Officer, with access to all sorts of secret documents and a private filing cabinet to which only the Town Clerk and I had keys. And I shan't reveal any of the secrets with which I was entrusted, except to say as a generalisation that it seemed to me that the whole scheme was designed to keep London in *running order* from the moment the enemy landed on our coast.

I shall at this point depart from chronological narrative to say that after I left the job, in 1944, I ran into the Deputy Town Clerk one day, who took me for a drink and after having had several himself said confidentially: 'I'll tell you something, Mrs Green. A week after you got to Poplar, the Town Clerk had a visit from MI5, who told him all about you.' They had paid checking visits throughout my stay at intervals, and on each occasion he had – bless his heart! – declared stoutly: 'She is doing her job all right, and that's good enough for me.'

So much for my cautious, 'non-political' airs and graces!

When Ena left I had found a delightful flat in the Temple – amazingly at a rent no more expensive than the Bloomsbury one. Aileen came to share it with me. She had been a nurse in Spain, not one of the volunteers from Britain but already living there, as Matron of a maternity home for foreign residents in Barcelona. On the outbreak of war, she had been given the choice of returning home, or becoming 'militarised', the hospital having been taken over by the government. She had chosen to remain. A true professional in the Florence Nightingale tradition, she had been nursing since the age of eighteen and was now in her late thirties. One of her military patients had been a German anti-fascist, rather older than the majority of volunteers, called Gustav, who had spent several years in the underground movement against Hitler. Like Aileen, he was of what is called 'the old school'. Neither of them, though they fell deeply in love, would have dreamed of starting an 'affair'. Indeed, Gustav felt impelled to ask permission of Winifred (in charge of English nurses' welfare) before becoming engaged to her.

When the war ended in Spain, Gustav found himself in one of those viciously inadequate camps which the French government had set up for anti-fascists of various nationalities who had no home to which they could return. Aileen went to France to rescue him, just on the outbreak of the World War. He was in hospital, with pneumonia and she was not permitted to stay. She returned to London and took a job as a factory nurse in a projectile factory – the first non-hospital job in all her career, and waited agonisedly for news.

After weeks of suspense, word came that he had managed to reach England and was in a military centre being 'screened' (a method of examining refugees to see if it was considered safe to release them). In a few days the lovers were united. Now a problem arose. Aileen was working in a projectile factory (war industry) from which aliens were excluded. If she were to marry

Gustav, she would become a German and might be without a livelihood. Live together, I urged her. But no, neither he nor she would agree to that. So for weeks and weeks Gustav spent the evenings with us, and Aileen then escorted him back to his Bloomsbury lodgings, both wearing metal helmets. This was one of the intensive periods of air raids on London and, being equally anxious for each other's safety, they sometimes saw one another home several times, back and forth. After long delay and much negotiation, the Home Office agreed that Aileen should be allowed to retain her British nationality and thus her job. All obstacles thus removed, they were married (with a remarkably esoteric wedding breakfast due to the peculiarities of rationing) and went to live in Gustav's lodgings. A month later, Gustav died; he had galloping TB, which had not been recognised by any medical authority to which he had been subjected.

It was not more than a few days after the wedding that the flat was 'bombed out'. Thanks to Mary Williams, the secretary of my trade union branch, I was not there when it happened. I had been to see her and stayed to tea. As I got up to go, the air raid alert was sounded and almost immediately Mary (living high up in Hampstead) looked out of the window and noted that flares were falling in the direction of my home. 'You'd better stay the night,' she said firmly, and made me up a bed on her living room floor. Next morning I went straight from her house to Paddington, to meet a young girl whose mother had written to ask me to see her through London, on a journey from Cornwall to Edinburgh, where she was to start her nurses' training.

'Come along,' I said when she got off the train. 'You can come home to my place for a bath and a meal and then we'll go to Euston to catch your next train.' There was no bath there, and no bathroom. The kitchen too had practically disappeared, my bedroom was a mass of rubble and broken glass and the walls of the living room next to it were intact though the entire ceiling had come down and the windows were blown in. In the far corner of the living room stood one of George's cellos, absolutely intact. Not two yards away stood a table with my typewriter on it, smashed into a tangle of twisted wires, with an enormous lump of rubble on top of it. Salvage men came and took such pieces of furniture as were not entirely wrecked, wrapping up the carpet with the plaster and rubble still in it, and taking it all away to be stored. I dared not let them take the cello, and emerged into the street, homeless, with a bundle of dust-impregnated clothing and a bulky violincello as my luggage.

There was no need for me to go to one of the 'Reception Centres' to which the local authorities sent the victims of what were known as 'incidents'. Again, as so many times in my life when I have been up against misfortune, friends offered me hospitality and comfort. The trauma of being bombed-out is intensified by silly little things, like finding oneself without a toothbrush, nail-scissors, face-cleaning things and a workbasket. I had noticed in the reception centres at Poplar that people tended to cling fast to some homely thing that they had picked out of the wreckage of their homes – a teapot, a birdcage – some familiar thing which linked them with ordinary life. Mine was a soup plate, which I had picked up because it had a neat hole right through its centre, and I was irrationally *cross* at having to buy and use new toilet things, none of which seemed quite right because of their newness. In a few days I had found lodgings in a rooming house near Baker Street station, from which I made my way to my job, mostly by Underground but sometimes partially on foot through the wreckage of East London and the City. It was by no means any safer than my previous place, being in the neighbourhood of three railway stations, a major target for the bombers. I hadn't been there very long when the house was partially destroyed by fire. I had been sitting, with one of my fellow-lodgers, under a very heavy kitchen table in the basement. We chatted and drank brandy as we listened for any nearby crunch, quite unaware that the top of the house was ablaze over our heads.

The chronology of the 'Blitz' is rather hazy in my recollection but I think I next went to stay in Hampstead Garden Suburb with Lizzie S., whose two sister-sharers of her house were both Civil Servants and had been sent outside London with their jobs. Lizzie's house had been knocked slightly askew by the blast from a landmine which had fallen nearby, and nearly all the doors and windows were a bit out of true and would either not shut properly or open properly. I went as often as I could to North Wales, to Llan Ffestiniog where Summerhill had moved for safety. Grandpa Green was living in Llandudno, having been given a job at the (evacuated) Ministry of Food, where he was vigorously conducting the Ministry's amateur orchestra (I think this must have been part of the reason that he got the job). So we used to go together to Ffestiniog, where the custom was, whenever a parent or parents visited the kids, they were taken out to tea at some nearby farmhouse and could invite their close friends to come too; thus Frances and Martin used to have four or five companions with them and we would have exuberant parties, striding over the hills and feasting on homemade scones and ditto jam. The going and coming were not pleasant: icy cold, crowded trains, corridors full of soldiers and their kit, the usual Sunday-night delays being exacerbated by war-time conditions – reaching Euston in the small hours with bombs falling all round ...

I never went to sleep down the Underground, as many Londoners did, having forced the unwilling government first to permit them to spend the night down there and later to put up three-tiered bunks on all the platforms (the main responsibility for the latter move belonging to the Communist Party, which campaigned brilliantly for the facility). It sounds silly but I remember being scared only once and that was while I was still in the Temple flat, when one night I was standing at the window and there was a tremendous crash from the neighbourhood of Blackfriars: I went to bed but found myself shaking horribly. 'I'm scared,' I thought but eventually got to sleep. Next morning I found that it had been a landmine which had exploded at the head of Blackfriars Bridge and scattered the entire contents of a big bicycle shop in all directions. Someone remarked – one talked to everyone after an 'incident' – that there had been a tremendous blast and I instantly recognised that shock was what had made me shake ... the fear went away at once. Did I regard myself as indestructible? No, but there was so much to do that one never had time to think about being hit. I think a very large number of London people were the same. Each morning on the way to work, if you were lucky enough to get a vehicle to go to work on, you exchanged narrow escapes and sometimes mythical horror-stories of happenings to the unfortunate ones, or the latest miraculous fulfilment of the prophecies of 'Lord Haw-Haw',[90] who always seemed (in legend) to have announced in advance exactly where last night's bombs were going to fall, though it was always a brother or an aunt or a friend who was reported to have heard him say so. There seemed to be a sort of glee in describing this infallible accuracy of Haw-Haw, though I don't think anyone really believed in it. Every third or fourth night I spent at the Town Hall, fire-watching, and was there on the night that Wally the Warden excitedly announced that he had seen 'a pilotless plane' come down over Bethnal Green – the first of the V-1s.[91] I was more distressed by the V-1s than by the straightforward bombing; not more scared because one got along by not being scared, or, rather, ignoring the danger and the bangs. But there was a moral twist with the V-1s that brought the distress. One heard them coming from afar off: the noise was not the same as that of an aeroplane. Nearer and nearer, and one knew that when the engine cut off, the thing would then fall to the ground and explode. The waiting seconds were hard to bear, but worse was when the explosion came and one realised that it had not fallen on you (relief) but on someone else (grief, shame and horror at one's selfish relief).

But before this, Sunday 22 June 1941 – I am losing my chronology again – came the day when we learned that Hitler had attacked the Soviet Union, tearing up all pacts and treaties and marching in without warning. I had, as I have mentioned, never felt comfortable with the 'Party line' that it was an imperialist war and that the concern of the workers was to defeat the capitalists who were making it, and had cheered up when I heard that Stalin in one of his speeches had referred to 'the just, defensive war' of the Greek people. Indeed, with some malice, I had gone around asking comrades, of whom I saw few at the time, 'If the Germans attacked us what would you do – fight?' Now it was plain sailing again. And when Churchill came on the air later that same day to say that Britain and the Soviet Union had one aim – and one single purpose – 'to destroy Hitler and every vestige of the Nazi regime', the ambiguity came to an end. 'Now it is a people's war, in which the people of Britain and the Soviet Union are fighting side by side,' said Harry Pollitt on 26 June, having become Secretary again. 'Sure, Churchill has not changed his spots, but he had changed his attitude towards the USSR. Political support of the Churchill government did not mean subservience to it, or the unquestioning acceptance of everything Churchill might say or do; it means getting rid of the men of Munich, demanding a unified strategy and a second front in Western Europe; India to be treated as a full ally and to have its own independent government, equality of sacrifice.'

I went on working at Poplar until the end of 1942; the Invasion Defence Scheme seemed less urgent; we did not believe that Hitler would try an attack both East and West but I had plenty to do with the re-housing of bombed-out families and requisitioning premises in which to store their rescued furniture, etc.

XI

It was at that time I was asked by the International Brigade Association to become its Secretary. Jack Brent, who had magnificently filled that post until then, was too ill to continue (he spent the whole of the rest of his life, after being severely wounded at Jarama,[92] in and out of hospital, battling with pain and disability until his death in 1952). It was a many-sided job. The foremost task was to continue to aid and encourage the betrayed people of Spain. Urgent too was to rescue and help those members of the International Brigades who had been unable to return to their countries (Nazi or Nazi-controlled). Jack, in a brilliant move, had summoned a conference of representatives of those countries which had representatives in wartime London: Belgium, Czechoslovakia, Norway, Poland and Holland – and caused them to demand the release of their nationals. (Prisoners of war in international law were due to be released six months after cessation of hostilities, but what was to happen to the German, Austrian, Turkish and other volunteers who had no country to which they could return?). Anyway, Czech, Polish and other fighters were eventually released and came to London. The International Brigade Association was 'official' enough to be held responsible for their future; I often signed a receipt for a *man*, handed over to me by a British sergeant, for whom we were thenceforth responsible. The great majority of them joined the fighting forces of their own country (but this was not fortunate for the Poles, necessarily. The Polish Government in exile was far from democratic and the Polish forces, officered by the old regime, were sternly against the anti-fascists who joined them –

particularly Jewish ones, whom they persecuted and threatened – 'You wait until we get back into Europe, you'll never see *Poland* again'. In the end we had to run a campaign to have them freed from the Army, in which Tom Driberg[93] played a splendid and memorable part). Those who hadn't got fighting forces to join found employment in war industry. There were a few, but a few only, who couldn't make up their minds to do honest work and expected us to keep them. A few too, who posed as International Brigaders but weren't. But they were anti-fascists, and we tried to help. It was, as I have said, a many-sided job.

Earlier, in the spring of that year, I went to live in Battersea, with Frank and Anita, who had taken a large ground-floor flat where they were accommodating Laura, a 'Basque child' and Balbino, a Madrileno. With their usual generous warmth, they found room for me there. In a partly furnished flat upstairs were two young men, both recently arrived in London from Worcester: Tom, a gifted engineering draughtsman, and Ted, a sheet-metal worker who had been involved in a strike at the Austin motor works and had come to London 'to seek his fortune'. Before long we combined forces with these two and I got my bombed-out furniture, what there was of it, from the storage centre to fill up their rooms. We organised what would in these days be called a 'commune' and eventually, having decided it was silly to go on paying rents for two flats and using only one kitchen, took another house nearby. (Doesn't it sound easy; but there was plenty of empty property in London those days!) Tom, who was an 'absent-minded professor', was greatly admired by his friend, Ted, who was a country-lover, only son of a widowed mother and a self-taught sheet metal worker. The 'commune' worked as such bodies usually do – with enthusiastically worked-out rotas about taking turns for cooking, washing up, cleaning etc. which would have fallen quite quickly into muddle if it had not been for Frank, who kept us more or less up to the mark, and Anita, who would have done everyone's turn if she had been allowed to. Laura too,

Spanish in upbringing, could not be prevented from doing most of Tom's chores and Tom, who had been brought up in a household consisting of his mother and three loving sisters, was not at all averse. When I tell you that though he was nearly thirty they all still called him 'Boy' you will realise that it was taken for granted by him. He also had some spinal trouble which made it easier for them to 'spoil' him. Ted liked long country walks and soon we were striding off into Surrey at weekends for a breath of fresh air and some good healthy exercise. Ted got a piece of metal in his eye, which had to be extracted by an operation; the other eye inflamed in sympathy and for a week or two he was nearly blind. I used to come home in the evenings and read the days papers to him. We took to going out into the country for day-long Sunday walks. Ted was a good walker, and excellent map-reader and planner of excursions, a nature lover and a pleasant untalkative companion for a day out ...

Sometime in 1942 my sister Elizabeth got married. Born in 1897, she had had the misfortune to belong to that generation of young women whose potential husbands and lovers were killed in the 1914-1918 war. She had always longed to marry a clergyman, and at the age of forty-five married a Canon of Coventry Cathedral. Since I was, in many ways, the Black Sheep, she was not sure of really wanting me at the wedding, and sent me a back-handed invitation, saying 'I don't suppose you will be able to come, but Father would like us all to be together ...' It was a bit spiteful, but I decided to go. Having just sold one of George's four cellos, I first bought new outfits for both Frances and Martin, and then a new and very smart one for myself with the only Bond Street hat I have ever had or wanted. (It lasted for *years*, that hat. I took off the velvet bows that trimmed it, and gave it to a Hungarian friend, who some time later gave it back to me with a shred of fur around it, which made me look rather like Davy Crockett.) Even my own brother didn't recognise me when I got to the wedding. A Bishop celebrated. Afterwards there was a breakfast at Kunzles, and there was a hitch in the arrangements so we all sat round the table waiting for the food to come. I scribbled a note and flipped it to my younger brother (Richard): 'Ask the Bishop to do a miracle!' and he let out such a guffaw that it was only with great difficulty we kept it from the company.

We were a good 'commune', with frictions of course, but nothing resembling antagonisms. Tom seldom did his fair share of the chores, coming from the home of a widowed mother and devoted sisters, who, as I said, still called him 'Boy' after his thirtieth year. Anita was too motherly to him, and Laura so devoted to him, in a Spanish sisterly way, as not to mind doing his chores when he neglected them. Frank was a superb cook and within the limits of rationing we ate remarkably well and NO black market. The bombing having come to a lull (before the V-1s) I brought the kids home for a short holiday, uneventful in my recollection except that I bought Martin a real bow and some arrows, with which at first attempt he split an apple, balanced on a stick at about 15 yards. I have never forgotten the look of triumph on his face and the exclamation that burst with difficulty from his smiling lips: 'Great...big...!'

Ted and Tom shared a bedroom. One night Ted knocked at my door and asked me to come to Tom. Tom, who had a cough, had spat up a quantity of blood into the bedroom washbasin and was in a state of advanced terror. Feeling the need to cool the situation I cast around for comforting words and some inspiration made me say: 'Nonsense, you've just burst a small blood vessel. That isn't from your lungs, it would be full of froth if it were.' I don't know how I thought of this, or knew if it were true. But it temporarily calmed Tom, and we got him to lie down. Soon, however, he became convinced that he was about to die, and eventually we sent for the doctor (a German refugee) who, failing to cure his hysterical moanings, eventually sent for an ambulance and whipped him off to hospital. In the early hours of the morning Ted came back having seen Tom to bed, and asked me to marry him – inspired, I think, by my efficient coping. I didn't answer. I wavered for a month or so.

I had long decided that I would not be a worshipping Widow, poor old Mum who because of her devotion would have to be cherished for the rest of her life, dutifully visited once a week, a D.H. Lawrence Mother, especially to my adored Martin, who was at that time in the stage of 'little sons' ('Mummy, will you look like this when I am grown up? You MUST look like this when I'm grown up') where mummy looms large. I wanted them to have a stable home after the war. I wanted security for myself and them. I had already had to wage a fierce battle at the Town Hall when, returning to work after two weeks in bed with flu, I had been blandly told 'We don't pay temporary workers for sickness'. (I turned into a termagant, saying that if I had been a man with dependent children, there would have been no question, and it had not been explained to me as a condition of employment that I should not receive pay for sickness, threatening to consult my Trade Union – it put the fear of God into the Council, which hurriedly passed a resolution that put things right, and back-dated it to before my sickness. It was brought round to all *temporary* workers and the man who handed it to them for signature told me: 'I am telling them all it is due to you, Mrs Green...' But living from hand to mouth as I did, it put the fear of God into me, too, or at any rate fear of destitution for the children if anything should 'happen' to me.)

I consulted Frank and Anita. Frank approved of Ted, an honest workman. Anita said 'Ted is a man who won't change.' I was *fond* of Ted as one is fond of someone to whom one has done a good turn (reading when he could not see). I did not love him, and he repelled demonstrative affection, which was daunting. But I admired him, his steadiness and uprightness, his determination to carry through every job he undertook and his refusal to undertake any job he knew he might not be able to do fully. And one night, after coming home from an evening meeting outside London in a darkened tube train and getting out at the station in pouring rain and having fallen over a railing in the blackout, coming home drenched, with scraped shins, tired and hungry, I went straight in and told Ted I would marry him.

We went to Ffestiniog to tell the children. It was one of those occasions when parents took their kids out to tea (there was a farmhouse over the hill where pre-war things like scones, butter and jam were plentiful and each invited four friends to accompany them). So we streamed over the hills; on the way I grabbed first one and then the other and asked them what they would think if I got married to Ted. Frances said, with a touch of dismay: 'Oh, why?' and then quickly answered herself saying, 'Well, I don't see why not. It's only Ted after all.' And ran off. Martin scampered past and I grabbed him with the same question. Without a pause he said: 'That's okay,' and galloped off. He can't have given it a thought. Later on Frances mused: 'It won't be like a real *stepfather* ...' She had evidently envisaged someone objectionable and having known Ted in the holiday at Rusham Road, found him friendly.

I think they were a disappointment to him. Brought up as they were at Summerhill to have a very free and unawed attitude to grown-ups (a mother of a new pupil at one of the end of term fiestas at the school said to me in distress: 'The difficulty is, I can't tell which are staff and which are older pupils') there was a sort of airy equality in their attitude to him which didn't please him. This I had cultivated in my treatment of them – I tried never to command them or even to ask them to do something I didn't *know* they would do. I recall Ted once saying at the breakfast table: 'Frances, I haven't got any butter.' 'It isn't butter, it's marge,' retorted Frances, and Ted got up to fetch it for himself. He would have liked both of them, and particularly Martin, to like the things he liked, not realising that when they came to London, after spending all their school time in the country, they were not enthusiastic about the long country walks he planned for weekends – they would rather be shut up in stuffy cinemas or eating synthetic ice-cream in Lyons. He got a bicycle for Martin, who didn't ride it, much less tinker with it (Ted, who had started life as a motor mechanic, loved engines and anything to do with tools). After they left Summerhill and came to live in London, they enjoyed the country walks and especially the walking holidays we spent (Malvern Hills, Dartmoor, Forest of Dean, down to Southampton; the Peak District walking perhaps twenty miles a day) and Ted established a sort of masculine, anti-woman relationship with Martin in the home. But as time wore on and Frances came to adolescence, she ceased to be affectionate towards him from sheer feminine revulsion for a man not her father.

I had a tightrope to walk, between giving the children their father by keeping his memory alive – especially Martin, whom, as I said, I once found lying in bed staring at the ceiling ('What's the matter, can't you sleep?' – 'I'm *trying to remember Daddy ...*') – and building a family relationship which would satisfy Ted, who buried his jealousy deep down but remonstrated with me for talking about George so much. 'It's unhealthy,' he said. I don't think I was entirely successful in this, and much later in life I asked two or three International Brigaders who knew George to talk or write to Martin about their recollection of him.

I was wrong perhaps to insist that I should pay the expenses of the children, buy their clothes and pay their school fees etc. out of my own earnings. I felt that this was only fair, not saddling him with the expense of a ready-made family. But it may have hurt his pride, I don't know. This was an ongoing problem. Meanwhile, there was another year of war to go through. Our admiration and love for the heroic Soviet people grew and grew. Stalingrad renewed and intensified our faith and admiration in the first socialist country: we listened to Stalin's speeches on the radio and dismissed the unease created by the trials of Radek, etc. in 1937,[94] or repudiated the comments on them as 'capitalist propaganda'. The nasty taste left behind by the 'confessions' faded: they confessed, right; so there must have been something, and anyway the Soviet Union said so. I am not sure that Harry Pollitt didn't have his pinch of salt, but no less a person than D.N. Pritt declared the trials were genuine, so who was I to say they were rigged?[95] (It was not until I read Artur London's *The Confession* that I understood just *how* they were rigged.) By that time, I had, in the words of Nazim Hikmet, 'unlearned blind faith' and replaced my rose-coloured spectacles by clear glass ones. But this was a long time ahead: filled with exhilaration at the Victories of the Red Army and with glad relief that the slaughtering was over, we celebrated VE Day with the rest of London, Britain and the world.

Ted and I had done our bit for Civil Defence, Ted manning the anti-aircraft guns (as a member of the Home Guard) in Hyde Park three nights a week, and I womaning the telephones in Poplar Town Hall against air raids. They were different nights; we seldom saw one another except at breakfast or evening meals.

XII

I spent the years from 1943 to 1950 plugging away as Secretary of the International Brigade Association. There was much to be done, particularly as Spain was not 'in the news'. Terrible things were happening in that betrayed, exhausted country as Franco mercilessly persecuted those who had fought on the side of the Republic and the Germans ruthlessly hunted down those anti-fascists who had got left behind in occupied France, unable to go to their homes; there was a group in *residencé forcé* in Portugal, there was a larger group who had been sent, together with Spaniards, to slave-labour on the trans-Sahara railway; there were Spaniards who had been conscripted into the British Army (Pioneer Corps) and at the end of hostilities were threatened with repatriation to Spain (and certain death). We had to keep our fellow countrymen aware of what was going on and stir up support for those in danger. Badgering MPs, raising money, seeking channels for sending cash and comforts to the destitute. Quakers, Red Cross and Unitarian Service Committees all helped but all insisted that our help should not be *earmarked* for those we wanted to help (must be 'non-political'). We published a monthly – *Spain Today* – the editorial committee was three, the despatch was done by me and anyone I could grab to tie up bundles or stick stamps on folders. That much of our help did reach those we intended it for I was only to know much later, and even now I don't know it all. I also helped the Spanish emigrant colony in London who not only ran a club for their compatriots in exile but issued news and trade union bulletins to be distributed in the Trade Union movement here. I translated these at high speed into English, straight on to stencils – and here is where casting one's bread on the waters has its reward: it gave me a facility at direct and rapid Spanish-English translation that stood me in good stead much later as you shall read. A Spaniard once said in my hearing to a newcomer to the Spanish Club: 'What, not know Nan Green? Every Spaniard who comes to London knows first Trafalgar Square and then Nan Green.'

But really I was just the hub. The former members of the British battalion in the army and out of it retained their loyalty to the Spanish people and their pride at having fought alongside of them; the Trade Unions movement gave tremendous support; the cause of Spain, though somewhat eclipsed by the events of the war, remained bright and *untarnished*, and the Spanish struggle was never forgotten (and isn't to this day). Soon after the war ended we were able to send relief to our comrades more easily; we sent what now strikes me as an amazing sum to our French counterparts to start their Association and give help to the large number of disabled Frenchmen who had fought in Spain, unpensioned by the French government at that time. We worked to save the Spaniards of the Pioneer Corps from being sent back to their country. We 'adopted' a hospital for the disabled in North Africa and sent funds to purchase artificial limbs for some of them.

In 1945, the Polish government invited our association to send two delegates to a ceremony at which those Poles who had fought in Spain (and thereby lost their nationality) were to have it ceremonially restored with due honours for their service to the anti-fascist cause. I went, with TM, a Scot. The ruins of Warsaw were horrifying. People were living in cellars, the halves of houses, in shacks made of stones and bricks. It was the eve of All Saints Day and over all the rubble were little cards with flowers, commemorating the yet-unburied dead in the ruins. But they were determined to rebuild the city which had been threatened by Hitler with total destruction (and they did, with magnificent success in the course of the next few years). A theatre which had remained undamaged had been decorated with red bunting and white paper-sculpture, and in it the moving ceremony took place in which our Polish comrades commemorated their fallen, decorated and congratulated the living and promised pensions of the most generous kind to those who came home disabled.

We also attend a first post-war Trade Union Congress in Warsaw. Here, I felt, was our socialist dream coming true. The top position, the highest honour, was given to the trace unionists of the mineworkers – the basis of Poland's industrial wealth. Their delegation was preceded to the platform by an escort of young people wearing national dress and carrying flowers, and a brass band played national tunes. We were in that state of euphoria that comes after victory, everything we had longed for was going to come true, though the enormous task of rebuilding that shattered country loomed ahead and the tears and grief of their losses had not been wiped away.

We visited Auschwitz and saw the gas-ovens and incinerators; but these were cleaned up. What remained was the horrifying sight of a huge pile of *shoes*: boots, slippers, little children's shoes, stripped from the victims, and another pile of small possessions: cigarette cases, nail scissors, even false teeth, trinkets, the useful or sentimentally valued things one carries around – the last pile of objects, which the Nazis had not had time to send to Germany ... I shall never forget those shoes and the people who, stripped naked, had gone to their horrible deaths to feed the glory of the maniacs who had fallen on innocent people.

Here was an incredible area where socialism had not yet dawned. Driving along a main road, we passed a long procession of men, women and children laden with pathetic bundles and small suitcases, heads down, feet dragging, tired and worn. 'Who are these?' I asked. '*Volksdeutsch*,' was the reply. (Poles who had claimed German nationality and worked with Hitler's forces during the war). 'Where are they going?' 'Who cares?' said my Polish companion. Brotherhood of man? 'But they are people,' I said.

He turned his head in disgust and made no reply. It was *too soon* for forgiveness. The Nuremburg trials, which purported to establish the blame for this inhumanity, had not yet taken place. I was *for* that, but could not reconcile that sad procession of ordinary people with my idea of socialist morality. Indeed, in the celebration of the International Brigades in Warsaw, when speeches were made by the various delegates from other countries that had fought in Spain, Hans, a renowned German anti-fascist and military leader in the International Brigades,[96] had included a mild plea for working class solidarity with the German people, and had been asked to *omit* it. It was *too soon* ...

My fellow delegate, the Scotsman, had already left when I was put aboard an aeroplane (an old-fashioned military job – a Lancaster, perhaps?) to return to Paris with some of the other International Brigade delegates – Belgians, French, a little Polish teenage orphan daughter of a Polish miner who had worked in France and had been killed in Spain, and had come to Warsaw to receive the decoration bestowed on her father. There were also some Poles who were on various missions to Europe – I recall an admiral who was journeying to France to try and purchase naval supplies (he spoke English, having trained with the British Navy before the war and spent the war in a POW camp for officers: very officer-and-gentleman and British navy he was, and attached himself to me, or sought to do so by slavish admiration for everything British, from 'Your wonderful dark blue passport', to his Dunhill cigarette lighter, none of which cut any ice with me).

The plane got into trouble. We were forced to land – at Magdeburg, which had been turned into a posting camp for troops and where the airfield was not yet entirely de-mined. We landed safely but had to wait several days for repairs, refuelling and some sort of military permission from Warsaw and Paris. The Russian military authorities put camp beds in two large offices, one for men and one for women. They gave us adequate meals and we tried to pass the time by playing cards, discussing various problems, and even playing simple round games (at my instigation). But we were a nuisance and an embarrassment to them and some of them were a nuisance to us – for example the 'other ranks' contained some extremely uncouth peasant types who were manifestly unused to modern sanitation and choked up the loos, and even on one occasion raided our 'woman's dormitory' with evidently ugly intentions. Discipline was summoned and all was well. The days wore on. We asked if we could have a bath. Now came a piece of extra courtesy which offset the disagreeable aspects of our stay. The Red Army commanding officer called with his wife, who presented each of us women (about ten as far as I remember) with a complete set of pure silk underwear to change into when we had finished our bath (which took place in a large tub, four at a time with plenty of really hot water and soap). The delicacy of bringing a woman to give us the underwear was striking – I am not at all sure that the RAF would have thought of this and I am sure the USAF wouldn't.

Eventually we reached Paris, to a tearful welcome from our French and French-Polish friends who had had no news of us for several days. From Paris I went to Toulouse, where I met Pasionaria, whose fiftieth birthday was about to be celebrated. I had brought with me a hand-printed white wool headscarf from Mexico. Paris was cold, Toulouse even colder if possible. There was no heating and for the few days I was staying there talking to the Spaniards who were all working in overcoats and gloves or mittens, I could only get to sleep by dashing to the nearest estaminet, drinking two glasses of cognac (inferior) in two cups of lukewarm so-called coffee, and running at top speed to the hotel where I was staying, leaping into bed and slowly freezing until morning. Pasionaria was wonderful – as ever. She and the whole Spanish community were confident that the end of the war meant the end of Franco (this was the time of the Potsdam

declaration of Attlee and Truman etc.)[97] and Enrique Lister offered
to take me over the border to an area where Spanish *guerilleros*
were waiting to advance. 'You will be perfectly safe,' he said. But
by this time I had been 'missing' for so long I decided I must get
back to London, and started off for the most horribly cold railway
journey I have ever endured. I kicked my shoes off in the train,
and could not get them on to my swollen feet when we eventually
reached Paris.

Now here is another example of casting one's bread on the
waters (and its coming back made of cake). Jacques Dulery, a
member of the French resistance, had during the war made several
risky journeys to England and because it would have been
dangerous for him to contact the Party, used the International
Brigade office as his port of call. (Whether this was really safe as
he thought, I don't know; at all events he came and went
unharmed.) I knew nothing of his contacts and the only things
he wanted from me were nutmegs and peppercorns. I used to
keep large bags of these ready packed for whenever he called.
They were absolutely unobtainable in Paris. Now, when I tottered
off the Toulouse-Paris train on my swollen feet, he met me and
brought me to his home, where I met his Flemish wife. They
gave me *boiled chicken* and pain d'épices with butter on it!
Furthermore, Jacques was working in the French equivalent of
the Ministry of Transport (whatever it was called)[98] and in
December 1945, when cross-channel boats were full of troops
and VIPs and places were unobtainable by civilians, got me a
berth on the next steamer. During the crossing by night I heard
an American voice saying to someone: 'We aren't going to give
the secret of the Atom Bomb to the goddam Briddish because
the goddam Briddish will give it to the goddam Russians.'

They were glad to see me at home and I did a radio broadcast
for a BBC chat programme which was called 'In Town Tonight',[99]
elaborating on the courteous and kind treatment of the Russians
at Magdeburg, with special emphasis on the silk underwear and

the Colonel's wife.

To the vast and bitter disappointment of the Spaniards, the Potsdam pledge to 'eliminate the last vestiges of Fascism from Europe' was not completed by any action at all against Franco and before long the US had given him a substantial loan and were building Spain as an advance post against the Soviet Union in the foreseen war (had we begun to call it the Cold War?). More work for the International Brigade Association. Frances and Martin both at home now and both went to Battersea Polytechnic, doing extremely well in most subjects but failing miserably in maths. Frances became a nursery nurse in a local day nursery, Martin took work with a newsagency in Fleet Street.

Throughout 1944 and 1945, people in Britain began to think about the kind of world they wanted to see 'after the war'. All over the country – and in the armed forces abroad – discussion groups began to be formed to thrash this out. Ted and I, in 1943, had moved into a LCC flat on the Larkhall Estate in Clapham, where among some 200 families we had a Party branch of thirty to forty members. We had begun to move from our earlier exclusiveness (sectarianism) and had begun to see the need for working amongst our neighbours. However, Blind Faith was still very evident – illustrated by the first visit of the Branch Secretary, who had worked in the Soviet Union before the war as a telephone engineering expert and believed with his whole heart that the Soviet Union and Stalin could do no wrong. He took an affronted step backwards before our bookcase, pointing to a copy of John Reed's *Ten Days that Shook the World*.[100] 'I shouldn't keep that book on my shelves if I were you,' he said. It had been 'put on the Index' (cf. Roman Catholic Church) in the USSR because of its emphasis on the role of Trotsky in 1917. We did not remove the book. The rosy tint was beginning to fade from our spectacles, faster in Ted's case, I think, than mine, since he was in the thick of things, trying to convince his fellow-workers that 'the Party line' had all the answers, whereas my task was to be among like-minded people, since Spain was still an issue on which almost all could agree: those who did not agree, including a small but influential group of poets and intellectuals, had found the anti-fascist cause too stringent in its demands on their delicate emotions – 'the God that Failed' was the God that had failed *them* ...[101]

At all events we kept John Reed's book prominently displayed, and helped to form discussion groups that met in our tiny flat almost every Sunday (sometimes as many as forty neighbours, sitting on the floor or on every available chair) to get our minds clear as to what the war was being fought for and what we wanted from our government after the end, which was becoming clear after Stalingrad.

These many discussion groups, I am convinced, played a tremendous part in the outcome of the 1945 election. Labour's victory was felt as a victory for a socialist future. 'I bet Old Joe's laughing,' said a bus conductor.[102] And, for a week or two, or a month or two, we experienced a surge of confidence in the future. Some members of our Party – I don't know how many but I know they existed – actually left and joined the Labour Party to hurry things along.

But the Apocalypse was yet far off.

There we were in the post-war world, a world filled with joy and relief at the defeat of fascism, but with no time to rest or to stop to mourn: the task all over Europe was to re-build, to repair the wanton, senseless, beastly damage that had been done to the work of man's hands, to economies, to agriculture and above all to men and women, to families, to homeless people (a new category came into the vocabulary – Displaced Persons, or DPs as they began to be called). The problems were enormous. We learned a new term, People's Democracy, for the governments that had been formed in various countries after the defeat of the Nazi occupiers and, we hoped, the removal of all those who had collaborated with fascism at the expense of their own fellow countrymen. I say 'we hoped' but we soon found that there were two viewpoints among the victors – mainly the British and United States 'occupation forces'. Known Nazis were reinstated in Germany on the pretext that they were the only ones who understood the running of things. Known reactionaries and collaborators emerged in France, Holland and elsewhere and 'posthumously joined the resistance', claiming to have been anti-fascist all along. In the countries occupied by the Red Army, on the contrary, harsh punishment was sometimes meted out to the Right and vengeance was wrought against all oppressors of the people during and even previous to the war. How could the resistance forces in Italy, Yugoslavia and elsewhere have built such tremendous and heroic movements for liberation without the broadest possible unity, forged in the death-defying long, grim years of battle? On both sides of the 'Iron Curtain', as it came to be called,[103] that unity was put under strain amid the post-war problems and on each side the victors strove to shape the new Europe according to their views of society. Churchill sent British troops to Greece to defeat the revolutionary force that had borne the brunt of the fight against the Nazis, for the kind of world they wanted after the war – the nature of which they had hammered out between various groups, parties and sects in the intervals of fighting.

Only in Yugoslavia, with Tito and his partisans, despite British endeavours to build-up and maintain support for Mikhailovich (until it became clear even to them that Mikhailovich had no intention of fighting the Nazis, but was biding his time and maintaining his troops to fight the people once the Germans had been defeated),[104] did the broad popular unity which fought such tremendous battles, hardly aided from either side, maintain that unity after the end of the war and carry it through into the new day.

'People's Democracy' was meant to be a form of government uniting the anti-fascist forces in each country. It was not meant to be fully socialist, but a progress towards socialism carrying with it the whole people. This is how we in the Communist Party of Great Britain defined it after considerable discussion and much effort to trace a line among the muddled, problem-beset forms emerging in the various countries liberated with the help of the Red Army, for which unstinted admiration existed among all the peoples.

With the Fulton Speech and the Marshall Plan the formation of two antagonistic 'sides' began to take shape. Harry Pollitt, in his report to the congress of our Party, spoke of the dangers of a new war – and was privately attacked by the French fraternal delegates, who said such a line would sow defeatism in Europe.

1951 saw a new sort of extraordinary Party Congress – a Congress of Communist Parties from countries coming within the sphere of British Imperialism. We gave hospitality to the delegation from Malaya (as it was then called). To represent the composition of the people of that country, three delegates were appointed: a Malay, an Indian and a Chinese. All had participated in the resistance movement and were still striving for freedom from colonialism and all three were quiet, modest, experienced and utterly without rancour towards us as representatives of their oppressors. The Chinese, Wu Tien-Wang, managed to get on a course at the School of Oriental Studies and stayed on for some months, sharing a bedroom with Martin. He became one of the family.

There is a sequel to this, which I shall now introduce, out of chronological order. When Martin was conscripted at the age of eighteen for military service war was being waged against the Malayan people still fighting for their freedom. At the end of his training, word went round that Martin's group (Signals) were to be posted to Malaya. Martin said: 'I can't go ... I can't fight against Wu Tien-Wang.' 'Okay,' I said. 'Refuse. I'll stand by you and send you cakes when you are in the glasshouse.' But it never came to that, fortunately for us all. Martin developed scarlet fever a week before the posting, and by the time he came out of hospital, his group had left. He was posted to *Woolwich*, where he did the rest of his military service, coming home every afternoon (except on days when he had Guard Duty), spending the evenings at home and rising in the early dawn to be back in barracks. I spent my military service, he said later, resisting being made into a murderer. What he got from it was an ability to mix with all sorts and conditions of men, facility in touch-typing and a knowledge of the Morse Code. His discharge report said he was a good soldier but apt to keep himself to himself. In his leisure time he edited and wrote, with a friend, Tristram Hull, a poetry magazine called *Nimbus*, which they sold personally to bookshops or by (scarce) subscription. It did not make, but nor did it lose, any money.

The years from 1943 to 1951 were far from humdrum domestically, with much coming and going – between the young people who permeated the house as friends of Martin and Frances and the hordes of American GIs – either ex-International Brigade or friends of theirs who called, spent their leaves, and incessantly discussed the war and the world we wanted after the war. We literally kept 'open house' for all comers (the key hung on a string behind the letter box) and I don't know how we managed to accommodate so many – or feed them, except that the GIs were accustomed (by order) never to visit a civilian home in England without offerings of food, which did much to offset the *rationing* that was in effect. Tins of peaches, packets of coffee, olive oil (a bottle of near-gold), soap, even khaki-coloured towels from the stores, all was grist to the Shipley House mill, and people sometimes lay like sardines on the bedroom floors to be wakened with cups of tea in the mornings. (I recall one experienced GI saying to the others, 'Go on, drink it, it's a good English custom.')

I recall running an English class for fellow students of Frances or Martin who found themselves, though proficient in English, inexpert in some of the requirements of English at Battersea Polytechnic (they'd never heard of *parsing*) – a once weekly session of hilarious discussion with me keeping one lesson ahead by mugging up the grammar book a day before ... I am glad to say they all passed in that branch of learning when the time came and I still possess a thick and beautifully bound cookery book (useless) which was presented to me by one of them in gratitude.

I think it was in 1949 Frances eloped. She had been to Paris for the Quatorze July celebrations and had there met and been fallen in love with by a young Frenchman (an architectural student) who declared he could not live without her and pursued her by a correspondence of which I was unaware. Drawing out her savings from her nursery nurse's salary, she packed her things and decided to leave on the morning train for Paris. But on the Saturday night she relented towards me, and announced her intentions. Dilemma. Ted insisted that since she was under-age I should confiscate her passport and forbid her to leave, as I had a right to do. My attitude was: SHE MUST GO. If ever in her life afterwards she was unhappy she would turn and rend me; that she must have her own experience and nobody could have it for her. My dear friend Jack Coward, who had loved George in Spain, was staying there that weekend. He agreed with me. 'She's your daughter, Nan,' he said. 'She'll be all right.' I said goodbye to her in anxious anguish. Thus Frances was off to Paris in 1949, full of unrepatriated US troops; with no job nor prospects of a job, and not more than £30 sterling.

Five agonising weeks followed, with no word. Eventually I wrote a short and unreproachful letter which I sent to the boy's address for Frances, saying that the fatted calf was ready for her at any time. She replied in a letter which began Dear Mummy – she had been calling me Nan for years – and ended, 'I realise that I have been a fool and I must now take the consequences of my folly', and she returned home within a few days. The lad had proved a man of straw – but can one blame him if his parents had refused to countenance his marriage to Frances before he had finished his studies? Both, I suppose, ended sadder – and wiser.

(Twenty-four years later the young man rang our number and asked for Miss Frances Green. William answered saying that he was her elder son. He did not pursue the matter further. Had he conceivably imagined that Frances was still waiting for him – or was it just a sentimental wish to talk over old times?)

Frances relinquished her near-completed nursery-nurse training and took a job in the telephone service. She had discovered a liking for the French language and found that if she joined the Continental Trunks service she would get free tuition in French, the 'international language'. Soon she joined the Party, saying that she needed it to know 'how to behave' with her fellow operators, very many of whom were refugees from Poland and other East European countries, all determined not to return to the new 'People's Democracies' and bursting with horror stories about Red Domination and the usual propaganda scares about confiscation of private property, brain-washing and slave-labour (which was some of it true, alas, as we discovered later, but which we dismissed wholesale as 'capitalist propaganda').

She had a series of boy friends, most of them foreign (I have noted, though it is not a good generalisation, being founded on too few facts, that girls educated in co-educational schools find their contemporaries too immature – their *English* contemporaries, I mean). Frances passed rapidly and with admirable coolness through brief affairs with a Dane, a West Indian, a melancholy guitar-playing Swede, at which stage she met Noël, an exuberant, terrifically energetic French-Mauritian whom she married in 1951 and to whom she is still, thirty years later, happily married. It is not my purpose to analyse their marriage here, but it is one of the very few happy, stable, and long-lasting marriages I know – there are all too few these days and, while I am glad that unhappy relationships are nowadays more easily dissolved, I tend to think that sometimes people don't *try hard enough*, blithely expecting to 'live happily ever after' (pernicious phrase), but not fully seeing that there is give as well as take in a marriage and it takes hard work to build something permanent.

Martin (as mentioned previously) was called up for military service in 1950. In those days it was compulsory and lasted two years, with three-and-a-half years continuation in the Territorials (with a camp once a year). He was not fortunate enough (wise enough, tenacious enough, clever enough?) – at any rate not *fortunate* enough to establish a satisfactory relationship until much later, as we shall see when I get to more recent times.

Events in the period I am dealing with (1943-50) continued the development of political understanding and brought some dusty answers, which clouded the rose-coloured spectacles. The Spanish cause, which was still my main responsibility in the Party, remained (and remains) untarnished despite the 'god-that-failed' desertion of those intellectuals who found they could not sustain conviction and spent subsequent years justifying their weakness, and, later, the far Left all-or-nothingers who wrote books, articles etc. on the 'betrayal' of the Spanish revolution by the Communist Party of Spain and the USSR for having striven to build and maintain the Popular Front.

But events there were that demanded 'the painful process of real thinking' – I recall all-night sessions in Shipley House when we strove to hammer out the 'Browder Line' with American and Canadian soldiers, the virtual dissolution of the American Communist Party and its fusion with an amorphous broad Left following the war and the victory of the Left in the post-war world:[105] for a time I sat on the fence and subscribed to the line of 'American exceptionalism' – but not for long. The Marshall Plan, disillusion with the 1945 Labour Government, the Czechoslovak upheaval of the early 1950's, the *British Road to Socialism* or the discussion that led to its formation, the formation of the Cominform and its denunciation of Yugoslavia in 1951 – how to *believe* that the Yugoslavians, who had fought fascism so heroically and with such unity, could turn over night into a 'nest of spies and traitors' – what had they *done*, except to try and build up their devastated country with help from all who would give it? The brides, the Soviet Doctors' trial and other sinister stories – thoughts went buzzing round like a fly in a bottle.[106]

Up to 1950, my main work and my main Party task was still concerned with Spain. In this period, it mainly concerned the struggles to save the lives and liberty of Franco's opponents, repeatedly sending British lawyers to attend the trials (by Military Tribunal) of Communist, Socialist and Anarchist figures who worked underground to build the resistance. If there were more Communists on our list it was because the Spanish Communist Party was the foremost and sometimes the only opposition force of any mark or merit. In the years immediately following the end of World War Two the Spanish Communist Party had maintained and organised *guerilla* forces which strove heroically to rouse the people (mainly in the countryside areas) to resist the fascist persecution and restore democracy. But the people were exhausted, the country bled white. Crippling poverty stalked the whole country and military action decimated the numbers of the *guerilleros*. A decision was reached to change strategy and tactics – to disband the *guerilla* formations and to enter the legal mass organisations, such as were permitted by Franco, and work from inside to build an opposition which could overthrow the hated regime, uniting not only those who had been on the side of the Republic but everyone who had reason to wish for change, regardless of their past.

Meanwhile our Association worked to arouse support for the persecuted, raising large sums of money to pay the fares of the barristers (who always gave their services with great generosity), observers and their interpreters, who had to be ready to leave at almost a moment's notice, since the Franco authorities did not announce the actual date of the trials until a few days before. Among these were Richard Freeman, Ian Mikardo and many others.[107] Sometimes arriving in time, sometimes too late, they pursued every legal aspect of the trials and reported on them. They could never be anything but 'observers' but probably their presence helped to modify the savage sentences demanded by the prosecution.

There were whole days of envelope addressing and duplicator turning.

In 1947 a Labour MP, Francis Noel Baker, made a clandestine journey to Spain and reported his findings on return in *The Times*.[108] The Franco authorities, through their embassy in London, cavilled at this, stating that there was no reason any Labour MP should not visit Spain openly and with full permission from the Spanish authorities. Just at this stage we learned of three women who were in prison awaiting trial, charged with forcing an organisation to help prisoners. I should explain that at that time, prisoners were fed and kept in cells but were not given prison clothing or any laundry service, their families having to provide these. Since many prisoners were in jails far from their homes, where families could not reach them, and since some had no family, organisations were formed to provide the help which was needed. These three women – a school teacher, a textile worker, and another – had been accused of forming an illegal organisation and sentences were demanded which jeopardised their lives. Leah Manning, who had been a firm supporter of the Spanish Republicans and had been one of the prime movers in the efforts to bring 2000 children from the Basque country when in 1937 the fascist forces were bombing and shelling civilians in their drive to cut off the Basque country from the Republican side, and was herself a Labour MP, took up this offer and invited Monica Whately, a prominent Roman Catholic and secretary, I think, of the Save the Children Fund,[109] to accompany her. They were accepted – it could not have been avoided by the Embassy, after their statement about freedom to visit. But neither woman spoke Spanish and I was asked to be their interpreter. We three applied for visas. I went to the Consulate to pick them up and the clerk said: 'I have permission for Mrs Manning and Miss Whately but nothing here for Mrs Brake' (my married name). 'That's nonsense,' I said. 'They can't go without an interpreter,' and I pushed my passport over to him with an imperious gesture – which paid off. He meekly stamped it.

We were furnished with an official interpreter by the Franco Foreign Office – a young man who had been educated at Hailebury (a Roman Catholic public school) and who escorted us everywhere. (Also, as I subsequently learned from a Cockney chauffeur at our Embassy, with a couple of plain clothes detectives, who dogged our unofficial footsteps on shopping trips, visits to restaurants etc.) Our 'hosts' pretended not to be aware of the purpose of our visit and expressed surprise when we asked to visit the three women in prison. But the interview was agreed in the presence of the prison governor and other officials, and of course the young man from the Foreign Office, all ears. The Franco authorities had long been denying that there were but a handful of political prisoners, and that these were all 'criminals', in the whole of Spain. I began, as we were crossing the courtyard to enter the prison proper, by casually asking the Governor how many prisoners were held there: he gave the number. And how many of these are political prisoners, I went on. About fifty, he said. This was more than a mere handful in one prison alone.

'They will tell you lies,' said the Foreign Office interpreter, before the three women were led in.

I began by introducing Leah and Monica, and then said: 'They would like to ask you some questions, but we realise that in the present circumstances there may be things which you won't wish to say. We shall quite understand.' Leah asked the sixty-four dollar question. Have you been tortured? There has been torture in this prison, they replied discreetly. They told us the reason for their arrest, and the sentences demanded – possibly the death sentence. Both Leah and Monica ended up with short speeches assuring them of our concern and solidarity and they were led away. We were then taken on a tour of the establishment (a 'show' prison, evidently) and shown the diet sheets, the cells, and the nursery for the children of mothers imprisoned there. Leah, with superb understanding, loitered deliberately, asking questions in corridors while I dashed into cells (all open because it was dinner time) quickly asking the four or five women in each, 'What are you here for?' There were no beds in the cells, only rolled-up mattresses. Everyone was working at knitting, crochet or embroidery – to sell, they told me, to buy the extra food they needed (so much for the diet sheets!). In the nursery, the spotlessly clean children were eating what looked like an excellent lunch. *Dear* Leah, who had taught in kindergartens in the course of her career, decided to puncture the discipline and walking between the tables began to roar with laughter so infectiously that the whole dining room was soon in an uproar, to the consternation of the wardresses.

When we got back to London, I wrote a feature article for the *Daily Worker*, which was of course signed Nan Green – I had kept this name as Secretary of the International Brigade Association. Leah paid a visit to the Spanish Ambassador, who was fulminating about my 'dishonesty'. 'But Your Excellency,' said Leah, 'what is dishonest about travelling in your *own* name with your *own* passport?'

The three women received relatively light sentences and the demand for the death sentence was dropped. I like to think that our visit was instrumental in saving their lives, or at least contributing to a milder sentence.

XIII

The threat of atomic war began to loom; the USSR took the initiative in starting the World Peace Movement (Paris, Wroclow congresses) which aimed to be broad and all-embracing but was distrusted by many because of its origins. A world-wide campaign was launched to collect signatures against the use of the atom bomb. 'Peace', because of the press campaign against the movement, had become a dirty word. I recall knocking at doors in a mean street in Battersea with sheets of forms for collecting signatures. It was dark. 'I've come to ask you to sign a petition against the Atom bomb,' I began. 'Come in,' said the woman who answered, 'Of course I'll sign that.' We went into the living room, which opened off the street and was lit by gas. At the head of the form were the words British Peace Committee. She drew back. 'Oh, if it's *anything to do with* peace I can't sign it,' she said.

The British Peace Committee eventually collected a million signatures against the use of the atom bomb, which may or may not (one has no way of knowing) have influenced the Attlee government when the Korean War broke out. It was decided to hold the next world conference in England, and Sheffield was chosen, as it had a very large Hall holding thousands of people. Suddenly the Party asked me to take the job of organising this, a huge and awe-inspiring task. Not that I was single-handed – behind me was the Peace Movement, the World Peace Council, our Party and the vast majority of the British people.

And I was given a team of excellent, efficient and devoted helpers – mostly members of the Party – to whom were allocated separate jobs such as arranging the travel, accommodation, feeding of the 2000 delegates from various countries, and the press and public relations and a thousand and one other aspects of the big event. I discovered that a good organiser is one who does nothing herself, but presents the tasks and the reason for them to those responsible and leaves them to do it – constantly checking to make sure that it is progressing satisfactorily. We all stayed in one boarding house, kept usually for travelling 'reps' by a young couple who knew little or nothing of our aims but became gradually inspired with enthusiasm far beyond their commercial interests, thought up ways of making our life easier and showed immense ingenuity in protecting us from the Press, which (mainly) was searching for scandalous items to denigrate the whole conference, sitting in cars outside our lodging to watch our comings and goings and even descending to such stupidities as describing our women as 'drably dressed, lacking make-up, all wearing flat heels' etc., which was manifestly untrue but another stick to beat us with.

We met for a check-up each evening. So many hotel rooms hired: Sheffield had not nearly enough accommodation and Maud, with great ingenuity, realised that touristy places like Buxton, which would have closed down at this time of the year, would be only too glad to have a fortnight of full beds. The catering problem – for midday meals and constant refreshments and snacks – was solved after vain attempts to find one or more restaurants by hiring a huge marquee, installing electric. coolers, chairs, tables, etc. and having it erected on a bomb-site near the Hall. The catering firm, scenting valuable publicity, entered into the problems of special meals for Muslims, vegetarians, etc. with enthusiasm. And all this was arranged by a team led by Jane, a *housewife* who discovered in herself powers of organisation she had never known she possessed. We hired ten Gestetner machines and operators. An electrician, whom we called Slim (because his name was Somerville)[110] undertook the wiring of the hall for simultaneous translation – and he had never done anything of the kind before, but produced a thoroughly efficient system despite the fact that the listening apparatus had to be installed during the night before the opening (because the Hall was being used for a concert the previous evening). Doris, a social-worker in ordinary life, used her extremely sexy charms to persuade the Police to set up big signs on the main roads leading to the hall with arrows pointing to the Conference. A feeling of pride began to be noted, as Sheffield attained fame as the venue of the World Peace Congress. Landladies in the city showed pleasure when we asked them to accommodate some of the hundred or so 'helpers' who would converge at the time – translators, typists, messengers, 'security' men (led by a seaman who had served in the International Brigade).

My other discovery was that a group of people all working for the same job in which they believed (knowing what they fought for, like Cromwell's soldiers) could become not merely invincible but *fast friends*, ignoring personal whims and fancies and antagonisms (one or two mavericks and grousers there were, but I am ashamed to say that I sent them back to London on the grounds that we hadn't time to sort them out). People afterwards praised me for having created a Team Spirit but it had nothing to do with me, it was the *job* that stretched us all and made us feel capable.

And then the blow fell. The Attlee Government took sudden fright, and started banning people from entering the country in a haphazard and panic-stricken fashion that showed their haste and hatred. Noted Continental Socialists, such as a French woman deputy who had lived in London throughout World War Two and been closely associated with Attlee himself, were turned back; equally noted Continental and other Communists arrived safely (including Picasso, the Soviet author, Fedayev and others).[111] There were twenty-four hours of utter confusion, and at last it was decided that the whole Congress should be moved elsewhere;

the Polish government offered Warsaw.

The day before the Congress was to open I received a telephone call telling me of the change of plans. But I was told not to make it public until press statements had been issued. That was one of the worst mornings of my life. I sat in my office (in a Church hall we had hired as headquarters) while one by one the team came in to report everything ready. I went to inspect the marquee at Jane's request: the tables were laid, menus printed in several languages, the band was rehearsing. 'Splendid, splendid,' I said. 'What's the matter?' someone asked me, 'You look pale.' I dashed back and sloshed some colour on my cheeks and went on ... at eight o'clock in the evening the whole team and all the newly-arrived 'helpers' were summoned to a meeting where I broke the news.

We decided to 'open' the Congress the next day just to show what it could and would have been like, while the organisation in London made superhuman efforts for the delegates to travel to Warsaw. Poor Slim, heartbroken at the blow, went into the hall from the meeting and started to dismantle his work. We sent after him to tell him to mantle it again for the 'opening'. He worked through the night, and his landlady sent him over a hot breakfast, carried by her son between two plates, to show her indignation; up to that time she had grumbled a good deal at his erratic comings and goings, but like the rest of Sheffield she was angry. Gestetner had started to prepare a publicity brochure entitled 'Gestetner at the World Peace Congress'. The catering firm made its own protest: over the Festival of Britain, scheduled for the coming summer, where were they going to be?[112] And subsequently they *relinquished* the substantial retainer we had paid them for the fortnight's catering. Landladies said goodbye to the 'helpers' and refused compensation ...

The meeting was held. The translation equipment worked perfectly. Speeches were made in a variety of languages and were translated. Picasso made one of the shortest contributions. 'My father was a painter of animals and birds,' he said, 'and as I grew up he let me help in painting the legs of birds. How proud he would be to know that my two modest doves have circled the world.'[113] The security worked: a group of provocateurs, closely watched by the press, endeavoured to start a fracas. They were removed and I watched little old Tony and a couple of others, all ex-International Brigade, *lean* gently but firmly on the press cameras trying to get pictures of the scuffle.

Next morning began the process of transferring the delegation to London there to be embarked on aeroplanes for Warsaw. The London end saw to that. I was left behind with Maurice, assistant organiser,[114] to clear up the confusion in Sheffield. A week later we too caught a plane to Warsaw, where the Congress had already reopened thanks to superhuman work by the Polish government.

The World Council of Peace held several Congresses in this and subsequent years and I think they did a lot of good in bringing together people of different nationalities and views and persuading people that peace was something that had to be striven for, hammering out policy statements (nightmare sessions where the leading committees spent hours perfecting phrases which expressed the united view of the participants). But there was always an atmosphere of distrust due to the origins of the movement and the fact that criticism of the Soviet Union was felt by those of Blind Faith to be 'capitalist propaganda' (which some of it was) or outright enmity. Courageous socialists, Quakers and others defied unpopularity and scorn by stating their views in open sessions and people like Ivor Montagu and Joliot Curie[115] exercised immense skill and diplomacy to maintain the precarious unity, but in my opinion it never really broke into a genuinely broad movement, the non-Blind-Faith element being peopled to some extent by those I eventually learned to define as 'professional peace delegates', like a Latin American (unfrocked) priest, an English Quaker, a Chilean painter, and others who found themselves in great demand in various countries' peace movements as a manifestation of this very 'breadth' they were striving for. A few of these had so many invitations to so many countries that they stayed away from home for weeks and months at a time and lost any connection they had had with the rank and file in their own countries, and were fêted to such an extent that they began to expect VIP treatment wherever they went.

The process of 'unlearning blind faith' was slow, with me, and went by fits and starts until 1953. I am not a quick thinker: indeed I don't know what I think until I have thought about a problem for quite a while. Gordon Childe, the historian,[116] once wrote of 'the painful process of real thinking' and there was usually some point at which it dawned on me, some turning point where I said to myself: '*That's* what I've been thinking for ages!'

There were many instances of events I did not like: the Soviet Brides, for instance. Young women who had married British and other foreigners during the war period and were forbidden to join their husbands when the time came for those foreigners to return home. We had such a neighbour, a civil servant who had held quite a minor job in the British Embassy in Moscow and returned to await his bride, who never came. All sorts of specious excuses were patted to and fro for this: to protect the women from the evils of life under capitalism for instance. But I couldn't make it sound right. The trials (and subsequent rehabilitation) of the Soviet doctors left a nasty worm burrowing in my consciousness. And then the discovery by the Cominform that the Yugoslav Communist Party was 'a nest of spies and assassins' which had to be expelled from the international movement.

Now, up to this time, having as my main and constant Party task, as well as my daily work, the building and maintaining of solidarity with the Spanish people, I had not been asked to do any task I disagreed with. In 1951 I was asked in the name of the Party to bring about the disbandment of a broad committee of Friends of Yugoslavia, of which I was a member. With a very sore heart I obeyed, putting forward the specious argument that since there was total disagreement in the entire Friendship membership we had better disband it for the time being. The non-Communists – good sincere people – saw that a split would leave them a minority (because most of the 'friendship' movements were staffed and kept going by Party members) and agreed. Leah, who saw through me with unerring clarity, said I was being 'disingenuous' – which I was. (Many years later, having unlearned blind faith, and having this on my conscience, I wrote to Leah and acknowledged that I had been dishonest. She did not reply, but as she was by then very old and died not long afterwards, I don't think she was unforgiving.)

After Warsaw, I changed jobs. There was some euphoria in the British Peace Committee after the success of the Warsaw Congress and it was decided to expand and I became the organiser of the London Peace Council, a separate but united (like the Holy Trinity) branch of the British Peace movement, which prided itself on having one or two elements of a 'broader' character than the parent body. Steering a course between the two was not an easy matter; some local peace committees in London affiliated to the British Peace Committee and some to the London Peace Council, and there was no homogeneity either within or among them. London possessed a small but vociferous group of devoted women who believed in furthering the spirit of peace by courting arrest and making tremendous speeches in magistrates' courts. (One went to prison and continued her propaganda, among her fellow inmates and wardresses in Holloway, where she had once been a wardress herself).[117] The parent body spent much time in holding tortuous conferences with other peace organisations, such as the Peace Pledge Union as well as others, finding points of unity. It was all rather amorphous and eventually a new policy came down 'from above' (the World Peace Council) for another world-wide signature campaign, demanding a Five Power Peace Pact (Britain, France, the Soviet Union, China and the United States of America). Thousands of forms were printed and handed out to supporters who, glad of something active to do, set out to collect names – some with immense success.

In the Summer of 1952 we began to organise for the next World Peace Congress, to be held in Vienna in the autumn. At the same time our Party received a request from China to send some technical helpers for a Peace Congress of the Asian and Pacific Regions, to be held in Peking. Stenographers and interpreters were requested. (China, never having had diplomatic relations with more than a handful of Spanish speaking countries, had no interpreters in that language.) I naturally volunteered to be one, but was slapped down by V D-J, the British Peace Committee's General Secretary:[118] 'You will be needed in Vienna, so put it out of your mind.' A week or two later Ted and I, together with a small group of others, were offered a holiday in Romania (it being the habit of brother parties in the socialist countries to provide restful holidays for active functionaries every year). We were James Klugan, Margaret, Bill and Molly, Allen Hutt and his current wife, Howard Hill and Mary – the Yorkshire organiser – and Ted and me.[119]

We were given embarrassingly lavish treatment – ten days in the mountains and ten by the sea, banquet-style meals ('Ah'm getting a bit fed oop wi' chicken,' remarked Howard), limousines everywhere and VIP seats at the National Day procession in Bucharest. (Handshakes from Georgiu-Dezh).[120] At evening parties we met resting functionaries from other Communist Parties and soon discovered that we were expected to *sing*. Now, all other nations seem to have national songs of impeccably patriotic quality but we were not prepared to groan 'The Red Flag', particularly as the tune belonged to a German hymn. So we developed two or three choruses which won applause from all – 'Pretty Polly Perkins', a Victorian ditty called 'You Take to the Boats, Boys', and lastly one which might be characterised as faintly revolutionary, 'Lillibulero'.[121] Since none of our hearers understood the words, they were taken as genuine British working-class sentiment.

Apart from slight unease at being given such VIP treatment –
by a Party which had undergone ten times the vicissitudes we
could have envisaged, it was a marvellous holiday. We flew back
to Prague where Roy Gore, an emissary from the headquarters
of the World Council of Peace, told me: 'You get off here. You
are going to China.' Remembering the stern injunction of V D-J,
I said: 'But I can't. I'm supposed to go to Vienna next month.'
However, it had all been arranged, our Party had been quite
unable to rustle up sufficient interpreters to fulfil the Chinese
requirements. All I had to do was to get my visas: transit through
the USSR and entry into China. This was easier said than done.
Daily visits to the Soviet Embassy met with unexplained delay. (I
am sure my passport was lying in some bureaucratic in-tray,
despite table-thumping.)

Ted went back to London, envying me the coming experience
and carrying two huge hampers of food and wine which our
Romanian friends had given each of us 'for the journey'. He
managed somehow to get them through Customs. After nearly a
fortnight of heel-kicking in Prague, I eventually got away, in a
group destined for Peking consisting of Ivor Montagu, a French
journalist whose name I may remember before I've finished this
tale, and George Jeffares, a teacher of Spanish from Dublin whose
strain of Irish humour enlivened the trip through the Soviet Union.
('My God,' he said when we were visiting a children's creche in
Gorky and saw the toddlers in a paddling pool, they even wash
the nappies with the babies in them!) We spent a couple of days
in Moscow and saw the Red Square, with a feeling of treading
on holy ground: in the Lenin Mausoleum we saw the embalmed
figure of the great man. A Colombian peasant – one of a group
of Latin American delegates to Peking – repeated over and over
again: 'To think I should become acquainted with Lenin!' The
queue to pass through the Mausoleum waited patiently, as it had
been doing without stopping for thirty years. But is it really

Marxist, said a nasty little grub in my mind, to make a dead body an object of worship and pilgrimage? I'm sure Lenin would have agreed with me. He lay there looking a bit amused ...

Air travel in those days was not a matter of jets. We Stopped at Krasnoyarsk, Nobosibirsk (where we went to a magnificent production of Ivan Susanin in the Opera House) and Irkutsk,[122] where we had to leave all our rubles in a Bank against our return, and flew off over Lake Baikal to the East. I have flown over Baikal several times since but never in such perfect weather, and saw the largest inland lake in the world.

XIV

Someone has since invented the term 'cultural shock' for the amazement and delight of changing civilisations as we did on arrival in Peking. To start with, the magical quality of the *light*, which is (was?) like that of no other city I have ever seen, enhancing the colours of the roofs (yellow for Imperial buildings, blue elsewhere), and the glowing red pillars of the palaces on this first occasion, too, the red silk lanterns, yellow-tasselled, hung out in preparation for the celebration of Liberation Day (October 1st). The populous streets filled with people all wearing dark blue, the thousands of bicycles (no trams as yet except for one short route in the centre of the City), the large-wheeled peasant carts drawn by one horse with a donkey for company (not to help with the pulling) and trains of laden *camels* stalking amid the traffic with a disdainful air. Pedicabs. Storytellers. Booths and street stalls. A funeral procession with bamboo and paper models of things for the deceased to take into the next world – a car, bicycles, chests, followed by white-clad mourners and gongs. Eyes and ears were assailed with new sights and sounds ... and people, people, people, everywhere – strange people all black-haired and dark-eyed, moving with grace and dignity and seemingly unhurried. The carters urging their horses on with piercing stouts of 'Yü, yü!' Cicadas carried about as pets in little straw cages, chirruping away noisily. Bicycle bells ringing, the horns of the scarce motor cars blasting away – pedestrians not taking much notice. Clicks – the click of the abacus, the click of the bones wielded by story-tellers, about whom little groups of passers-by stood, the tock-tock and brass disks of the street vendors. The cries, which I did not learn to identify until much later, of the menders ('I mend wood,' 'I mend leather shoes,') ... it was overwhelming.

George Jeffares and I, having received bouquets of gladioli from a posse of welcoming schoolgirls, were driven to the large house where the British interpreters and stenographers were lodged. There, with immense cordiality, we were greeted by a group of English-speaking Chinese students who had been charged with our welfare for the period of the Peace Congress. I have never experienced such solicitude, such unostentatious concern for our wellbeing.

Only a few days were left before we were to begin our duties. There were, I found, plenty of interpreters for the other languages in which the congress was to be conducted (Japanese, Chinese, Russian, English and Spanish) but we were only *eight*, of whom three could translate but not interpret, two knew only pidgin Spanish and could only assist the delegates by telling them this way, mind the step and so forth, and three could actually perform the simultaneous interpretation required for the whole Congress. We had two quite supernumerary French speakers, whose job was to help the two French representatives of the World Peace Council who were attending – and they were engaged in *vying* to be the most useful and self-sacrificing. (I have noted at this and other congresses in which I have engaged that there is an occupational disease of some interpreters – Ostentatious Self-sacrifice – they insist on doing more than they ought to show their devotion to the job, forgetting or ignoring the fact that *fatigue* can attack interpreters after a relatively short space of time – I believe the turn-around among interpreters at the EEC or United Nations is less than an hour – and render them less efficient.) These two French-speaking English women had little to do and their rivalry was comical to watch. The rest of us got organised. The important thing was to get someone into the interpreters' cabin who could 'pick up' from whatever language was spoken at the rostrum – or from the nearest translation: for example, if the speaker made his speech in Spanish, every other interpreter had to wait for us to put it into English, Russian, Chinese, Japanese in succession. It was slightly easier if the speaker submitted his speech in writing beforehand so that it could be studied. I recall with some pleasure a young Russian interpreter who knew some Spanish, coming to me and asking if I could identify what seemed to him a quotation: 'Father, forgive them for they know not what they do ...'[123]

A huge hall had been created (out of an enormous roofed-in courtyard) for the conference. But a few hours before it was to open, the Chinese Peace Committee decided to hold a banquet – and there was no other building large enough. Every seat intended for delegates to the conference was ripped out, all the electric wiring for the simultaneous interpretation (on which we had been practising) was dismantled, and the hall cleared for tables and the feast, at which I saw Mao Tse-tung for the first and only time.[124] And throughout the night it was *all put back* by the work of I don't know how many workers and electricians. Large tubs containing cassia trees were set everywhere in the approaches to the congress hall. Their fragrant scent even now recalls those days to me.

We were led to the banqueting ball through a garden whose walks were lined with young Chinese people – all holding out their hands to greet us and shouting 'Long Live Peace' (the first Chinese words I ever learned). The smiles, the welcome, the enthusiasm and greeting hands, the shouting were an emotional experience I had seldom undergone. With tears streaming down our faces (I wasn't the only one) we shook the outstretched hands and shouted '*He Ping Wan Sui*,[125] tore badges off our bosoms and exchanged them a few yards further for other badges as we eventually reached the banqueting hall.

Now, it must be remembered that this was only four years after the announcement of the Liberation had been made in China, the post-revolutionary euphoria was still in existence. If we drive out the Japanese, if we drive out the Americans and Chiang Kai-shek,[126] if we achieve the revolution, then the new day will begin. And indeed it had begun. Life had begun to improve for the vast majority of people: here was no more starvation, the landlords were being eliminated, honest government had been introduced (at least at the top) and this had been achieved by the Communist Party of China, mostly identified in the minds of the peasant majority with the Red Army – the 'Old Eighth Route' they called it,[127] which had become identified with the liberation because of its *presence*. Most peasants still personified it by the term 'Che-Mao' – Che Teh[128] and Mao Tse-tung – it was not until a few years later, when I began to understand a bit of Chinese, that I found peasants still referring to the Old Eighth Route, but this being translated into 'Thanks to Chairman Mao Tse-tung and the Communist Party' ... But that was still to come. We didn't meet peasants on this first occasion.

Aurora, Jeffares and I had three tasks – checking written translations, simultaneous interpretation and what was called 'whispering' – sitting among a small group of confercs (in specialised sessions) and interpreting either in a low voice what was said so as to keep the discussion going, or loudly in a high voice when one of 'our' group wanted to make a contribution to the discussion. One of my most difficult 'whispering' assignments was to participate in the discussion on Germ Warfare, which was believed to be (and I still don't know rightly or wrongly) being perpetrated in the Korean War. I didn't know sufficient medical or chemical terms to be efficient.

Our group, interpreters and stenographers were all lodged in a Chinese-style home, with rooms built round a central courtyard and a 'devil screen' facing the main entrance – hostile spirits in old China were believed to be unable to travel except in a straight line and consequently the devil screen prevented them from entering the home. We were cared for with unparalleled consideration and affection by a group of English-speaking students whose task it was to see that we lacked nothing that would give us comfort and rest, and who strove with all their might and attention to anticipate our every wish.

(Towards the end of the Congress, when the preparation of resolutions in several languages became an urgent matter, I undertook to work through one night and when someone asked if I could do it I said airily: 'as long as I have some black coffee I'll be all right'. The young man who had special responsibility for my welfare sat up all night with me and whenever the cup beside my typewriter was cold or empty, he refilled it with boiling hot coffee. One night later, when Aurora and I were preparing final versions of the resolutions for the conclusion of the Congress, we worked until midnight and decided to snatch a bit of sleep before finishing. We asked for an alarm clock which we set for 5 a.m. and Aurora's 'nursemaid' went to sleep beside it. It went off and we awoke, but the poor girl didn't. At 8 a.m. she came actually *weeping*: 'I have not done enough for you!' she sobbed.)

The warmth of their friendship and courtesy, the glorious surroundings, the colour, the light, the scent of the cassia (where did they get so many trees?), the strange but delicious meals, the happiness of our friends, whose joy at the 'new society' was everywhere, put most of us into a state of similar euphoria, making the strenuous work of the Congress a labour of love and fostering a team spirit such as I have described for Sheffield. One or two of our number never recovered from the millennium feeling, the 'honeymoon' spirit of that experience, and later became ardent Maoists for whom China could do no wrong (Mao Tse-tung was *their* Stalin). But in those days I was congratulating one of the Chinese/English interpreters, a very beautiful and intelligent girl who had lived a long time in the USA, on how wonderful it must be to work here. Her reply was a bit sobering: 'Nan, *it isn't always like this.*'

The celebration of Liberation (afterwards called National Day) on 1 October, which preceded the opening of the Congress, was a shattering experience which I tried vainly to describe in letters home. In the great square before the Imperial Palace, over half a million people paraded before reviewing stands which were decorated with enormous portraits of Marx, Engels, Lenin and Mao Tse-tung and with red silk lanterns and a huge banner saying '*Workers of the World Unite*'.[129]

Precisely at 10 o'clock, Mao Tse-tung, Chou En-Lai, other Chinese leaders and the heads of the foreign delegations to the Congress emerged on the reviewing stand while four military bands struck up the Chinese anthem (Xi Lai!) and the Internationale, and the thousands of schoolchildren with red pioneer scarves released a cloud of white pigeons and the Day began.[130] Che Teh, on a white horse surveyed the troops who began the procession: the cavalry on little Mongolian horses (in after years it was tanks and armoured vehicles, but this year they didn't have many of those, and what they had were nearly all captured from the Americans as one could see from their markings (– a delighted US delegate standing near me said in my ear: 'No wonder Forrestal jumped out of the window ...').[131]

And then the people.

For four hours they streamed through the Square in a river of joy and colour, carrying banners, flags, flowers, slogans and giant portraits – workers, peasants, 'national capitalists' (the business community which had chosen to stay and build up China rather than go with Chiang Kai-shek), religious groups – Christian, Muslim, Buddhist, Taoist, etc., students, athletes and sportsmen, theatrical groups and circus groups and acrobats, and all as they came before the saluting stand shouted 'Long Live Mao Tse-tung', waving their arms and jumping up and down and singing and shouting ... with flags, vermilion, gold, blue, green, fluttering in the light breeze (they were all of silk, not bunting, and rippled in the sunshine). It was an emotional experience of tremendous impact, people wept for sheer joy.

In the evening there were fireworks, and dancing in the Square; we were drawn into the circles of dancers who smiled and took our hands. Eyes sparked, there seemed no unfriendly face. And so to bed, to rise early and prepare for the tasks of the Peace Conference.

My recollections of the next few days are tangled between cabin-work (simultaneous interpretation), interpretation in committees and small groups (the ones we called 'whispering') and eventually the gruelling work of preparing resolutions, which had to be expressive of *all* viewpoints and couched in language which meant the same thing as in all the others. On the last day but one, one delegation – (I think from India, but I forget) – cavilled at one of these and with superb wisdom Feng Chen (Mayor of Peking) suspended the conference while the question could be talked over in private sessions or groups. *Unanimity* was the aim. How it was arrived at I don't know (or don't remember) but it was achieved and the Conference ended a day after with everyone satisfied, Aurora and I, as I have recounted, sitting up all night for two nights running to get the translation into accurate Spanish and typed ready for stencilling and handing to the delegates the next day.

The bulk of the delegations set off the next day on conducted tours of China. Aurora and I stayed in Peking, however, with a small group of Latin Americans, to put the whole proceedings into Spanish for a full report which was to be issued. Three Chileans (including VT[132], afterwards a member of the government and, later still, a refugee), a Guatamalan, a Colombian, Aurora and myself, built a marvellous fraternity – such as I have described in relation to Sheffield – working against time to achieve a job we all believed in. Then they, too, the job finished, were taken on a tour of China, but I refused, thinking I had been long enough from my job in London. So I went back, carrying with me a small green silk banner on which they had all inscribed their names (I still have it).

But I did not know that I was followed by a request from the Chinese Communist Party, which had somehow developed an admiration for what they called my 'style of work', to return to China and assist with the formation of a permanent Peace Centre in Peking. I now know, though I did not at the time, that there was a highly nationalist ambition to divide up the leadership of the Peace Movement with the USSR and big plans were afoot to form an alternative centre for this.

One of my last tasks before leaving Peking was to act as interpreter in a conversation between Chou En-lai (Foreign Minister) and a Latin American who was not only a delegate to the Conference but a diplomat in his own right, charged with negotiations to establish diplomatic relations between his country and the new China. The conversation took place in the Foreign Ministry and there were two interpreters – one Chinese-English and one (me) English-Spanish. The proceedings were highly cagey – we recapitulated every few moments (I am to understand what he has said, and he is to understand what I have said). It began with *feelers* ... could relations such as exist between such and such a country and China be acceptable? or such and such a country? At one stage the question of relations between Britain and China entered the suppositions: would relations between Britain and China ...? Chou En-lai became very positive. 'On no account. The British maintain a Charge d'Affaires in Peking but also recognise the so-called government in Taiwan. This is hypocritical ... On we went, arriving at a sort of definition of the possible.

As we left the meeting, Chou En-lai followed the Chinese interpreter into the vestibule and gave him some instructions: his words were, 'The Foreign Minister wants me to say that when he spoke of the hypocrisy of the British government, he did not wish to reflect on the British *people*, and hoped he had not hurt your feelings!' This is the only time in my life as an interpreter that I have been treated as a *person* and not a machine and my respect for Chou En-lai, which stems from far more than this, was raised sky-high.

So back in London I was faced with a choice. Frances was married. Martin in the Army. Ted would not say yes or no (he had been the first to urge me to apply for Peking at the very beginning). I was not exactly happy in my role as London organiser of the peace movement, having reached the conclusion that what was needed was a sort of federation of the multifarious and multi-motivated local groups which formed the peace movement in the capital, allowing some allegiance to the broad movement but differing in 'breadth' and all, as in the London Peace Council, clinging jealousy to their Quakers, their Anglican or Methodist ministers, their 'non-political' local figures and pacifists who illustrated the 'breadth' of the movement we were all in favour of.

'You want OUT!' said Scottish Peter flatly when my return was discussed with the party. I nearly burst into tears. I did want out, but I also wanted something satisfactory to do, something which I thought was useful (and appreciated).

So I went back. The delay in Prague was even longer than the previous one and I was caught up in the immediate aftermath of the Trials, with the result that a further tint was wiped from my rose-coloured spectacles by the characterisation of the condemned as 'of Jewish origin' – what was this, coming from a socialist country in which anti-Semitism was unthinkable?[133] There was *unease* among British friends who were working at that time in Prague, but enough 'can't-help-thinking' among them to prevent an outright stand. I recall talking with an English girl (widowed?) who had a child born in Czechoslovakia, who felt she ought to leave but said she didn't want her daughter to be brought up 'under capitalism', at which I retorted: 'But a hell of a lot of us HAVE to bring up our children under capitalism and some of them still turn out good socialists.' (She later returned to England.)

Back in Peking I expected and hoped to be plunged into work

right away. But delay followed delay. When do I start work? I kept asking. Well, you see, we are having a 'Movement' at the present time (the 'Five Antis', I recall).[134] In desperation my Chinese colleagues found me some translation – left-over speeches from the Peace Conference – and I embarked, with the aid of 'my' interpreter on the translation into English of a new 'picture book' explaining the new Marriage Law ...[135]

But no real work.

At this stage I had the good fortune to be brought into contact with Rewi Alley, who taught me an enormous amount about China past and present. A New Zealander, he had lived there since about 1922. Following World War I, he had failed as a sheep farmer and shipped out as an engineer to Shanghai, where he stayed, becoming eventually a factory inspector in the British concession (also a Fire Chief if I remember rightly). Quite soon, having become appalled at the ghastly exploitation of the Chinese people – for example the little girls in the silk factories – he had taken the side of the Chinese people and been drawn into the revolutionary movement. He was one of the major movers in the Chinese Co-Operatives (Gung Ho) which supplied the resistance movement to the Japanese.[136] Intensely *practical*, he stormed all over the hinterland of China on foot, by bicycle, by camel, by cart and by truck, setting up co-operatives for making blankets, uniforms, shoes, small arms, anything that was needed in the devastated countryside and that could be made by small or increasingly larger groups of inhabitants. He ended up the Headmaster of a school for derelict, abandoned boys (and a few girls) in Kansu province: here, with some 1000 children, he ran a community. Half-study, half-practice, it made its own buildings, its own clothing, its own machinery (running a truck repair service), its own agriculture and cattle raising, its own paper and exercise books, in a system like that developed in the USSR by Makerenko (of whom Rewi had not heard until I sent him his book, *The Road to Life*).[137]

After the Liberation and at the time of the Peace Conference he had been brought to Peking. His school, the apple of his eye, had been transformed into a part of the new educational system and become an institute for oil technology and Rewi himself had been put upon a shelf to remain as a sort of international Peace Worthy, of whom there were some staying on in Peking after the conference. It slowly broke his heart and I was a witness to it, though he never spoke a word of it to me.

Rewi approved with the utmost whole-heartedness of the New China despite the heartbreak; he loved boys and all young creatures and as long as they had freedom and *challenge* (freedom to tackle any job they thought they could do) he approved of the measures the new government took. Having dedicated fully, fully, fully, his whole adult life to the Chinese revolution he was unable to see major flaws (minor ones he saw) in the subsequent events and faithfully followed the Chinese Communist Party policy (to the time of writing) in spite of contradictions and slights and changes. A great man – 'an engineer with the soul of a poet', wrote Joseph Needham[138] – he became for a time my mentor as I stayed sitting around for the work that never materialised. I learned the history of the revolution from him, and the history of China, which he taught from a marvellously practical viewpoint – not that of dynasties or monarchs but of *people*.

Stalin died in 1953 and I had enough idolatry left (in spite of revulsion at his plaster-Christ image in the post-war films – which may have been one of the reasons why Mao Tse-tung never allowed himself to be presented in historical films, or maybe he didn't have a Gelovani?)[139] – despite uneasy suspicions that he did perhaps know what deeds were being committed in his name; despite these and other doubts, but because of what we all understood to be his leading role in the magnificent resistance of the heroic Russian people to Hitler, I felt grief and a sense that it was a loss to the world. Dutifully I joined a long mourning procession through the Soviet Embassy in Peking to bow before

his portrait and 'sign the book' ('*Take off your hat*' hissed my
guide and interpreter, Mr Weng in a shocked voice ... the woollen
hat I had put on specially with a feeling as if entering an English
cathedral, which even in those days insisted on women keeping
their heads covered and men taking off their headgear). And the
following day in the Main Square, Heavenly Peace, I began to
think, probably because, standing there amid thousands of other
mourners, with my legs freezing to total numbness, listening to
interminable speeches in Chinese and Russian which I did not
understand, I had nothing else to do. For God's sake, he was just
a human being and subject to death like anyone else! what's so
awful about it? Others will have to take his place. And that evening
in the cinema witnessing a Chinese newsreel with shots of *whole
classrooms* of children weeping, presumably to orders and not at
all inscrutable, the last bit of idolatry dissolved in the salty tears
of the poor kids.

A great man, I still thought, and not the great criminal he was
subsequently presented to be by those only too eager to throw
out the baby with the bathwater. Both views I have modified but
I have yet to read a really objective estimate of his good and bad
qualities (can there ever be one in our lifetime? and is history
ever totally objective?). It was to be two more years before
Kruschev, with admirable if partial courage, opened the window
a crack and let some of the light in.[140]

Total admiration for Mao Tse-tung remained for a time
unflawed. *He* was modest. He took only the same salary as his
leading 'cadres'. No streets or cities were named after him (the
first Chinese-built locomotive left the sheds bearing his name, but
we were told he didn't approve of it). He lived frugally, dressed
like everyone else and his famous wart appeared in all the
portraits. (But was it humble to have so many portraits? I never
asked myself, not at that stage anyway.)

(All the foregoing is tinged with hindsight, for though I have
tried to be honest I am sure I have also tried to be self-justificatory.

Let it stand. The process of unlearning blind faith with me was slow and mixed and wavering.)

I have said that I am a slow thinker. It took me the best part of that year to realise that there wasn't going to be any job. That there wasn't going to be a Chinese centre – an Eastern as opposed to a Western centre – for the World Peace Movement (Soviet/Chinese battles must have been going on behind my back, only some murmurings of which I was aware of). I did lots of translation and lots of editing (from 'Chinglish' into English) and wrote pages of criticism on request from English-language Chinese publications, none of which I think were ever given any consideration. But I felt supernumerary and asked, and was given, permission to return to England, which I did in December 1954. What remained was the Peace Liaison Committee, which still exists.

But before that, in the late summer, I asked the Peace Committee (feeling perhaps that they owed me something for keeping me kicking my heels so long – just a mild blackmail) to invite Ted for the October celebrations, to which miscellaneous foreigners always came. My request was granted; all the arrangements were duly made, except that the Chinese in London forgot to tell Ted about it until the eleventh hour, which meant that he arrived a day late for the National Day celebrations.

These were preceded by a Peace gathering, which began to form one of the annual tasks of the peace movement in various countries; called 'Giants of World Culture', anniversaries chosen by various countries for these celebrations. This year's giants were Avicenna, Chü Yen, Rabelais, José Marti, the Cuban liberator (a rush of work for me, translating his typically wordy writings)[141] and a fifth whose name I can't remember. Representing France on this occasion was the writer Vercors (Jean Bruller),[142] who came with his wife and was disconcerted by the simultaneous translation: he made a light-hearted and humorous speech but found his jokes were reaching the audience at different intervals, so a ripple of laughter at his last crack came from one or other part of the audience as he embarked on the next sentence but one ...

After National Day Ted and I were joined to a party of Distinguished Foreign Guests: an Australian Senator and the two Brullers, Jean and Rita, who were enchanted with their first experience of the East. It was all superbly arranged to give us VIP treatment. Wherever we stayed, an official welcome awaited us, with five little girls carrying five bouquets, visits to factories and famous beauty spots, a banquet and a special coach on the train on which we travelled. (The Australian Senator, a railwayman, found the sleeping compartment which he was allotted too luxurious, and after bumping about on the well-cushioned berth, chose the floor – to the consternation of his interpreter). This was my first and only sight of Canton, a crowded and bustling city whose back streets were an infinite source of interest and enjoyment. Much industry was still in the handicraft stage and Ted was very eager to get photographs of sheet metal workers hammering away in little workshops of a Dickensian type. Our interpreter tried hard to prevent this – China never wanted foreigners to photograph anything which they (the Chinese) regarded as 'backward' – a mistake in my opinion because this illustrated the magnificent achievements they had made in the four years since the liberation with most inadequate tools and equipment (foreigners entering China from Canton, their minds filled with glossy magazine pictures of laughing tractor-drivers and smiling factory workers or builders, took the long train journey to Peking and saw probably nothing but fields of peasants crouched over their short-handled hoes or operating primitive irrigation machinery). To have virtually eliminated starvation in four years by sheer hard human labour (and the equitable distribution of its results) was a tremendous feat, the magnitude of which could not be appreciated without the evidence of the shortage of all kinds of machinery. Peasant life was getting visibly better and nearly all of it achieved by do-it-yourself methods. The Australian Senator exclaimed every few minutes, 'Aren't they marvellous people'

(Ted got his photographs by sneaking out of our hotel a couple of times when the interpreter wasn't looking.)

We left the Senator in Canton to continue his journey home and returned to Peking, forming a warm friendship with Jean and Rita, which has continued to this day. Jean wrote a delightful book, *Divagations d'un Français en Chine*,[143] describing this interlude. Ted went back to London in early November and I, having worked out my time, followed just before Christmas.

From first going to China I had taken the most scrupulous care never to 'come the bloody foreigner' to all our Chinese friends, burdened as I was with the recollection of British arrogance from the Opium Wars to the notice in the Shanghai parks (dogs and Chinese not allowed). But I did once lose my temper and that was in an interview with Liu Ning-yi, the head of the China Peace Council, where I complained that they might have told me when it dawned on them that there wasn't going to be any real job for me to do. I cited occasions when they had given me *sops* – useless jobs which turned out to be impractical or immediately forgotten. I did not at this stage quite realise that no Chinese likes to give a flat refusal or impart unwelcome news; instead, the polite thing is to tell a manifest lie, which you are supposed to recognise as such and take as the refusal he doesn't wish to give. Liu Ning-yi, speaking through an interpreter (though he understood some English), tried to explain this by saying it was 'the Chinese way'. Something went pop, and I said loudly: 'Bloody hell, it isn't the Communist way!' – at which the interpreter turned deathly pale and the interview closed with great courtesy and no reply.

XV

Despite this enormous bloomer, I was again followed to
London by a request for me to work on one of the
publications sent out by the Foreign Languages Press, with some
Spanish as a sideline. And Ted was invited too. He hesitated for
a long time, and I refused to go back without him, though I
wanted to return very much. Here, I endeavoured to persuade
him, was his chance to learn a new job. He had said hundreds
of times that he didn't want to end up as a sheet metal worker
and I had several times offered to continue working for us both
while he took some sort of university or other course (which
would have been difficult but not impossible). But he argued he
didn't know what he wanted to be instead. Finally, in August
1954, we went back to Peking. Ted was given a job almost
instantly with the Trade Union movement (All-China Federation
of Trades Union), where he did an extremely efficient job working
on editing English language publications and – on his own
initiative – making a study of conditions in various branches of
industry which he turned into articles for trade union journals in
English-speaking countries, workmanlike articles without any of
what Dickens called 'enthusy-moosey' which were just what trade
unions in other lands wanted to know about. Having edited his
own trade union's journal (the *Sheet Metal Worker*) for several
years, which involved, as always with such publications, writing
most of it himself, he was skilled at this and amassed a large
book of press-cuttings from Britain, the United States and
Australia. As a hobby he took up, with characteristic determination
and perseverance, the study of Chinese porcelain (with the help

of old Rewi Alley) and became something of an expert on dynasties, kilns, markings etc.

Meanwhile, though I did not know it, there had been a somewhat delaying battle between two organisations for my services. I only learned afterwards that the Foreign Languages Publishing House had wanted to employ me but also *China Reconstructs*, a magazine published under the auspices of Soong Ching Ling.[144] All I saw at the time was a bewildering clash of welcome banquets and a muddle about where we were to be housed (each organisation having its own accommodation for foreign staff) and we were taken to several 'courtyards', the drawbacks of which were pointed out by rival organisations, including of course the All-China Federation of Trade Unions, which was involved. Meanwhile we stayed in the Peace Hotel in a poky little room and relative luxury: *China Reconstructs* won the battle for my services and the trade unions won the battle over our accommodation. We took up residence in a courtyard of an old-style Chinese family house (with bathroom and modern plumbing as well as a devil-deflecting screen at the outer gate). The other rooms in and around the courtyard were occupied by functionaries of the All-China Federation – the head of the Teachers' Union and his family, and a retired member who was suffering from a deteriorating illness (Graves' disease?) with his family – his wife being an educational worker. We were happy and fortunate to live there; fortunate because most of the foreign community were subsequently placed in a huge hostel called Friendship House, where the various language groups lived together for ease of communication and staff were trained in the various languages and ways of life. Thus they lived quite apart from the ordinary Chinese, ate specially prepared food of their own national sort and never had to go out shopping, ride in buses or pedicabs, or buy what the Chinese call 'daily necessities', like toothpaste, cigarettes, drawing pins, a bottle of ink, shoe polish or notepaper, in Chinese or sign-language. Moreover our courtyard neighbours and their children and our excellent and energetic housekeeper, Liu Yung-taui, spoke only Chinese, so we had to get along as best we could – it did wonders for my spoken Chinese and even Ted, who could never get the 'tones' of the words, being almost tone deaf, got quite adept.

Liu Yung-taui, a poor relation from an Anwei 'clan',[145] had been recommended to work for us by a wealthy branch of the same clan, because she knew some 'foreign' ways of cooking (she proudly displayed boiled beef and carrots whenever we had guests). She felt humiliated if I ever did anything for myself – she was deeply offended when I once began to darn some of Ted's socks, sat down beside me and produced a perfect darn in the heel and then said: 'Here you are. I can do it as well as you.' (Chinese patch socks with calico patches but she knew how to darn.)

At the Chinese New Year following her coming to work with us, knowing that it was the time for people to visit their families, I asked a colleague at *China Reconstructs* how long it was customary to give as a holiday for the occasion. There was a shocked reply: '*Servants* don't have holidays!' 'Well, ours will,' I said, and made arrangements for her to go to Anwei. At this stage I discovered that, a widow, she had an eight-year-old son living with his grandparents and proposed that she bring him back to Peking with her. A day later she came to me with a sorrowful face. 'They say I ought not to do this,' she said. 'Who says?' 'They' were the rich family to which she belonged. 'Then I say,' I replied, 'that children should be with their mothers!' So our household was increased by Chou Hai-chin, a bright little boy who never understood that I could not speak Chinese and thus conversed with me without the slightest hesitation. A great boost to my acquisition of the language, since he was that kind of voluble kid who has to pour out his experience at every move. If he went to see a film, he would come back and tell the entire story without condensation: 'Well, there was this man on a train and another man came along...' reminding me of Mamillius in *A Winter's Tale*.[145] He always wound up, since the majority of films at that time were straightforward tales of victory – not by any means unvarnished, but glossy with heroics, 'and WE CHINESE' (whereat he always pointed to his own nose), 'smashed the enemy, won the day'. It was perhaps natural, though nonetheless distressing, that there wasn't a single film which did not depict the 'cadres' of the Chinese Communist Party as anything but smiling, not to say grinning heroes or defiant heroines, and never in my experience showed the Japanese as anything but double-dyed villains and cowards – though there had been decent ones who helped the Chinese revolution and even may have had enough working-class solidarity not to fight the Chinese ... There was no Marxism in Chinese films of the 1950's.

Chou Hai-Chin, by coming to live with his mother, gained an education of which Liu Yung-tsui intended he should make full use. She *beat* him if he did not persevere in his homework and rejected my protests saying, 'If it were not for Nan and Ted and Chairman Mao he would still be sitting on the back of a buffalo', and embarrassingly brought him to BOW to us at New Year.

My other language teacher was Mr Li, who spent his days going from house to house giving hour-long lessons to foreigners. He was a Roman Catholic and had learned his method (Berlitz style, using nothing but Chinese) from the days when the Jesuit missionaries had come to China directed, unlike missionaries from other denominations, to like the Chinese people, to eat their food and wear their style of dress. They must also be able to preach a sermon in Chinese by the end of their first year of stay. (Not *all* other missionaries, I must explain. The evangelical sisters, Cable and French[147] crossed inner Mongolia and the Gobi desert over and over again, wearing Chinese dress and sometimes travelling by camel, sometimes pushing carts, taking Bibles and teaching hymns wherever they went. Healing, too, for they were not the type of evangelical that neglects the body to save the soul.)

I take my hat off to the Jesuits for this. Mr Li in consequence provided a sort of crash-course of one year and thereafter his pupils had to work out what they wanted to know or be able to say.

I never got to be really fluent, though I had a lesson a day from Mr Li for the whole of the time till I left, but I learned very valuable things from him; we chatted about every day life in early post-liberation Peking. He was extremely enthusiastic about the new government, which was, he said, actually putting Christianity into operation. His children all went to school, free. There were things in the shops which had been unobtainable before (though there were shortages too – I shall never forget the gratitude with which he welcomed my gift of a book of 100 needles for his wife – one bought needles one at a time in those days and they were of inferior quality). A very moving and memorable example of his reasons for supporting the new government came a bit later. His mother died and he called to say he would be away from Peking for a few days to attend to her funeral, etc. During his absence, thinking there might be some conventional words to utter or behaviour to perform for the bereaved, I asked a Chinese friend what I should say: just say you are sorry, he replied. And he will *smile* because it is not proper to inflict one's grief on others. On his return Mr Li was not smiling, he was beaming and could barely listen to my condolences. Instead of burying his mother in a mound above ground, he had been given a burial plot in what the government called an 'ancestors' co-operative' – there was a mass drive over the country to do away with the old-fashioned mounds, like stone-built igloos, which not merely disfigured the countryside but took up valuable agricultural land and made the use of tractors difficult, not to mention the pooling of land in the agricultural co-operatives, which were beginning to spread throughout the countryside. ('Communes' had not yet been introduced.) Mr Li expatiated at great length on his mother's resting place: in the middle of a dual carriageway on which shrubs had been planted and through which drains or pipes did not pass, being at the sides of the road. I don't know how widespread this move was, but it showed a practicality and a sense of consideration for people's feelings and traditions which I found notable.

Mr Li, though his language course (first year) was not really adapted to the new day and he taught me some terms I wasn't likely to need (virgin birth, for instance), was practical as well. He told me excitedly that the State Store had just received a consignment of knicker-elastic and I'd better hurry there if I wanted some; he called more than once with packets of candles when there had been radio announcements of power-cuts in our neighbourhood; and he once cycled off into the country around Peking to fetch me honey, which had been prescribed for my diet when I developed hepatitis and which one could rarely buy because, though it existed in the villages, there were no jars in which to transport it (we supplied him with our empty jars from the imported jam mainly sold to foreigners).

He told tales about the 'bad old days' as well, recalling how in the worst of the inflation, one had to pay in advance for a ride in a pedicab, on which the driver stopped at the first opportunity and bought *grain* because the price might gallop higher before the journey was complete. Dear Mr Li. He was persecuted in the 1960's, when xenophobia became prevalent in ruling circles, but he did not, I think and hope, lose his livelihood altogether.

So rich in incidents of this kind was my life during the years spent in Peking that I could not tell it all in a million words and will have to come to some generalisations. (I wrote Frances a weekly letter of impressions, trying always to recount everyday life as it was lived in the new China from my own impressions, which she kept. In the course of time this letter was duplicated, triplicated, quadruplicated – as other people asked for copies – until I was making eight copies, all the typewriter would hold, for distribution to various parts of the world. A clergyman in Sheffield used to post them on his parish notice-board. An elderly friend in Geneva – friend of a friend, I never met her – used to sit down and make six more copies, which she sent to the United States.) I think their tone was a bit starry-eyed, but I sought to take the dread out of post-revolutionary life, to counteract the horror stories about 'regimentation', hardship and absence of freedom, and show what I *saw* – that life was getting better for the majority of the people. Sure, there were shortages, hardships, conflicts and quarrels, broken marriages and bereavements; but there was no fear of the future, of *not having enough to eat*, of destitution in old age (at least, not that I witnessed, except among older people who kept urging the younger ones to have more and more children to take care of them in their later years).

There was a general air of tranquillity and it was 'thanks to Chairman Mao and the Communist Party' as everyone repeated. But it was also thanks to the hard work, the practical wisdom, the resilience and the *unity* of the whole nation, with the single aim of building socialism, which at that time seemed easier and easier to define than it afterwards became.

Meanwhile at work there was the deep satisfaction of being intensely busy at something useful – editing translations from what we called Chinglish into clear, concise and informative English. We were called 'polishers' (there were four of us at *China Reconstructs*, three of whom had English for their mother-tongues). China was anxious to tell the world what was happening – but it was no use sending it out in the Chinese script, which not one in ten thousand, not one in a hundred thousand, people in the rest of the world could understand, and which cannot be *cabled* or telexed, or coded without immense and time-consuming labour. (One could, I discovered later, send simple telegrams, because a number of gifted clerks in the post office had learned to use *numbers* for a minority of frequently used words.)

So I polished and polished and polished with great satisfaction

– the simple satisfaction of helping to make China known to the rest of the world – articles, pamphlets, speeches, captions, even programme-notes for concerts given to foreigners – and with nearly everything I polished in the first period I agreed. For an hour or two every morning I taught English to my fellow workers, and this gave rise to a slight contradiction in them. You see, it is almost impossible not to resent someone who alters the words you have so painfully produced from your mind (I did and still do to anyone who edits my translations). It was not long-lasting resentment, usually only momentary and there were arguments on the lines of 'But that's what it says in Chinese, Nan.' 'But it doesn't make sense in English...' On the other hand there is a deep tradition of respect and love for teachers among the Chinese, so we always started the day with affectionate relations and diluted these as the day went on.

After a while one was conscious of stereotyping; the articles had a dismal tendency to follow the formula: 'China for thousands of years produced ... (many, or beautiful, or abundant) ... Under the Kuomintang these ... (disappeared, deteriorated, were vulgarised) but since the Liberation, hurrah, hurrah, hurrah ...' No harvest was anything but 'bumper'. And up to the mid-1950's the ending (which we nicknamed the Doxology) included the formula: 'Thanks to the selfless help of the Soviet Union and its experts ...' And then the argument was: But is it really necessary to put this six times in one issue the magazine? And the reply: This is what the author wishes to say! It was not until the late 1950's that one also had to cavil at the inevitable prefix to the name of Chairman Mao: Our Beloved and Respected Leader. Could he really want this? Where was the modest figure we had met with in our first experience? (The term Great Helmsman had not been introduced by the time I left, in 1960). But don't you think that such ceaseless repetition may bore and antagonise foreign readers? It is what we *want to say*, comrade (and to hell, I suppose, with the foreign reader).

I won a satisfactory and single-handed battle for 'pure wells of English undefiled'.[148] My three colleagues were accustomed to use American-English and I fought constantly for the English spelling of things like Flow, Program, and for the abolition of transport*ation* and the other '-ations' they fancied, on the specious grounds that if we were going to oppose American imperialism (as China did, fiercely at that time) we had better not commit 'cultural aggression' and offend our English readers in other lands.

We foreign 'experts' were not really much involved in the various 'movements' which from time to time hindered ordinary progress, such as getting the magazine out on time. We studied and discussed them, as we studied and discussed the *Works of Chairman Mao* and the other writings which were meant to indoctrinate communists from other lands (*How to be a Good Communist* by Liu Shao Chi was widely read in other Parties: later, when Liu was disgraced, he was deeply criticised because he hardly mentioned Mao).[149] The Three Antis, the Five Antis, the Anti-Rightist Movement, the Hundred Flowers etc. were the subjects of intense discussion among our colleagues, our neighbours and the groups of people we could see gathered together in courtyards, back streets, railway stations and workplaces, patiently waiting until everyone had had his or her say and *unanimity* (the pre-requisite) had been achieved.[150] Sometimes at *China Reconstructs*, and I expect elsewhere, it took days, the work in hand grinding almost to a standstill while we foreigners, accustomed to buying the March issue of a monthly magazine in March, ground our teeth in exasperation. I tried to make our colleagues picture the disappointment of booksellers, newsagents, friendship societies and individuals subscribers and their difficulty in trying to sell the March issue in May. But the colleagues were loftily sure that nobody would mind. It took a long time for me to realise that I need not have worried quite so much. The bulk of the magazine was sent to India, Israel and Indonesia, where much if not most of it was given away ...

We did of course participate in the practical movements – helping to make backyard steel and to keep our homes and offices free from rats, mice, bugs and fleas and, I am ashamed to say, I spent part of one Sunday banging saucepan lids to scare sparrows (someone having worked out (i) that they were a 'pest', since they ate grain and (ii) that if they were kept in the air their hearts would fail after a time and they would drop dead).[151] Subsequently it was decided that sparrows also ate flies and insects, which were themselves pests, and so the campaign died out (as Mr Li said, of other campaigns of this sort, 'a lion's head and a snake's tail' – beginning with a bang and going out with a whimper). It never really worked, even in Peking, because the Indian Embassy, for Buddhist reasons, refused to participate and I think a lot of the sparrow population took refuge there while the rest of the city filled with people 'making a joyful noise'.[152]

The steel campaign seemed to me a bit like Charles Lambs' story of Roast Pork.[153] It did hinder all sorts of production (handicraft things like umbrellas and baskets almost disappeared for a time). But it did, in the countryside, give rise to the discovery and development of sources – iron ore, for instance, hitherto undiscovered: sometimes in small quantities, sometimes in larger, and this was of immense benefit to peasant communities, which could set up their own forges, put ball-bearings on their carts and wheelbarrows and do all sorts of repairs which had previously had to be carried to the nearest town or further. 'Step by step'[154] made an immense difference to the countryside, as peasants learned to make their own chemical fertilisers, build primitive little turbines for irrigation, without having to wait for giant steel mills and chemical combines, tractor factories and hydroelectric power stations. Many Third World countries have not yet learned this lesson: relying on 'aid' programmes which start by building palaces and providing limousines for government figures and *never get down* to those in real need.

But these were practical, not political matters. We did, however, discuss endlessly and intensely the political direction of the 'building of socialism'. And here I have to speak of the other half, as it were, of life in Peking for us English: a small group, some members of the Communist Party and some not, but all feeling a deep interest and involvement in the Chinese revolution. I have spoken already of the tendency to admire and gain encouragement from a *successful* revolution and to apply its lessons to one's own situation. (Hence the tendency among the 1920's and 1930's communists to follow the Soviet revolution, the works of Lenin and so forth, as if to do what *they* did was to guarantee our success. It happened later with the Chinese one, then the Cuban, not to mention the altogether admirable Vietnamese.) The trouble was that we, or later they, were not Marxists enough to relate them to our own histories, political situations, or even our own *people* and to see that emulation was not by any means enough. It gave rise to what in the end I learned to call the 'Holier than Mao' syndrome, which made itself felt, in the main, mostly among comrades who had not done much real *mass* work in their own countries. (Ted never succumbed – he had always done mass work.) I recall (this by way of illustration) a British Party member fixing Harry Pollitt, visiting China, with a stern gaze and asking him, 'What are you going to do to raise the consciousness of the masses in England?' I recall a couple with two children, to whom I suggested that to stay too long in China might be to deprive their kids of their own cultural heritage and being told: 'My children will inherit *proletarian* culture.' The fact of the matter was that we British communists *had no masses* with whom to put our half-baked theories into practice. Stalin, who spoke many untrue words, spoke truly when he likened the ivory-tower people to Antaeus, whose strength diminished as his feet were separated from the earth.[155] A good communist, and it took me a long time to learn this, will remain sterile and isolated as long as he isn't among *people*, testing Party theories and learning from their reactions, their opinions and their wisdom, listening to them as well as telling them.

And our tiny group of British Marxists (Communists) *had no masses* except ourselves. It turned us inward, as it had turned all exile groups, and one had to fight against two tendencies – cynicism and Holier-than-Mao-ism, between which tendencies there grew hostility and antagonism (cf. the backbiting and hostility between the Russian exiles in Geneva, Paris and elsewhere) which were unavoidable in the circumstances. Not altogether unavoidable, for the French Communist Party, wiser than ours, sent members to help in China for not longer than three years at a time, rotating one a year so that continuity could be maintained and the newcomers did not have to start from scratch. I don't think that this affected our work for the Chinese much, in various spheres, for we all sincerely wanted to be a credit to our Party and help the Chinese revolution to the best of our ability. But within the group it sharpened personal failings, ambitions, attitudes and other tendencies.

There were things to be cynical about. In my over-simplified thinking (and in Lenin's words) the difficulties began when the revolution is at last victorious.[156] We have been promising ourselves that once we have won (power?) everything will at once begin to get better. It doesn't, as history shows. Some things do improve at once (life for the Chinese peasant, for instance, *visibly* improved during the first four or five years of my stay). But just try legislating for 800 or 900 million people in a backward economy (or an advanced one for that matter) and many things will not happen *immediately.* Moreover, those who have the responsibility to put the new society into practice are, many of them, sincere and devoted people but they have no initiative and above all no flexibility. So policy is worked out at the top (on the basis of unique experience of the struggle) and passed to those sincere, devoted ones who dare not for the life of them deviate from the given word. There are also some, less sincere and more devoted to their own 'little brief authority' and advancement.

And we have them too. You have only to go to the labour exchange or the social services to watch them in operation.

'From the masses, to the masses,' was a favourite slogan.[157] But 'from the masses' has a long way to get to the top, while 'to the masses' slides down with little obstacle. And those who have not experienced the instant fulfillment of their pre-revolutionary dreams may grumble, and become dissidents: and a dissident quite rapidly becomes an enemy, to be silenced or labelled or persecuted.

(We used to tell a joke story which has a ring of truth. A soap-box orator at Hyde Park Corner is holding out apocalyptic promises, including: 'Come the revolution, the workers will eat strawberries and cream every day.' A voice from the crowd shouts: 'I don't like strawberries.' The orator: 'Come the revolution you'll eat strawberries and cream every day and *like it*, or else ...')

Hence the Anti-Rightist movement, hence the Hundred Flowers campaign. Hence, but after the time when I left China, the Cultural Revolution ...

We build the new society on the remnants of the old. The very day after the victory is won we have to start. The structures which we have inherited from the old days are used without much change. The new always has elements of the old in it. Notice the resemblance in the new motor cars of the 1900's to the horse-drawn carriages they supplanted. Notice the vestigial three legs (sometimes merely bumps) on Chinese porcelain or earthenware pots. Notice, as I noticed, the gradual change from the 'arranged marriage' by virtue of a go-between, to the semi-arranged marriage by *organisation*. (I noted and participated in at least three at *China Reconstructs*, where the Party Committee debated and discussed suitability of partners and made its findings known before the actual wedding took place; it is true that the ceremony began with the question: Is anyone making you marry this man/woman?) Two of the marriages stuck, one failed.

So the new society proceeds from one problem resolved to a new problem (the solution of one problem gives rise to another). China, in my witness, solved its problems with varying degrees of success, 'thanks to Chairman Mao and the Communist Party' as they said, but also thanks to the selfless help of the Soviet Union and other socialist countries, and thanks above all to the fantastic hard work, cheerfulness, perseverance and united effort of her people.

Kruschev's speech at the 20th Congress of the Communist Party of the Soviet Union[158] disturbed our foreign group more, I think, than it did the general run of the people of China, for they knew little or nothing about it. First our group was flattered by the rumour that there had been such a speech. Then extracts from it reached us in such foreign newspapers as we received (always late). Could it be yet another bout of anti-Soviet propaganda, as our starry-eyed die-hards instantly characterised it?

All too soon it was confirmed and we had to re-examine our attitudes to a hundred aspects of the past and the immediate past. We asked ourselves if all this was going on, why did not the rest of the leadership protest? How had the 'violations of socialist legality' been concealed from fraternal parties? Were there really slave camps? Gross injustices? Were all these show trials from 1937 onwards a sham? Beria was executed:[159] was he at the bottom of it all? Some could not even ask themselves these questions, let alone try to find answers for them. Did the revolution devour its children?

It has taken years to find the answers and even now there are those who can't accept them. For me, but slowly, slowly, it was like the lifting of a stone from my heart. At the following October celebrations I asked John Woods of the Scottish Miners, member of a Trade Union delegation from Britain, what effect the revelations had on his members. Not much, was his reply. They knew it was true all along.

It is immensely difficult to change long-standing habits of thought. Looking back, I am reminded of the effect of the discoveries of Darwin & Co on the Church of England and its members. There were those, like the father of Edmund Gosse (*Father and Son*),[160] who simply could not accept the thought the Book of Genesis was not the word of God.

XVI

In 1957 I had a brief experience of another and distant part of that vast country, of which even to this day little is heard – Sinkiang (or the 'new territories'). I did not choose this for myself – indeed it will be seen by now that, of all the remarkable experiences I have had, I didn't select any of them for myself. I may be the captain of my soul now and then but I haven't been the master of my fate...

It came about this way. Old Rewi had at last gained permission to go back to the scene of his earlier work, and decided to go first to Lanchow, where the conventional successor of his immensely creative school had been set up (now an Oil Technology college) and where one of his adopted Chinese sons was now the Headmaster. From there he went to Sinkiang on an exploratory trip to see how the new day was affecting the multinational population there.

Now, old Rewi Alley was a prolific writer of reportage, very comprehensive but totally undisciplined. I had already edited for him a book on the Peking Opera – built it out of his random scraps of information: he used to sit down once a day and write his thoughts and lump them together in no sort of order, chronological or otherwise. He wanted to write something about Sinkiang, but knew he'd need an amanuensis, to gather his impressions into shape. So he persuaded Ching Ling's representative on *China Reconstructs* to persuade the leadership of the paper that I needed a holiday – it is true that I had not had a holiday that year, having held the fort while three out of the four other 'polishers' had theirs ... Two days before Rewi left

Lanchow, CHS rang me up early one morning and said: 'It is all arranged, you will leave for Sinkiang in two days.'

Whoopee! this sounded a lot more interesting than those rather conventional seaside holidays provided for foreign 'experts' every now and then. It took three days, but I was off to the Far West on my own, without an interpreter, told that I would be attached to Rewi on arrival in Lanchow. Alighting from the aeroplane there I found no one to meet me and no one who had ever heard of my arrival. This was unheard of – foreigners weren't allowed or expected to roam around on their own. Summoning up my Chinese, I explained the situation and suggested they should ring up the Oil Technology Institute and ask the Headmaster what had happened. 'We can't,' they said, 'It is Sunday, and there won't be anyone to answer.' 'But it isn't Sunday, it is Thursday.' 'They have their Sundays on a Thursday,' was the reply (the staggered week).

After a couple of hours of frustration, during which I imagine there must have been some forceful telephoning, I suddenly became a kosher traveller, lodged in a hotel and arrived with an interpreter/guide, who explained to me that Rewi (in his usual impetuous way) had gone on to the next stop – Urumchi – and I should catch him up, but not for two days because there was no plane to Urumchi until Saturday. I was 'shown' round Lanchow, but not, I think, the whole run-around for visitors, because the interpreter, a nice elderly man who spoke good English, kept getting car-sick so I cut the tour short.

On to Urumchi, with vast tracts of Gobi desert seen from the plane and the Tienshan mountains, snow capped, on the right. You have guessed what happened. Rewi had gone on to Kashgar, and the plane to Kashgar went only twice a week. Kashgar or bust, I said. But it was bust. I never got to Kashgar. Rewi was due to arrive back in three days, before I could start out in pursuit. So I stayed around Urumchi, a fascinating place, inhabited by some of the thirteen nationalities that made up the population of Sinkiang. It was a great relief to be in a place where Western noses, curly hair and European clothing did not call attention: I have never got used to the embarrassment of being stared at by Chinese children whose mothers hushed them if they exclaimed in my hearing, 'Ta bidze!' (high nose). But here there were all sorts of noses, complexions, clothing and hair, from the dark curly hair of the Uighurs to the flaxen hair and blue eyes of a colony of Russians who had fled over the border in 1917 or 1918. I was anonymous in the street!

I wrote some impressions in a letter – which Frances has kept. I shall include it here because it gives an impression of what I felt at the time.

'"It was ... a plucky journey for a lady to undertake. But Mrs Thompson Glover is one of the world's courageous women, plays a good game of polo, and is an intrepid traveller not likely to be daunted by the hardships and discomforts of a journey through Turkistan." (*Journey to Turkistan*, Sir Eric Teichman.)[161]

'With this enchantingly fruity piece of British upper-class travel talk I open my greeting to you from Sinkiang, Chinese Turkistan, farther than any country from the sea, fabulous heart of Central Asia, traversed by the Old Silk Road down which Marco Polo made his way, along the bases of snow-covered mountains, from desert oasis to desert oasis, past the ancient kingdom, Khotan and the now-vanished waters of Lop Nor. Place of nomads and tribesmen, Khazaks, Mongols, Kirghiz, Uzbecks, Uighars and Chinese Muslims. Strategic hinterland where, at the end of the last century, British and Russian "explorers" – watching one another with suspicion and apprehension and occasionally putting one another under arrest – were roaming about, trying to discover whether there was a pass over the Pamirs, the Karakorum or the Himalaya, from which "the brightest jewel in Britain's Crown" could be invaded with artillery. (There wasn't) ...[162]

'I am writing this from Urumchi, the capital, my first stage in a journey that was meant to be made in company with Rewi Alley; but he left Peking in advance and due to a series of errors and miscalculations we seem to have got into two different machines, his grinding him through each place about three or four days in advance of me, and telegrams getting there late and aeroplanes being held up here and there. I failed to catch him up in Lanchow, I failed to catch him up here, and I could have gone on to Kashgar to join him but by that time he was almost due to proceed to Kucha and back here. Though I would have loved to see Kashgar above all else, it seemed an awful expense for one day only. And now *he's* been delayed two days by planes not flying ... keeping a stiff upper lip, Mrs Thompson Glover set off to explore Urumchi single handed, down its mysterious alleyways and crowded bazaars, peering into shops and staring, fascinated, at the people who throng the streets. An extremely pleasant thing about Urumchi is that people don't stare at foreigners as they do in Peking. I experienced a sudden delightful feeling of anonymity, because about half those one meets have "high noses" anyway, and there are enough White Russians for one's hair to get by and one to be mistaken for one of them quite easily.

'Since the majority of the Sinkiang people are Uighurs (formerly called Turki), the province is now the Sinkiang Uighur Autonomous Region. Their language is used, all squiggly, alongside Chinese on all the buildings, streets, bus-stops, posters, theatre tickets and notices. Chinese (Han) government workers who come here to help with administration and development have to learn the Uighur language and must at all times respect the Muslim Religion and its practice. Last Monday and Tuesday was the Courban Festival (a big religious holiday after a feast) so I was able to see the full splendour of national costume on the streets, for it was a public holiday.

'Everyone, of whatever nationality, was out in their gayest clothes, wandering up and down the streets and thronging the beautiful park with tall trees, a boating lake (where naked brown urchins were swimming. in the shallow water), tea-places and a small zoo with a sad-looking leopard, an entrancing baby bear, a wapiti, some wolves, cranes, eagles and a peacock which was kindly spreading its tail for the crowds to look at. There was a smell of mutton on the streets and in the park – being sold by the skewerful (shish-kebab) with noodles or not as you choose, cooked in little open air booths and stalls. It's quite another world.

'But I also got a sense of familiarity. It began on the drive from the airport, which is about eight miles out. At first there are no houses, but what struck me at once was the carts, the shafts of which are joined over the horse's back with that high wooden arch they use in the Soviet Union. Then big drays, drawn by three or four large horses, loaded high and driven by tall, burly, handsome, bearded' brown men wearing white embroidered blouses, baggy trousers thrust into high boots, and round embroidered caps on their heads. Next, a white-turbaned patriarch in a long gown on a mincing, disdainful camel; then a four-wheeled buggy with a canopy on top, carrying a whole family whose women folk have their heads tied in untidy kerchiefs. And then you come to buildings, painted pale blue, pink and apricot, with smallish windows, double-glazed for winter cold – why, you think to yourself, this might be Novosibirsk or Irkutsk, or at the very least the pages of one of the Soviet glossy magazines.[163] Sure enough, the Russian influence is very strong, and there are geographical and historical reasons for it.

'Geographical: there's a good route from Sinkiang into Soviet Central Asia and after the Turksib Railway was built it came almost to Sinkiang's back door, whereas the 'front door' to what people here refer to as the Eastern Provinces starts with a thousand miles of desert that formerly took weeks to cross by camel caravan. Historical: A great number of white Russians came and settled here after the October Revolution;[164] next, during the civil war that took place in Sinkiang in the early 1930's the Chinese Governor asked for, and received, Soviet help suppressing it – the Soviet Union permitted troops who had retreated into Siberia after the Japanese invasion of "Manchuria" to come back into China through the back door via Soviet territory and furthermore sent arms, tanks and aeroplanes, and some sort of semi-volunteers called the Altai Army, to help (who incidentally fought quite well alongside the White Russians, Red and White in complete amicability). This was common sense on the part of the Soviet government because the Japanese were trying to get through Inner Mongolia and drive down from there to grab Sinkiang and cut the Soviet Union off from China. The Soviet Union also sent doctors, teachers, experts in livestock breeding and others to help the people advance. But in 1943 when Sinkiang's relations with the Chungking government were normal (and Chiang Kai-shek was an ally), they stepped right out of the picture again, troops, technicians and all, much to the amazement of those who had been hollering about "Red Imperialism".

'Potted history. However, you feel yourself in Siberia or the pages of one of the Soviet glossies – until you notice the smaller houses, and see that they are just ordinary Chinese mud-brick such as you see everywhere in China; and notice that among the gaily-clad people in the streets women in baggy trousers and billowy shirts, short jackets and embroidered caps, young girls in vividly patterned flowered silk – and embroidered caps, white-turbaned old men, old ladies in flowing robes and vestigial veils of white or brown, burly black beards in long coats and conical fur-rimmed hats, jaunty young men in floppy trousers and shirts – and embroidered caps – among them you notice the (Han) Chinese, trim and sedate in their blue trousers and white shirts, just as if they were in Peking. What a lot of beautiful girls with deep-set eyes and "high noses", some with chestnut curls; and dark-skinned, black-eyed babies, and even fair people with blue eyes (who strike even *me* as strange after living in Peking so long). I'm only sorry that the beautiful guest-house where I am staying is not on a main street; indeed it's right outside the city. This is an earthquake area, so the buildings are none of them more than two stories high, with a lot of space all round and thus the city sprawls with what looks like a complete extravagance to my tight-little-island eyes, and means you have to walk long distances – but it's common sense of course.

'Besides prowling about the street I have so far seen (i) the new textile factory ... (ii) the new Medical College, not yet complete, with 60 acres of buildings ... (iii) the truck repair depot that overhauls 2000 of the 10000 trucks ... and (iv) the new power station that supplies the town ...

'In each place I asked: "What is your main problem" and in each place the reply was "We can't keep up with demand!" – partly for reasons of technique and partly for reasons of lack of machinery etc. The manager of the power station hopes that now the embargo is being lifted they may get turbines from Britain, whose workers, he said, were very "creative and skilful" and can make bigger turbines than China can make yet; the textile mill sells its stuff as fast as it is produced, and is shortly going to start building another entire mill to try and keep up with demand (in the province alone).

'A boom city, where no "salesmen" are needed. The number of silk frocks on the streets during the holiday would amaze you. I don't think I've ever seen so many all in one place. (Silk is made in a new mill further south).

'I have decided to be a nomad. At any rate, in the summer. The place I have chosen is just over the top of the pass that leads from the Dzungarian basin to the Ili region; after grinding across the desert, climbing slowly for hours and hours and hours (in my case from 4.50 in the morning to 3.50 in the afternoon with a break for breakfast about 10.30 a.m.) pushing on past dark blue gray mountains looking at you forbiddingly from under white eyebrows of cloud, and after stopping, towards the top, *every kilometre* because the radiator was boiling and the driver "'adn't brought no wa'er wiv 'im", – and in one place the road had been washed away by a storm for about six miles and you had to drive right across the desert – after all that, as I said, you go through a high, cold, windy, misty pass palled Fir Tree Pass and then simply glide down into the Promised Land.

'A huge blue lake comes into sight on your right, while the mountain slopes turn green, instead of greyish-brown, on your left and higher up there are *trees* – the first you have seen all day except for a few willows and poplars where a spring of water comes to the surface in the desert. And across the lake are mountains too, hazy blue lavender, with the blue sky above, and the lake going from pale green through cornflower blue to indigo – it's like Switzerland, only better. And down the shore are some *yurts* (the round tents nomads live in), one with a red flag on top, and the sun picks out that speck of red, and the vivid red-chestnut of the horses standing by, while a man comes towards you on a horse, driving a herd of sheep and goats, idly, as if he couldn't care less where he got to.

'In the lake, about a quarter of a mile from the shore, is a small barren-looking island with a small mud hut on top of it. There, they say, lives an old Taoist monk, who spends the summer in contemplation and only comes back to the mainland when he can walk there; it freezes up for about five months in the high, chill place. There are no fish in the lake, cos why? Because a woman once washed some of her clothes there! That's what they say, but actually it is chock full of salts and only a very thin, small shrimp, not worth shrimping, can survive that Krushcen feeling.[165]

'We got out of the car and capered madly for joy. That's what hours of desert does for you. Alas, alas, the haversack with my camera was in the jeep miles ahead – the jeep hadn't needed cooling coming up to the top and had long been lost to sight. And anyway it wouldn't be much good without colour film. Rewi took 24 pictures straight off, but he's the kind of photographer who just lifts up the camera and points it at something, and 23 may very likely be failures.

'And all along past these tall fir clad mountains (you could walk up to the snow line in an hour) on the green lower slopes are yurts, with horses, sheep, cows, goats and camels grazing around – all of them with young ones and baby camels are the stiltiest little sillies you ever saw. And people are just lying in the sun, either sleeping or drinking kumiss[166] (or else tea out of actual real proper samovars) and kids are herding little flocks of sheep-and-goats (they make so little difference here in China that it's the same word for both) or else playing football or lying around in the sun too – well wrapped up because it's cold too. And a few women are doing a sort of slow bustle round outdoor fires. It's like heaven. I stood on the short turf and without moving my feet picked myself a nosegay of thyme, forget-me-nots, purple vetch, small buttercups, scarlet pimpernel and a yellow spiky thing the name of which I don't know. (As we afterwards discovered, it was a herdsmen's co-operative – like an agricultural producers' co-operative but no land, only animals for shares.) But, as they were Kazaks and nobody in our party could speak Kazak, we couldn't talk to them – an old man rode up on a brown horse with his silk-shawled wife on a white horse, and demanded to be photographed, but we understood him from gestures rather than speech. And did he pose proudly!

'At each turn in the road the scenery got grander and statelier, the mountains taller and the fir trees on them darker and more imposing. The colour was something entrancing – if I could only send you my eyes! there's no way to describe it – and as we proceeded down the road a stream ran by its side, clear as crystal and tumbling over the rocks, instead of the grey mud-coloured water that ran through the villages over the other side. In a place part village and part encampment, a bit further down, there were some more yurts and three or four low, mud-built houses, one of them a restaurant. There we found the jeep with the others, who had ordered paotzes for us (dumplings stuffed with meat, rather like ravioli, only bigger) and mutton. A crowd of friendly Kazak kids streamed up to see us – little girls wearing strings of amber, red leather boots, and gay kerchiefs on their heads and sturdy, grubby boys with Uighur embroidered round hats or peaked caps (Russian Kazak style) and bare feet. Oh, and it's here the men wear those white felt hats with black or brown velvet turn-up brims one sees in the Minority Hats Department of the Peking department store, and very handsome and dashing they look too, mostly with beards, flashing black eyes and long noses.

'A woman like a Murillo madonna stood on the doorstep of the house next to the restaurant holding an armful of fat baby. The baby wore a cap with owl-feathers stuck upright on top of it. This is to make them brave, and I saw it many times subsequently, but also sometimes sewn on the back of the baby's coat near the shoulders in little tufts. We were shown into the eating part of the restaurant – the cooking being done outside under a sort of awning – and listened to the proprietor, who wore a butcher-blue tunic, a velvet cap of sienna red, and top boots, counting the paotzes in a sort of high song, I suppose in Kazak. On the other side of the room from us was a long table and on it, I said *on* it, sat four men, cross-legged, before a smaller, lower table, eating mutton with their fingers. The driver of the jeep, who is a Kazak, suddenly came into his own and started talking volubly to everyone in his own language, and took the driver of the car (a Han) off to a yurt to drink mare's milk. We ate paotzes (provided by the restaurant) and bread, tinned fish, some peculiar coffee of the "instant" kind that sinks to the bottom of the cup unless you stir constantly and brandy – highly welcome to me – provided by our own commissariat.

'Every so often a group of horsemen galloped by, just galloping for the hell of it, or a rickety cart would pass carrying churns of mares' milk – and once a family moving camp – OR a ten ton truck would come groaning up, bringing machinery for the Karamai oilwells from over the border in the Soviet Union. Twentieth century meeting fourteenth.

'Lower down it opened out into a wide plain with huge expanses of cotton and maize growing on it – an army farm of which I shall have more to say in a letter which I shall call Swords into Ploughshares – and here, bowling along a smooth stretch of road with trees ahead on the plain that reminded me of coming off Salisbury Plain into Salisbury city, the road was *entirely* bordered with white hollyhocks and a sort of purple spiky flower I can't name, like a bordered carpet, and the sun shining at that moment right through the white flowers and making them glisten fit to dazzle you. My eyes were so full of colour and loveliness that I almost wanted to die so that that could be their last sight of earth.

'After that it got hot again and we came to villages which were half like the Bible and half like Romania, with tall poplars planted thickly along the street to make shade to walk in, high walls enclosing the houses, white-veiled women sitting on the doorsteps nattering, with kids playing around them, and men coming home on donkeys with sticks in their arms. Sometimes it reminded me of Spain, sometimes of Romania.

'Then one more stop, in a village with the inevitable stream in the main street, where everyone sat on the ground watching life go past – old women wearing a sort of white cotton wimple like a Nun's, but embroidered round the face, and bearded old patriarchs in fur-trimmed hats and long black coats, and younger women in very gaily coloured clothes and kerchiefs and rakish men in cotton in those little round caps, squatting in groups playing cards, while a HUGE cotton-picking machine, brand-new and just arrived from *Hungary* was towed through by tractor ...

'And so to Ili, a city full of tall, tall poplars and pleasant shady walks and dusty, unmade roads, and shops painted pale blue and white – hot, and busy in a slow sort of way but nobody moving fast. And stalls and stalls of fruit – cherries, apricots and rose apples, and at the end of the street a Mosque and a Chinese temple side by side.

'I haven't told about Karamai, back in the desert. Take all the wild west, oil-rush films you have ever seen: smooth off the gambling dens, the sinister men and the impossible blondes in tights, and you have Karamai. Last September there were no houses, only some tents, some caves and a few gushers. Now there are 110 buildings, most blocks of dwellings but also offices, drawing offices, small factories and a meeting hall, all low and painted pale pink, crude and rough, but dwellings because the families of the oil-men are coming here to live. Water has to be brought from thirty-seven miles away! Last summer, before they had started the city, it was brought up on trucks and rationed but now it's piped, though still scarce. And all around you, as far as the eye can see, right up to the distant mountains, is grey, dusty desert with only camel-thorn on it, and derricks in every direction. The drillers have a pretty exciting time because they may strike oil in as little as five days' drilling, and then they pick up the whole derrick with tractors and cart it off to the next place. But the men who mind the gushers, it seems to me, must feel rather like lighthouse keepers. All they have is – not even a pump, which is something to keep when oil is not gushing but needing to be pumped up – all they have is just some pipes and bends and bolts and nuts and a sort of meter thing to show how fast it's coming, and a tank; and the oil simply goes quietly slopping into the tank at about 25 tons a day, and once a day or more a tanker comes round and carts it off to be refined in Tushantze, miles away. The men on the wells have to build their own accommodation, and it has to be a cave, for the winter is sometimes 30 below zero. The vegetables come from 40 miles away and the roads are terrible. And everyone is roaringly excited and energetic and happy because this is a newly discovered oilfield and the extent of it is not even yet determined, but it is probably bigger than the Romanian ones and certainly China's biggest yet. We went to the place of the seepage, where an old Uighur man, one of the few inhabitants of this wild place, found bitumen and some black grease that he took off and sold to use to grease carts with – this was the sign of the millions of tons of oil below. For a very long time to come, these men and women are going to have to put up with an immensely tough time, the majority of them separated from their families, because only the toughest families will want to come to that place, with no amenities and no facilities and two days to get to any place with a proper road even ... all so that China can be rich and her people have a better life. I was very exhilarated to be at a performance by a theatre company sent specially by the All China Federation of Trade Unions to "honour the workers of Karamai" – a bunch of about fifty actors and actresses and musicians and singers and dancers as finished and polished as (and more original and with more musicianship than) any I've seen in Peking or elsewhere, putting on a magnificent show in the only hall Karamai has, which had a minute dressing room so that they had to do most of their changing and make up outside in a little space curtained off with canvas which kept falling down, much to the delight of the dozens of kids – all of them that one could see was rows of bottoms sticking through the available gaps in the canvas, if you know what I mean.

'I am now on the last lap of my journey back to Peking, having left Rewi in a place called Chiuchuang where, in the Han dynasty (I think it was), a general of the Imperial army put wine in the springs to let his troops drink in celebration of a victory over the Outer Barbarians, hence the name (*Chiu* means wine, like the name of the street where we live in Peking, Wine and Vinegar Street). He's writing a book about it all, which you may one day be able to read in far greater detail than I can tell you. (A note which should be added to the first page of this letter in justice to Rewi is that my technique with the camera is to lift it up and point it at things too: only I don't do it quite so often as he does, being thrifty enough to hope that I might get six out of 24.)

'Even when I caught up with Rewi, who was accompanied by

an interpreter, I didn't get much help with the language, because the interpreter has been down with diarrhoea most of the time (Mrs Thompson Glover NEVER has diarrhoea – and she was the only one of the entire party, including the various representatives of peace committees and other bodies who accompanied us at different stages, who didn't get *some* form of travel sickness) and had to manage by myself for most things and glean a lot of conversations by a process of grasping the words you know and using intuition with the ones you don't; which didn't always succeed because if Uighurs were speaking their accent was so unfamiliar that I often failed to catch a word, and the Chinese interpreter who helped us out from Kazakh to Chinese was himself a Kazakh – and sometimes I thought he was talking Kazakh when he wasn't. ANYWAY, what I began this involved sentence to say is that it's done my self-reliance in the language a power of good and I have just astonished myself by arriving in Lanchow, getting myself fixed in the hotel again, booking my ticket to Peking, arranging to be called in the morning, ordering a meal and so forth without a moment's hesitation ...

'I have an even more thrilling story to tell about Kazakh than the purely visual description I began with. For three days after we got into the Ili region over the Fir Tree Pass, we actually went to visit some herdsmen in their summer pastures high, high up in the mountain (past the level where conifers stop growing) and SPENT THE NIGHT IN A YURT, and were royally entertained by having a sheep killed – the absolutely unbreakable custom when strangers come – being given the best carpet to sit on, drinking kumiss ceremonially from a double-bowled cup made of carved wood, and having a talk and a sing-song until long after dark; and next morning went to another herdsmen's co-operative where they *also* killed a sheep, served kumiss, etc. etc. But that HAS to await another letter. Or maybe I'll write an article about it for *World News*.[167] For the moment all I can say is that it is an experience I will never forget and one Mrs Thompson Glover never had in her life, going up and down perpendicular slopes in a jeep with about fifty horsemen galloping beside it – and meeting the chauffeur, whom I thought so taciturn because his eyebrows met in the middle and he spoke so little (not knowing much else) ON A HORSE, grinning from ear to ear and laughing like mad when our jeep (the second one) got stuck in the beds of streams while he just skipped lightly over on his horse. The babies are absolutely *bedecked* with owl-feathers, beads and silver ornaments, and the women – especially the married ones – look like something out of Henry V, with wimples they don't take off, even to sleep in. And I passed round cigarettes in the yurt, and before I could stop myself held out the packet to the *Mullah* (they neither smoke nor drink by religion) and he took one!

'I bought Turfan raisins and Uighur caps for presents for various Peking friends, and last night the Urumchi Peace Committee presented me with raisins and caps. The excess on the aeroplane has made them cost like gold.'

Rewi eventually turned up before I returned to Peking with pages and pages of impressions for me to arrange in some sort of order. He typed a couple of pages or so every evening and stuffed them into a folder which he handed over to me. He has an astonishing capacity, which I have never seen equalled, of absorbing facts and impressions: we would arrive in a distant village; Rewi would get out of the jeep and start a conversation with the first old man he met; in fifteen minutes he would get back into the jeep and tell me the history and present condition of that village (that district) and some recondite facts which it took him a couple of hours to put on the typewriter that night. We travelled (by jeep) right up to the border with the Soviet Union (Ili) where I, still naive, was astonished to find sentries of the most armed and hostile kind facing one another across the well-defined border. (Yet didn't we understand that the greatest friendship existed between the two countries?) Did we not daily meet groups of schoolchildren, who approached us on seeing our 'high noses' and clapping their hands, about 'Soviet Auntie, Soviet Uncle!'

From Ili we went up into the mountains, to meet the (Chinese) Kazak people, nomad herdsmen who welcomed us with a typical feast of lamb, kumiss and odd little pastries. In two days we underwent three of these traditional feasts, always ending up with *sandwiches* of fat from a fat-tailed sheep, with liver in between, after which, as instructed, we went through the gesture of wiping our long beards and saying '*Armat*' (thanks).

There was a long history to this turbulent area. Turkic people fighting Chinese, both fighting Russians, all fighting English and Iranians, everyone wanting hegemony and control of the borders with India or else, or in addition, the sources of *oil* with which the area was endowed. We visited the Karamai oilfields, where some years before an old carter had greased his wheels with some black stuff that came out of the ground, unknown to the outside world. It was being exploited partly by Soviet oil prospectors, and because the Gobi desert lay between Sinkiang and Peking, the easier route for the export of oil, hides, agricultural products etc. was Westward ... all this was the subject of negotiations still at that time. Old Rewi attempted to sum up the extremely complicated history of the region and the complicated present situation and I tried to make sense of his summary; but it seems that Peking had not yet reached a consensus. Who had liberated whom from whom in 1949? (Rewi's book never did appear, at the end of the day.)

XVII

Leaving Rewi to complete his visit, I returned to Peking, to find myself in the midst of the *Great Leap Forward*, whereby China was to hurtle over the socialist system into full scale communism in record time.[168] 1958 was a year not only of good harvests but of startling achievements from the policy of 'step by step'. More areas of China were brought under irrigation than ever before in the same period of time. There was euphoria around.

For some weeks I had been engaging in some part-time work editing a translation of the history of Chinese films (subject later to a fantastic slander campaign against the author, which I learned about only afterwards). For this part-time work I was paid, eventually receiving a wad of money I didn't know what to do with. It occurred to me that I might blow it on a trip to Mauritius to see Frances in her new home (since I could buy the ticket in Chinese currency by virtue of the financial agreements between China and India, all I would need in hard currency was the bit between India and Mauritius). So I set about fixing the journey towards the end of 1958. Some months before, Ted and I had made the acquaintance of a very great South African, Cecil Williams,[169] who came on a Peace visit to Peking. We corresponded after his return to his country. I mentioned that I was coming to Mauritius and he wrote inviting me to fly from Mauritius to South Africa during my visit (with immense generosity offering to pay my fare).

The Chinese Communist Party did not raise any objections to this project, hoping that I would carry propaganda messages to the people of South Africa, and stuffing me with 'facts' (only some of which were true) on the effects of the 'Great Leap Forward' and in particular with copies of the pamphlet, 'Imperialism and All Reactionaries are Paper Tigers'.[170]

Mauritius was a heavenly interlude. Air travel was not, in those days, as direct and speedy as it is now and I travelled via Rangoon, Calcutta, Bombay, Karachi, Aden, Nairobi, Madagascar (Tananarive), Reunion and Mauritius. I was 'seen through' as far as Bombay by the Chinese authorities in the various places, and was moved to be greeted in Rangoon by one of my former pupils for English lessons with the greeting 'venerable professor'!

Of Rangoon I remember little except the stern notice in the temples, FOOTWEAR PROHIBITED. I stayed there only two days. Calcutta and Bombay were shattering. I had never seen such poverty, misery and suffering, nor felt so powerless to give anything but sympathy. The pavements were thronged with camping people, gathered round stand-pipes for access to water; people lay sleeping – alive or dead? The agony of the dark bony *hands* which stretched into the car windows whenever the car (provided by the Chinese Embassy) stopped at the traffic lights, accompanied by soft cries for charity ...

The seafront quarter at Bombay, with street after street of tiny booths, each the width of its door, containing a prostitute, displaying her wares for seagoing visitors. Oh what can be done, what can I do? It was a horrible experience.

Aden, smelling of oil and salt, where greedy visitors bought watches and other duty-free goods, with not a glance at the inhabitants.

Nairobi – where I scarcely saw an African other than waiters; there the hotel was full of brash, aggressive, Hemingway types shouting 'Boy!'

And Tananarive, where I spent only an hour or so, where the balmy fragrant air nimbly and sweetly recommended itself to my gentle senses. After Reunion, black lava rising from the shore, journey's end in Mauritius, where Frances, Noël and two of their by-now three children awaited me, and drove me to their little house, to be greeted by a great string of fire-crackers, ignited by their servant, Antoinette, to a vast outburst of barking from the neighbouring dogs. A bewildering panorama of nationalities – Indians (Hindu and Muslim), Creoles, Chinese, Whites (French and English) and 'people of mixed descent'. Street signs in French, English, Chinese, Arabic; temples, mosques, churches and pagodas; cars, bicycles, carts drawn by horses and some by zebus – I needed eyes all round my head to take in the picture.

Frances and Noël (a poorly-paid civil servant in the Forestry Department) were 'having a struggle to make ends meet', as the saying goes. I made the acquaintance of my second and third grandchildren, William, a redheaded little boy of three, and John, two years old and a very robust and energetic blond. Noël went to see a Chinese friend, owner of a photography shop, and mentioned that I had come from Peking. He closed his shop on the instant, took us to a nearby restaurant and invited us to a 'snack' consisting of about twelve Chinese dishes, and then to the office of one of the two Chinese-language newspapers (one of which supported Mao Tse-tung and the other Chiang Kai-sheck) where I gave an interview and arrangements were put in train to address various gatherings of Chinese – the secondary school, a group of doctors and others, winding up with a social-and-dance and finally a banquet given by a very rich Chinese businessman who served whiskey in tumblers and had friends in various parts of the room primed to ask me leading questions, such as: 'Does the wind blow from the East or the West?' (a current slogan from Peking). (I did not distribute any of the Paper Tigers pamphlets.)

Christmas Day was spent on the beach where Frances and I swam in the warm blue sea.

Then early in January I flew on to Johannesburg. The Communist Party of South Africa was already banned and to protect my anonymity Cecil did not meet me at the airport. Instead, a beautiful blonde girl approached me and asked if I were Nan

Green, and drove me some miles down the road where Cecil and Phyllis Altman (who had also been in China and was one of the secretaries of the SACTU)[171] were waiting – a joyful reunion. The girl was the daughter of Bram Fisher, a man whom I am proud to have known.[172] We drove to Cecil's flat, which he was vacating while I stayed there, and spent an hour or two with other friends, arranging my programme for the next fourteen days. I have never before or since seen such breathtakingly efficient organisation. Twenty-seven meetings were fixed, with their assignations, split-second timing, locations, escorts and transport, and every single one of them was carried out to the minute with no telephone nor missed appointments. I went to 'townships' where Whites were not supposed to be (after dark), was smuggled into factories, attended one day of the 'Treason Trial' in Pretoria,[173] wearing a fashionable little white hat with a veil, and carefully surrounded by Molly Fisher and her daughters so as to foil the press photographers, and to private houses in roads patrolled by friends on the lookout in case the police came by, noting down car numbers (mixed gatherings were prohibited and the police watch for them).

In Pretoria, in the lunch-time interval of the Treason Trial, I talked to Chief Albert Luthuli, a very great man and a Chairman of the African National Congress.[174] We had to drive round the streets because there was no place in Pretoria where I could sit down with a black man for a meal or a drink. Among other things I told him about China was the story of the 'ancestors' co-operatives', which intrigued him very much because above-ground burial was traditional among his (Zulu, Xhosa?) people and he saw its wasteful character. At two subsequent meetings – one at his son's house in Durban – he asked me to repeat this.

I told my audiences how life was getting better in China, expatiating, I am afraid, about the Great Leap Forward, which later turned out not to be as great as I'd been told. In pitch dark garages in one of the townships, where about fifty people sat on the floor and all I could see was the whites of their eyes, that brave and wonderful woman, Lilian Ngoyi[175] asked: 'But Nan, tell us what to *do*, which twisted my heart. It was no use telling *them* that imperialism was a Paper Tiger. I never gave away any of those pamphlets. That meeting was I think the high spot of my whole visit. Before they dispersed they *sang* in their own tongue a revolutionary song, softly in harmony, ending up with a whispered 'Mayibuye, Afrika'.[176] The hair went up on the back of my neck and I shook the dark extended hands, weeping.

Albert Luthuli, Bram and Molly Fisher, Lilian Ngoyi, Joe Slovo, Ruth First, Fatima Meer, Rusty Bernstein and his wife Hilda, Cecil Williams and Phyllis Altman, Helen Joseph – in whose house I ate hot scones while she went out to take part in a woman's demonstration against the Pass Laws (it wasn't safe for me to be there), Winnie Mandela – these are some of the names of those heroic, determined, open-eyed, truly glorious people who fought and are still fighting as I write, for freedom in Africa.[177] I am proud to have known them. (Some have already died – Cecil, Lilian, Bram, I shall not forget any of you, steadfast unto death). I am ashamed to have done so little for them, but when I said this, at Cecil's funeral, to Julius Lewin,[178] he said: 'But you've been fighting on your own sector of the same front,' which was a scrap of comfort.

The humiliation of having to use Whites-only doors, lifts, post-office counters and park benches burnt me up. But with the help of our friends I was able to cock a final snook at the government. The *Rand Daily Mail* was at that time as near progressive as one could get, in the circumstances, and on the day before my departure I gave an interview to one of its reporters, on condition that he did not publish it until he was sure I'd gone. He actually came to the airport to make sure, and took my photograph secretly behind a newsstand in the last few minutes. The next day the interview appeared, beginning – 'A British Communist woman has been touring South Africa ...' and giving my name as Nan

Green. I had of course entered with my passport, which said 'Brake'. The authorities did track me down as far as my real name, but never discovered where I had been staying or with whom associating, because the name and address I had given (by arrangement) on my entry-form was that of a friendly woman who allowed me to use it while she was out of the country. The authorities interviewed her husband, who was not so friendly and indignantly denied any knowledge of me and proved that his wife had not been at home during the time of my visit. The African comrades were overjoyed.

I had addressed a total of twenty-seven meetings in my fourteen-day stay. Back in Mauritius, I now relaxed and enjoyed the company of Frances and family. Then back to snowbound Peking, where within a fortnight I was discovered to have an attack of hepatitis, told to rest and put on a horrid diet of glucose, honey and plenty of meat. Not easy, since it was rationed, but the neighbour in our courtyard (the Graves' disease sufferer, who could only shuffle as far as the nearest lake in one of the parks) set himself to *fish* and brought me carp and other delicacies at least twice a week, while Mr Li, as I have recounted, cycled out into the countryside with jam jars to fetch honey.

I managed, when the original fever had died down to persuade *China Reconstructs* that one could 'polish' while resting, so they brought me work to the house, avoiding boredom. Some of the English group, in which hostility had now sharpened, criticised me in a meeting for irresponsibility because I went on working and had been seen, in defiance of doctors' orders, *walking fast* along the street. Ted unexpectedly leapt to my defence: 'If anyone has never seen Nan walking slowly, it's more than I have,' he said sharply.

It took nearly two years for me to be pronounced cured, but in the meantime I had gradually gone back to activity and felt no ill effects from exercise. (At the end of 1960, back in England, I had a check up at St Thomas's Hospital and was confirmed as free.)

Clouds began to appear on the horizon: on my horizon anyway, though some of them had begun looming for two or three years. The first, 'no bigger than a man's hand', was the sentence that kept cropping up in conversation: 'There comes a time when the pupil knows more than the teacher'. The 'doxology' about the selfless help of the Soviet Union had gradually disappeared from the articles we edited, but in this respect I thought they had at last heeded our protestations about boring repetition. But now there was a surprising phenomenon – loftily hostile criticism not published in our press but earnestly debated among our Chinese colleagues, of a recent film from the Soviet Union which had, through a sentimental love story, stressed the horrors of war and the human suffering it caused. (I never saw the film but this was what I was told about it.) Wordy critiques of the film appeared in the press. J.D. Bernal came on a visit; his recently published *World Without War* was muttered against,[179] and he was given a barely perceptibly cold reception, which puzzled us. We only sniffed this from friends of Chinese/European, Chinese/Canadian or other mixed nationality, who, for language reasons, were working in Peking Radio. There was no open hostility, but one was given to understand that the book would not be translated into Chinese. Then T M-c, whom I had known as a Chinese Communist Party representative in the Peace Liaison Committee, and seemed to have a sort of watching brief over the affairs of the British 'cadres', said to me one day, quite breezily: 'Well, let them start an atomic war. We will not be the first. They may kill a couple of hundred million people, but we shall still have four hundred million and then we'll smash them. The world will know that we are not the aggressors.'

My blood ran cold. 'You are inhuman!' was all I could gasp. He turned the conversation, and I brooded about it, though convinced that his was a personal opinion and he was merely fantasising. It was not until 1961, when I was back in England, that I discovered that this was the viewpoint of the Chinese Communist Party and had been manifested at an international gathering in Moscow of communist parties in the 1950's.

Ted went to London early in 1960. Though quite amicable, our relationship had deteriorated and he merely asked me what I should do, neither urging me to go too nor suggesting I should stay. He was in fact already in early negotiations to return as a correspondent of the *Daily Worker* (A.W. having left to go to East Berlin).[180] I knew that I would return to England but I did not know when: it was the summer period, when the four English-language 'polishers' took turns for their holidays, and I was forth-holding for two of them (man and wife) so felt a strong sense of duty to the magazine.

But now appeared a pamphlet, translated into several languages and bound in scarlet and gold: 'Long Live Leninism'.[181] The text consisted mainly of quotations from various writings of Lenin, but its implication was clearly to be read between the lines – criticism of the Communist Party of the Soviet Union and all those other communist parties which were concentrating on ways to build peace and avoid the horrors of atomic war, already seen to threaten mankind. This was practically stuffed down our throats and our Chinese friends eagerly asked: 'What is your opinion?' An African communist working in Peking came on a visit, palpably *sent* to invite me to utter anathemas against the Communist Party of Great Britain. My reply in all cases was that I was a member of the British Party and adhered to its 'line'. I.E., born in Poland but brought up in China and the USA, took me out in a boat in Peihai Park (he had taken Chinese nationality some time before) to propose to me that I should remain in China – 'for the rest of your life, Nan. You will be taken care of in your old age', which finally and decisively put my hackles up and decided me.

'My Party will look after me in my old age,' I said (knowing full well that it could not). Blithely treating the whole conversation as a personal one – knowing that it was 'official', though unadmitted – I thanked him for a pleasant afternoon and went home. There I wrote instantly to dear Margaret,[182] indicating my urgent wish to be *sent for* – so as not to cause even a tiny rift between our Parties, but putting it in disguised words (for fear of censorship) which I knew she would understand, thus avoiding rancorous explanations.[183]

Notes

1. See Lewis Carroll, *Alice in Wonderland*, London: Macmillan & Co., 1865, chapter 12.
2. Arding and Hobbs, Clapham Junction, London SW11 is a long-established department store.
3. The reference is to Jane Austen's *Emma* (1816): 'One accompaniment to her song took her agreeably by surprise – a second, slightly but correctly taken by Frank Churchill' (Chapter 8)
4. 'Riding on Top of the Car' was written by Fred W. Leigh and V. P. Bryan and composed by Harry von Tozler. 'My Girl's Promised to Marry Me' (1909) was arranged by J. Chas. Moore and E. W. Rogers.
5. Benedicite: a canticle (a song drawn from the Bible but outside of the Book of Psalms – the Benedictus [Luke, 1:68-79] and Nunc Dimittis [Luke 2: 29-32] being the two best known). Its source is The Book of Apocrypha v. 35-66. The rise of Anglo-Catholicism was stimulated in the nineteenth century by the Oxford Group (or 'Tractarians') – a group strongest in East Anglia. A key figure in this movement was John Henry Newman, whose *Tracts for the Times*, 1834-1841 (with others) proved influential and controversial. The words 'Erred and strayed from Thy ways like a lost sheep' come from the *Book of Common Prayer*, from 'The Introduction to Morning and Evening Prayer'.
6. *Punch*, a humorous, sometimes satiric magazine, first launched in July 1841.
7. *The Strand Magazine* was begun by George Newnes in 1891, ceasing publication in 1950.
8. Arthur Mee (1875-1941) published his *Children's Encyclopedia* from 1908. The series continued into the early 1960s
9. The *Illustrated London News*, the first illustrated newspaper, was founded in 1842 by Herbert Ingram.
10. Bernard Partridge (1861-1945), cartoonist and regular contributor to Punch, became its chief cartoonist in 1901. His

conservative cartoons were very harsh on the Trades Union Movement. He was knighted by the Conservative Prime Minister, Stanley Baldwin in 1925.

11. A reference to the creation by James Thurber (1894-1961) of Walter Mitty, an ineffectual daydreamer. See 'The Secret Life of Walter Mitty' (1941) reprinted in '*The Secret Life of Walter Mitty' and Other Pieces*, London: Penguin: 2000.

12. Samuel Butler (1835-1932) composed *The Way of All Flesh* in 1885. It was revised by R. A. Streatfield and published in 1903. The reference here is to the cruel and disciplinarian parents of Ernest Pontifex (particularly the bullying Theobald).

13. Lloyd George (1863-1945) proposed a system of National Insurance, a contributory system against illness and unemployment, in 1908. Herbert Asquith (1852-1928) ensured his Liberal Government enacted the National Insurance Act in 1911. The suffragettes found their key beginning in 1897, when Millicent Fawcett (1847-1929) founded the National Union of Women's Suffrage. The suffragettes' pressure and tactics of direct action helped lead to the passing of the 1918 Representation of the People Act, the start of female suffrage in Great Britain.

14. The Excess Profits Tax was levied in Great Britain from 1915-1921, and was aimed at increasing government revenues in times of distress (particularly the hardships created by World War One).

15. The 1918-1919 influenza pandemic, the most devastating in history, killed more people than died during World War One. M & B was an early kind of antibiotic.

16. BSA (British Small Arms) manufactured bicycles and motorcycles from 1912-1973.

17. The 6th Form is the name traditionally given to the class in which school students aged circa 16-18 are placed.

18. The *News Chronicle* was a right-of-centre paper founded in 1930 by the merger of the *Daily News* and the *Daily Chronicle*.

In 1960 it merged itself with the *Daily Mail.*

19. H. G. Wells (1866-1946), author, essayist and political commentator; D. H. Lawrence (1888-1935), poet, novelist, playwright and freethinker; George Bernard Shaw (1856-1950), playwright, essayist, polemicist: James George Fraser (1854-1941), author of *The Golden Bough* (1922); Tom Paine (1737-1809), radical propagandist and revolutionary; Thomas Beecham (1879-1961) founded the British National Opera in 1915 (as the Beecham Opera Company, becoming the BNO Company in 1920); W. S. Gilbert (1836-1911) and Arthur Sullivan (1842-1900), were the librettist and composer, respectively, of light operetta. The first three people in this list all exhibited socialist leanings more or less consistently during their lives; Tom Paine relatedly, was, earlier in history, a strong supporter of the rights of the common man, most famously in his *Rights of Man* (1791) – a defence of the French Revolution.

20. The phrase 'Troubles of Ireland' is a reference to the conflicts between Great Britain and Irish nationalists resisting its imperialist aspirations or presence in Ireland over the last five centuries.

21. The Hallé orchestra is the longest established professional symphony orchestra in the UK, founded in Manchester in 1858 by Charles Hallé (1819-1895).

22. 'Lift Thine Eyes to the Mountains' comes from *Elijah* (1846) by Felix Mendelssohn (1809-1847).

23. Voting rights for women aged 21 was established by the Equal Franchise Act of 1928.

24. The Fabians were established as a left-wing debating society committed to social justice and a belief in the progressive improvement of society. In 1900 it joined with the trades unions and the Independent Labour Party to form the Labour Party, to which it is still affiliated. Early members included George Bernard Shaw, Sidney and Beatrice Webb, Emmeline Pankhurst and H. G. Wells.

25. Bradley Headstone, a character in *Our Mutual Friend* (1864-5), by Charles Dickens (1812-1870), is an obsessively jealous schoolmaster, prepared to descend to criminal depths to get his way: 'You could draw me to fire, you could draw me to water, you could draw me to the gallows, you could draw me to any death, you could draw me to anything I have most avoided, you could draw me to any exposure and disgrace' (chapter 32).

26. The Lickey Hills, an area of woods and heathland, is located eleven miles south-west of Birmingham town centre.

27. Mrs Wilfer is another character in Dicken's *Our Mutual Friend*. See chapter 5, in which Mrs Wilfer explains to her husband how their 'daughter, Bella, has bestowed herself upon a Mendicant' by marrying 'Mr John Rokesmith'.

28. These words spring from the lips of Catherine Earnshaw, when endeavouring to explain to Nelly how her love for Heathcliff is qualitatively superior to her love for Edgar Linton, in chapter nine of *Wuthering Heights* (1847).

29. William Ewart Gladstone (1808-1898) was Prime Minister of Britain on four occasions (1868-74, 1880-1885, 1886 and 1892-1894).

30. The Independent Labour Party was founded in 1893 by James Kier Hardy (1856-1915). In 1900 the ILP joined with the Fabians, the Trades Unions and the Social Democratic Federation (a Marxist Party established in 1881) to found the Labour Representation Committee. This entered candidates with some success in the 1906 general election, after which time the LRC was known as the Labour Party. The phrase 'to secure for the workers by hand or by brain' occurs in Clause IV of the Labour Party constitution, adopted in 1918: 'To secure for the workers by hand or by brain the full fruits of their industry and the most equitable distribution thereof that may be possible upon the basis of the common ownership of the means of production'.

31. Evil-Knievel (b. 1938) was famous in the later decades of the second half of the twentieth century for his daredevil motorbike stunts – especially his long-distance motorbike leaps.

32. The cartoon referred to is by J. F. Horrrabin, and was printed as a poster in 1912 by Twentieth Century Press Ltd., London.(with thanks to the Working Class Movement Library, Salford).

33. The *New Leader* (1922-46) was the successor to *Labour Leader*, founded in 1891 and from 1893 an organ of the ILP (and itself a renaming of *The Miner*, founded in 1996 by Kier Hardy). In 1946 *New Leader* was retitled *Socialist Leader*.

34. The National Government was founded on 24 August during the economic and financial crisis of 1931, which split the ruling Labour government (1929-31). The so-called National Government consisted of a few Labour politicians, led by Ramsay MacDonald, the Conservative Party, and most Liberals. Though led by MacDonald, the National Government was seen as Conservative-controlled and MacDonald was regarded as a traitor. The National Government lasted until the 1945 election after World War Two.

35. Jack Hilton and his Dance Orchestra was a swing band that begun life in 1927 and lasted into the 1940s.

36. The first Lyons Corner House, a development of the Lyons Tea Houses that begun in 1894, opened in 1909. Upmarket tea rooms, Lyons Corner Houses often featured live music by small dance bands. They were closed down during the 1970s.

37. Jon Kimche (1909-1994) was a member of a Marxist group in the ILP that, during the period 1933-36 was attracted to Trotskyism. He subsequently edited *Tribune*, the independent Labour weekly, and worked on the *Jewish Observer* and, during World War Two, on *The Observer*. Karl Marx (1818-1883), Friedrich Engels (1820-1895) and Vladimir Ilich Lenin (1870-1924) are three of the major political theorists of Communism.

38. Geoffrey Grigson (1905-1985) edited *New Verse* (1933-1939).

39. John Strachey (1901-1963) wrote *The Coming Struggle for Power* (Victor Gollancz, 1932) with the aim of making communism seem practical and logically necessary. The book formed part of the Left Book Club series. Strachey was one of Beaverbrooks' 'Four Horsemen of the Socialist Apocalypse' (the other three being Victor Gollancz, Harold Laski and Kingsley Martin).

40. Engels published *Anti-Dühring* in 1877-78. This was an attempt to survey and define the Communist world-view (to which dialectical materialism was central).

41. 'Forward ye workers' can be found in the undated song-book, *National Agricultural Labourers and Rural Workers Song Book* (Norwich: Caxton Press). 'Comrades, come rally' is part of the Internationale: 'Comrades, come rally/ And the last fight let us face,/ The Internationale unites the human race'.

42. Sigmund Freud (1856-1939) is generally regarded as the father of psychoanalysis. A. S. Neill (1883-1973) founded Summerhill in 1921 as part of the Neue Schule, an International School in Dresden run by idealists who fenced children in with regulations. Neill favoured children leading their own lives, with the freedom to be themselves and develop at their own pace. He moved his school first to Austria, then, in 1923, to Lyme Regis and, subsequently, in 1927, to Suffolk. The Russian Revolution is probably best dated to October 1917, when troops mutinied, Moscow backed rebellion and the tsar abdicated (to be assassinated). However, unrest had long been developing, to gather in momentum steadily from 1905, when a substantial, unsuccessful revolution occurred.

43. Ken Campbell (b. 1941), playwright, broadcaster and performance artist.

44. Lilian Baylis (1874-1937), sometimes described as the grandmother of national theatre in the UK, was the driving force behind the establishment of the Old Vic and the founder of Sadler's Wells.

45. Agit prop is a contraction of the words 'agitatsiia' and 'propaganda'. In the Soviet Union, agit prop denominates a mode of post-Revolutionary artistic expression designed to inculcate Communist values. After the revolution, the Communist Party of the Soviet Union (CPSU) annually elected a 27 member Central Committee. But this was soon felt to be too large and in March 1919 was therefore replaced by a five

man Politburo (increased to nine in 1925 and ten in 1930). Its first members were Vladimir Lenin, Leon Trotsky, Joseph Stalin, Lev Kamenv and Nikolai Krestinsky. In 1952 the Politburo was replaced by a presidium of thirty-six members. After the death of Stalin, this was reduced to ten members. *For Soviet Britain: the Programme of the Communist Party* (London: Communist Party of Great Britain, 1935) was a pamphlet outlining the CPGB programme adopted at the XIII Congress, 2 February 1935.

46. Maoists were people espousing the political philosophy of Mao Tse Tung. Fidel Castro (b. 1926) led an unsuccessful invasion to liberate Cuba from the dictatorship of Batista in 1953, and a successful invasion in 1956. His land reforms and other measures alienated the USA, and its growing hostility pushed Castro into alliance with the Soviet Union. Che Guevara (1928-1967) invaded Cuba with Castro in 1956. After a spell in the Castro's Cuban government, he went on to fight other guerilla campaigns, only to be ambushed and killed in one of these, in Bolivia in 1967. Ho Chi Minh (1890-1969) was an organizer of resistance to French rule in Vietnam, then to the invading Japanese during World War Two, and then to the French once more after the war. This phase of resistance culminated in the division of Vietnam into the North and South in 1954. But when the South refused to hold elections, fearing a Communist victory, Ho Chi Minh, as head of state of North Vietnam, helped organize guerilla resistance in the South, via the National Front for the Liberation of South Vietnam, firstly against the French, then, as it became drawn in, against the USA. This resistance culminated in US defeat in 1975.

47. Adolf Hitler (1889-1945) founded the National Socialist Workers Party (the Nazi party) in Germany in 1920, evolving it from the German Workers Party, which he had joined shortly before. He became German Chancellor in 1933 and led Germany into World War Two. Benito Mussolini (1883-1945) joined the *fascio* early in the Italian Fascist party's history, in

1914, and became Italian premier in 1922. In 1936 he led Italy into the Axis alliance with Germany. Mussolini perpetrated a murderous, victorious campaign against Abyssinia in 1935-36, including the bombing of remote villages. Chiang Kai-shek (1887-1975) was leader of the Koumintang nationalists campaigning against Japanese invasion during the 1930s, his resistance taking him into alliance with Mao Tse Tung and the Communists. After World War Two this alliance broke up, and after some nationalist resistance to the Communists, Chiang Kai-Shek fled to Formosa (Taiwan) in 1949. The Japanese during the late 1930s and early 1940s killed hundreds of thousands of Chinese. Oswald Moseley, elected as a Conservative MP, crossed benches to the Labour Party. Resigning in 1931, he formed his 'New Party', and then, in 1932, the British Union of Fascists. The party uniform included black shirts, hence the nickname, Blackshirts. At its high point, in 1934, the party had almost 40,000 members.

48. The Suez crisis of 1956 was precipitated by the decision of Gabal Abdel-Nasser (1918-70) to nationalize the Suez Canal (supported by Communist Russia). This move was opposed by Britain and France, who, despite the USA's indifference, invaded Egypt. This invasion failed ignominiously.

49. *The Daily Worker* was established in 1930 by the Communist Party of Great Britain. It was boycotted by newspaper wholesalers and therefore set up its own distribution system. It was banned during World War Two (in 1941).

50. The Pindar of Wakefield is a common name for pubs (premises licensed to sell alcohol) in the United Kingdom. The League Against Imperialism, a peace organization, was founded in 1927 and continued until 1957.

51. The Unity Theatre movement consisted of circa 250 group before World War Two, loosely linked to the Left Book Club Theatre Guild. Largely amateur, it sought to promote the labour movement by making theatre accessible to all. *Waiting for Lefty*,

first produced in 1935 in the Group Theatre and starring Lee
J. Cobb and Elia Kazan, was written by Clifford Odets. Its subject
was the lead-up to a taxi strike and detailed the injustice and
corruption afflicting working men.

52. The phrase 'glad, confident morning' comes from the poem
'The Lost Leader' (1845) by Robert Browning (1812-1889): 'Life's
night begins: let him never come back to us!/ There would be
doubt, hesitation and pain,/ Forced praise on our part – the
glimmer of twilight,/ Never glad confident morning again!'

53. Coram's Fields is an area of approximately seven acres of
largely open ground, the site of hospital founded in the 1740s
by Thomas Coram for destitute and abandoned foundlings. It
was converted into a children's play area in 1976 when much
of the hospital was demolished, leaving the park largely
surrounded by low Georgian architecture.

54. The London County Council or LCC was created in 1889 to
provide unitary direction to London's development. It was
replaced in 1963 by the Greater London Council.

55. The 7th World Congress of the Communist International
occurred in 1935. Georgi Dimitriov (1882-1949) was one of the
founders of the Bulgarian Communist Party in 1919 and became
Bulgarian premier after World War Two (1945-1949).

56. William Gallacher (1881-1965) was the first Communist to be
elected to Parliament, in 1935 (after several previous attempts).
He was a strong supporter of the anti-Franco Left in Spain. The
Front Populaire was France's first socialist government, under
Léon Blum, from 1936-38. Moseley's blackshirts sought to stir
up confrontation by marching an anti-semitic demonstration
through the East End of London in October 1936. Their attempt
to do this was blocked by anti-fascist campaigners in the so-
called Battle of Cable Street.

57. The 1870 Foreign Enlistment Act was revived by the British
government in January 1937 in an attempt to reduce the flow
of volunteers, many of them recruited by the Communist Party's

efforts, to fight for the Republican Left against Franco's fascist Nationalists during the Spanish Civil War (1936-39). This attempt proved unworkable, but was symptomatic of the British government's desire to maintain a non-interventionist stance during that war.

58. Wogan Philipps, The Lord Milford (1902-1993), a dashing, dilettante aristocrat and painter, became a Communist (attaining notoriety in 1963 as the only sitting Communist peer). He married Rosamond Lehmann in 1928, leaving her at the time of the Spanish Civil War.

59. Wilfred Roberts (1900-1991) was a Labour MP from 1935-60, and a leading figure in the Basque Children's Committee and other Spanish relief bodies, which came together in the National Joint Committee for Spanish Relief, for which he served as Secretary from 1937-40, and which raised money for various Spanish relief causes. Medical Aid organized the sending of medical supplies and nursing and auxiliary volunteers to Spain

60. The incontrolados, or uncontrollables were usually anarchists, especially in Catalonia, who opposed the centralization of power the Spanish Communists sought to establish via their Control Commissions.

61. Angela Guest was the daughter of Carmel Guest, a former suffragette and Dr Haden Guest, a Labour MP, once Minister of Health under Ramsay MacDonald.

62. Julian Bell (1908-1937), was a poet and nephew of Virginia Woolf. Izzy Kupchik, a German refugee and Somme ambulance driver, was killed in action in Spain during the Spanish Civil War.

63. Otto Jesperson (1860-1943) published many books on language and linguistics. His *Essentials of English Grammar* was published by George Allen and Unwin in 1933.

64. Dorothy Lowe, or possibly Dorothy Low, was part of the Aid Spain Movement: the Aid Spain Committee in Britain helped co-ordinate aid to Spain, such as volunteers for the International Brigades and medical aid and assistance (via Medical Aid). See

Jim Pyrth, *The Signal Was Spain: The Aid Spain Movement in Britain 1936-1939*, London: Lawrence and Wisehart, 1986. Pyrth's book also makes extensive mention of Nan Green.

65. The Popular Front, or Frente Popular, was a pact signed by various left-wing organizations in Spain, including the Communist Party of Spain (PCE). The Frente Popular won the 1936 election in Spain, prompting Franco's coup d'état and, consequently, the Spanish Civil War.

66. Leon Trotsky (Lev Davidovich Bronstein, 1879-1940), an ardent disciple of Marx, led one (Menshevik) faction in a split of the Russian Communist Party in 1903 (Lenin led the other, Bolsehvik wing). Although this rift was healed, beneath it lay Trotsky's greater commitment to an international perspective and international socialist revolution. After Lenin's death, Trotsky was a candidate to replace him, but he lost out to Stalin, was expelled from the Soviet Union, founded the Third International in 1938 and was then assassinated in a cowardly attack sponsored by Stalin.

67. Egon Erwin Kisch (1885-1948), prominent member of the Defence Association of German Writers (SDS) and Communist Party member, was forced into exile in Paris from Nazi Germany. From there, he became a newspaper correspondent in the Spanish Civil War's International Brigades, a force of volunteers recruited internationally and sent for training to Albercete before being deployed. A total of 59,380 volunteers from fifty-five countries served, including 10,000 French, 5,000 Germans, 5,000 Poles, 3,350 Italians, 2,800 Americans, 2,000 British, 1,000 Canadians, 1,500 Yugoslavs, 1,500 Czechs, 1,000 Canadians, 1,000 Hungarians and 1,000 Scandinavians. Battalions established included the Abraham Lincoln Brigade, the British Battalion, the Connolly Column, the Dajakovich Battalion, the Dimitriov Battalion, the Mackenzie-Papineau Battalion, the George Washington Battalion, the Mickiewicz Battalion and the Thaelmann Battalion.

68. Leah Manning, anti-Franco activist, was elected Labour MP for Islington East in 1931 and Epping (1945-50).

69. Artur London (1915-86), who fought in the Spanish Civil War with the International Brigades, had his *L'Aveu (The Confession)* published in 1969 (Paris: Gallimard), following his experiences in the Prague Trials of 1952, an extension of Stalin's anti-semitic campaign against 'rootless cosmopolitanism'.

70. Juan Negrin (1892-1956), member of the Frente Popular in Spain, became a Commuinst sympathiser. Resistir es Vencer can be translated as 'To resist is to win'.

71. 14 July is Bastille Day, celebrating the fall of the Bastille prison in 1789, during the French Revolution. Its fall came to symbolize the struggle against oppression and for liberty and democracy

72. Dolores Ibarruri, La Pasionaria (1895-1989) Communist leader, activist and inspirational orator, became especially prominent during the Spanish Civil War. She coined the phrase, 'No pasaran!' ('They shall not pass') in 1936.

73 The crossing of the Ebro in 1938 was part of a Republican Army offensive, led by General Sebastian Pozas, that quickly broke down after limited initial success. It is often regarded as a turning-point in the Spanish Civil War, marking the onset of the collapse of the Republican Army.

74. The Schick test detects immunity to diphtheria.

75. Sam Wild joined the International Brigades in 1936. He commanded the British Battalion during 1938.

76. Enrique Bassadone, or possibly Enrique Basadone, was a Spaniard from Gibraltar. See Pyrth, p. 134.

77. The Spanish third person (usted), rather than the second person (tú) was at that time used when speaking to someone older or subjectively viewed as in a higher position in society. It was not wholly dissimilar to the distinction in France, in which 'tu' was only used when a certain level of friendship and intimacy had been reached, with 'vous' otherwise preferred in polite society. Recently, in both Spain and France, these

kinds of distinctions have begun to erode.

78. The Munich pact between Hitler and Neville Chamberlain (1869-1940), British Prime Minister from 1937-40, sought to secure 'peace in our time', in Chamberlain's poorly-judged phrase, by surrendering the Sudetenland in Czechoslovakia to Germany behind the backs of the Czechs. The Munich pact is now regarded as the archetypal modern act of appeasement.

79. Peter Kerrigan was an International Brigade volunteer and journalist with the *Daily Worker* in Spain from 1937 to 1939.

80. The word alpargatas at that time referred to flat cloth shoes with straw soles, mostly worn by the working class. Since then the word has come to refer to many kinds of slippers.

81. Wife of Neville Chamberlain, Anne Chamberlain's maiden name was Anne de Vere Cole.

82. Isabel Brown was deeply involved with the Spanish Medical Aid committee during the Spanish Civil War. Hannen Swaffer (1879-1962) was a prominent British journalist. Lady Violet Bonham Carter (1887-1969), journalist and drama critic, became one of Britain's 'great and good' in the post World War Two period. Sir Peter Chalmers Mitchell (1864-1945), was a zoologist and left winger. His experience of Spanish fascism is recounted in *My House in Málaga: Reminiscences of Spain and the Spanish Civil War* (London: Faber & Faber, 1938). William Francis Hare, Earl of Listowel (b. 1906) became the last Secretary of State for India in 1947.

83. Sir Richard Rees (1920-1970), writer and one of the editors of Bloomsbury's left-wing journal, *The Adelphi* (1922ff.), was a close friend of George Orwell. Orwell unflatteringly satirized him as Philip Ravelston in *Keep the Aspidistra Flying*. The National Joint Committee mentioned here is the National Joint Committee for Spanish Relief.

84. *catedracticos* is the Spanish for University lecturers.

85. In 1941, in Operation Barbarossa, 3 million German soldiers and 3300 tanks crossed the Russian border in a blitzkrieg attack.

86. Nazim Hikmet (1902-1963), Turkish poet, playwright and novelist, traveled to Russia in 1922, attracted by the Russian Revolution's promise of social justice. After his return to Turkey, Hikmet was imprisoned in 1938 for anti-Nazi and anti-Franco activities. Released in 1950, he lived and travelled in Eastern Europe.

87. Harry Pollitt (1890-1960) was General Secretary of the Communist Party of Great Britain (CPGB) from 1926 until 1956, then Chairman from 1956 until 1960. His *How to Win the War* was published by the CPGB in 1939.

88. St George's Hospital, Cranmer Terrace, London SW17.

89. The phrase 'testifying in season and out of season' refers to Timothy 5.2; 'preach the word; be instant in season and out of season'.

90. 'Lord Haw-Haw' was the pseudonym of William Joyce (1906-1946), born in New York and raised in Ireland, who moved to England in 1921 and joined the British Fascist organization in 1925 and the British Union of Fascists in 1932. He became famous for his pro-German propaganda broadcasts from Germany during World War Two. He was executed for treason in 1946.

91. Also known in Britain as the Flying Bomb or Doodlebug, the V 1 (short for Vergeltungswaffe 1 FZG-76, or 'Reprisal Weapon') and often called the 'Buzz bomb' because of the sound of its early jet engine, was aimed at London. When it reached its target, as calculated by its automated navigational system, it went into a final dive, the angle of descent then cutting off its engine. This last characteristic allowed the V 1 to generate much anxiety, as the population below listened out for the moment when the engine cut out, fearing that its final dive would bring it down on their heads and only able to relax when the noise had passed over. It was later complemented by the more sophisticated V 2, which caused less panic, since it traveled so fast that no-one heard it coming.

92. In February 1937, at Jarama, the British Battalion of the International Brigades lost half its numbers whilst capturing and then desperately defending 'Suicide Hill'. The Lincoln Brigade, the American unit in the XV International Battalion, saw its first action at Jarama.

93. Tom Driberg (1905-1976), journalist, and Labour MP from 1942-74.

94. Karl Radek (1885-1939) helped write the 1936 Soviet Constitution. During the Great Purges of the 1930s he was accused of treason and confessed, first under duress and then at the 'Trial of the Seventeen' (the Second Moscow Trial, 1937). He died in prison.

95. D. N. Pritt, socialist and communist, was expelled from the CPGB for unknown reasons in 1941.

96. Most likely this is a reference to Hans Beimler (1895-1936), a member of the German Communist Party, a renowned German anti-fascist, was arrested by Hitler and sent to a concentration Camp, from which he escaped. He joined the International Brigades and died during the Spanish Civil War. Otherwise this may be an American, Hans Amlie, who fought in the Lincoln-Washington Battalion.

97. The Potsdam Conference occurred in July-April, 1945 and discussed the arrangements for Allied control of a defeated Germany and such issues as reparations, the Oder-Neisse line and how Russia might join in the war in the Far East. The initial British representative was Winston Churchill (1874-1965), replaced by Clement Attlee (1863-1967) after Labour's triumph in the General Election of 1945. Harry S. Truman (1884-1972) was U.S. President from 1945-1953.

98. The Ministère des Transports.

99. The BBC's 'In Town Tonight' ran for twenty-seven years on BBC radio, from 1933 onwards. In 1954 a television version commenced, but this folded after only two years.

100. John Reed (1887-1920), journalist, socialist and revolutionary

writer, visited Russia in 1917 to witness the Russian Revolution's progress and write reports for the radical periodical, *The Masses* (1914-1917). Whilst there he witnessed the crucial days of the October 1917 Revolution and wrote a book about these, *Ten Days that Shook the World* (New York: Boni and Liveright, 1919).

101. *The God that Failed: Six Studies in Communism* (London: Hamish Hamilton, 1950) included essays by Arthur Koestler, Ignazio Silone, André Gide (presented by Enid Starkie), Richard Wright, Louis Fischer and Stephen Spender with an Introduction by Richard Crossman.

102. Joseph Stalin (1879-1953), exiled for life to Siberia for his opposition to the Czar, returned in 19127 after the Czar's overthrow. He supported Lenin, and after his death in 1924 succeeded him, remaining in power until his own death. 'Old Joe' was an affectionate nickname given to Stalin in Britain during the time Britain and Russia were allied in their fight against German fascism.

103. The phrase 'Iron Curtain' was coined by Winston Churchill in his so-called 'Iron Curtain' speech, delivered on 5 March 1946 in Westminster College, Fulton, Missouri. In this speech Churchill described how 'From Stettin on the Baltic to Trieste on the Adriatic an iron curtain has descended across the continent. Behind that line lie all the capitals of the ancient states of Central and Eastern Europe ... in what I must call the Soviet sphere'.

104. Josip Tito (1892-1980) was Secretary General and later President of the Communist Party of Yugoslavia (1939-1980), supreme commander of the partisans fighting the Germans (1941-1945) and Premier (1945-1953) and then President (1953-1980) of Yugoslavi. Drazha Mikhailovich (1893-1946), a World War One hero, launched 'chetnik' resistance raids against the Germans during World War Two, but his dislike of Communism, and hence of Tito's partisans, finally led him to fight his own fellow Yugoslav resistors to Axis occupation. Though uneasy

collaboration was intermittently negotiated and restored, the underlying drift was towards breakdown, accompanied by betrayals, even leading Mikhailovich into obtaining aid and arms from the occupying Italians and Germans in order to oppose Tito. Mikhailovich was executed for treason in 1946.

105. The 'Browder Line', a line of argument advanced in the mid-1940s within the Communist Party of the USA and named after Earl Browder (1891-1973), General Secretary of the Party from 1930 and its leader from 1932, at first advocated organizational steps to establish Stalinism and displace Marxist-Leninism in the US Communist Party and then its 'Americanization'. Browder eventually argued, in 1944, that Communism and Capitalism could co-exist. The American Communist Party was founded in 1919, and established the *Daily Worker* in 1924. In the 1932 Presidential election its candidate polled 102,991 votes – the high point of its support. After World War Two, decline was rapid, with the Alien Registration Act being used in order to arrest leading Communists, and its deterrent effects being intensified by the work of the House Un-American Activities Committee and the activities of Joseph McCarthy (1908-1957), the infamous anti-Communist. The victory of the Left in the post-war world refers primarily to the return of a Labour Government in Britain in the 1945 general election.

106. 'American exceptionalism' argued that because of the USA's relative 'newness' as a Western nation, its immediate adoption of democratic government and it constitutional guarantee of liberty, the USA stood distinct from other Western nations – indeed, was *exceptional* in both senses of the word because of these legacies. This argument was to fall into increasing disfavor around the turn of the second millennium. The Marshall Plan was the USA's attempt after Word War Two to aid the recovery of Western Europe and reduce its suffering and poverty (and so shore it up from any influx of Communism). Devised by George C. Marshall (1880-1959) at Harvard

University on 5 June 1947, the plan lasted four years. Disillusion with the 1945-51 Labour government developed in the CPGB because of Labour's compromises (e.g., with doctors during the foundation of the National Health Service, with the setting of National Insurance contributions at very low levels, with decentralization of the economy, flotation of the UK pound and reductions in welfare in order to secure U.S. loans, and with the introduction of rationing). Czechoslovakia, following its takeover by the Communists in 1948, saw Stalinist-style purges and arrests of dissident elements in the late 1940s and early 1950s, especially affecting the Catholic Church. *The British Road to Socialism*, published by the CPGB in February 1951, outlined the Communist Party's political and economic programme for Britain. The Cominform (Communist Information Bureau) was a Soviet-dominated organization of Communist states, founded in 1947. Yugoslavia was expelled from the Cominform in June 1948 because of the defiance of Tito in the face of Soviet supremacy. The relatively liberalizing broadening of the Left in 1951 was precipitated by the cancellation of Yugoslavia's failing farm collectivization policy, a Soviet blockade begun in 1949 (Tito soon feared Soviet invasion), and the USA's consequent shipping of weapons to Yugoslavia, creating substantial Soviet anxiety. In 1956, as a gesture of reconciliation to Tito, the Cominform was dissolved. The brides scandal revolved around the maltreatment of British women entering Communist Eastern Europe, especially Czechoslovakia, as the wives of men returning to their homes after World War Two, and the refusal of Soviet Russia to allow any Russian wives of British soldiers and civilians returning to Britain after the war to leave with their husbands. The Soviet Doctors' Plot of 1953 involved action by Stalin against a group of doctors (mostly Jewish) accused of plotting against the State. Stalin died before the trial was completed and the doctors were exonerated.

107. Ian Mikardo (1908-1993) was a left-wing Labor Member of

Parliament.

108. Frances Noel Baker (an MP from 1950-1969) wrote a number of articles about Spain during 1946, including 'On the Spanish Republican Government in exile', 20 February, 8c and a series of columns 'On Spain', 8 June, 7b, 13 June, 2b and 15 October, 8f. The reference is probably to the column that appeared on 8 June 1946.

109. Monica Whately, a social activist, became prominently active in the Save the Children Fund, founded in 1919 as response to conditions in Europe after World War One, when allied policies led to many German and Austrian children starving. Save the Children soon gained a reputation as an effective relief agency, both in Europe and within Britain. It rose to increased prominence following World War Two and the relief work needed at that time. Subsequently, its relief work became increasingly global in range

110. Slim Somerville (1892-1973) was a movie actor whose career started as a Keystone Cop and evolved into comedy character acting.

111. Pablo Picasso (1881-1973), the world famous artist, prominent in many modernist art developments, most specifically, Cubism. Alexander Fedayev (1901-1956), Russian novelist and leading exponent and theoretician of proletarian literature, was also a prominent Communist functionary.

112. The Festival of Britain ran from May to September, 1951, and was intended to celebrate British achievement over the ages, so providing some respite from post-World War Two hardships and austerity.

113. Picasso designed a dove for the World Peace Movement's first international congress in 1949. It has become an iconic symbol of peace.

114. Maurice is likely to be Maurice Carpenter, left-wing poet and author of *Blade Ballad and Love Poems*, Downham Market: Quaker Press (Contemporary Norfolk Poets Series), 1971.

115. Ivor Montagu (1904-1984), left-winger and Communist, was at the centre of UK film activity, founding the London Film Society in 1924. Irene Joliot Curie (1897-1956), who won the 1935 Nobel Prize in Chemistry in recognition of her and her husband's work on the synthesis of new radio-active elements, was a member of the world Peace Committee. Her husband, Frédéric Joliot Curie became a Communist in 1946 and was president of the World Organisation of the Partisans of Peace. It is unclear which of the two is referred to here. It is probably Frédéric.

116. Vere Gordon Childe (1892-1956), a left-wing archeological historian.

117. Holloway Prison, begun in 1849, became London's main prison. From 1903 it became a female-only prison.

118. The British Peace Committee was founded in 1949. V. D-J is possibly V. (Vincent?) Duncan-Jones, a 'sleeper' member of the Communist Party of Great Britain

119. Allen Hutt is probably G. Allen Hutt (1901-1973), editor for several years of the National Union of Journalist's *The Journalist*. He also edited and completed William Rust's *The Story of the Daily Worker* (People's Press Printing Society) and was the creator of Allen Hutt's Working Library of the British Labour Movement, Anglo-Soviet Relations and the Theory of Marxism-Leninism. James Klugan is probably James Kluggman, a stalwart of the CPGB at this time. Howard Hill is the author of *Freedom to Roam* (Ashbourne: Moorland Publishing, 1980).

120. The city of Georgiu-Dezh is the administrative centre of Liski rayon (sector) of the Vorenezh region, Moscow.

121. 'Pretty Polly Perkins of Paddington Green' was written by Harry Clifton (1832-1872). The repeated line, 'You Take to the Boats, Lads' comes from 'A Gallant Ship Was Sinking', a

traditional ballad. 'Lillibulero' is a popular Irish broadside song, probably originating from the seventeenth century, espousing Irish Nationalist sentiments, yet one also frequently expropriated by regiments as a marching tune and by parodists.

122. Krasnoyarsk is the capital of the Krasnoyarsk region in central Russia. Nobosibirsk is another central Russian region. Mikhail Ivanovich Glinka (1804-1857), often regarded as the father of Russian music, wrote *Ivan Susanin* in 1836. Irkutsk is a city in Eastern Siberia.

123. 'Father, forgive them for they know not what they do' are Jesus Christ's dying words on the Cross. See Luke 23:34.

124. Mao Tse-Tung (Zedong) (1893-1976) helped establish the Chinese Soviet Republic in China and was elected Chairman in 1931. In 1934 he led the 'Long March' away from the advancing Japanese, saving the Chinese army. After the Japanese defeat in World War Two, the Communists defeated their rivals, the Kuomintang, and established the People's Republic of China. Mao became Chairman and enacted the Great Leap Forward of 1958-1960 and the Cultural Revolution (1966).

125. 'He Ping Wan Sui' translates, roughly, as 'Long Live Peace'.

126. Chang Kai-shek (1887-1975), after a prominent military career, became leader of the Kuomintang in 1927, when he finally abandoned attempts at rapprochement with the Communists and initiated a long civil war. After World War Two Chang Kai-shek's Kuomintang lost to the Communists and retreated to Taiwan (then Formosa) in 1950.

127. The 'Old Eighth Route' is the nickname of one of China's main military forces, named after is nominal designation in the Chinese Army. It was famed for its ability to infiltrate the Japanese forces during World War Two.

128. Che Teh (1886-1976) was one of Mao's fellow revolutionaries, and was often known as the father of the Red Army.

129. 'Workers of the world unite', one of the most famous rallying cries of Socialism, is a phrase occurring in Marx and Engel's

Communist Manifesto of 1848.

130. Chou En-Lai (1899-1976) was a prominent Chinese Communist, rising to become Prime Minister in 1949 when the Communists were victorious over the Nationalists. 'Xi Lai' translates (roughly) as 'Stand Up!' (as in 'Stand Up for the Revolution!'). The Internationale was written in 1888 by Adolphe Degeyter, using words written in 1871 by Eugène Pottier. The transnational anthem of the left, it became the Soviet national anthem, 1918-44.

131. James V. Forrestal (1892-1949) became the USA's first Secretary of Defense in 1947, but after his behavior became increasingly erratic he resigned in 1949, defenestrating himself that same year.

132. VT is probably Vlolodia Teitelboim (b.1916), Secretary General of the Chilean Communist Party from 1945 until 1994, elected to the Chilean Senate in 1965, re-elected in 1973, and exiled by Pinochet. Teitelboim won the Chilean National Prize for Literature in 2002.

133. The Prague Trials of the early 1950s centered upon anti-semitic prosecutions, and were a symptom of Stalin's growing anti-Semitism.

134. The Three Antis were introduced by China during the Korean War to combat corruption, waste and bureaucracy. They were succeeded by the Five Antis in 1953, a campaign aimed against bribery, non-payment of taxes, fraud, stealing government property and spying.

135. The new Marriage Law of 1850 gave women full equality with men in matters of marriage, divorce and property ownership.

136. Gung Ho was the slogan and nickname of the International Committee for the Promotion of Chinese Industrial cooperatives, 1937 ff. The project was founded by Rewi Alley. Gung Ho translates roughly as 'work harmony'.

137. Anton Semyonovich Makerenko (1888-1939), Russian

educationalist and author, strove to integrate democratic principles into education theory and practice. His two-volume book on education, *The Road to Life* subtitled 'an epic of education', evolved out of his work with Ukrainian delinquents in his 'Gorky Colony' during the 1920s. Rewi Alley (1897-1987), born in New Zealand, arrived in China in 1927 and by the mid-1930s was supporting the Chinese Communists. In 1937, working against the Japanese, he founded the Gung Ho co-operative movement, before switching his focus onto education, especially technician training. He traveled widely in China as a writer and poet in his later years. He achieved recognition in New Zealand only after New Zealand recognized China in 1972.

138. Joseph Needham (1900-1995) published numerous volumes in the *Science and Civilization in China* series (Cambridge: Cambridge University Press, 1954ff.).

139. Michail Gelovani, the actor, played Stalin in the propaganda film, *Padeniye Berlin* (*The Fall of Berlin*, 1950).

140. A reference to Kruschev's denunciation of Stalin in 1956 in a speech to the Twentieth Party Congress, 'On the Cult of the Personality'.

141. Abu Ali al Husain Ibn Abdallah ibn Sina (Avicenna) (980-1037), Arabian physician and philosopher; Yen Jo-chü (1636-1704), Chinese scholar from the early period of the Ch'ing dynasty who made decisive contributions to the formation of evidential procedures in scientific study, applying Chinese and Western astronomical techniques to his reading of the classic Confucian text, *Shu Ching*, so proving that a key segment of this text was a forgery; François Rabelais (1483-1553), French humorist and writer, famous for his (Rabeleisan) imagination, typified by coarse humour, physical excess and satirical mockery of religion, and for his books *Pantagreul* (1532) and *Gargantua* (1534); Jose Martí (1853-1895), a Cuban national hero famous for his struggle to secure independence, including

leading a rebellion against the Spanish and his consequent martyr's death, and for his writings, including *Our America* (1891), an essay opposed to U.S. dominance of the Americas.

142. Vercors was the pseudonym of French Resistance activist, author and illustrator, Jean Marc Bruller (1902-1991), who helped found Editions de Minuit as an underground publisher. His most famous work is *Le silence de la mer* (Londres: Le Cahier du Silence, 1943), a novel of resistance to German occupation.

143. Bruller's *Divagations de un Francais en Chine* was published by A. Michel, in Paris, in 1956.

144. *China Reconstructs* (1952-1989) eventually became *China Today* (1989ff.). It was intended as a propaganda vehicle for promoting the Chinese Revolution and Chinese Communism.

145. Anwei is a province in south-west China.

146. Mamillius, King Leontes' and Queen Hermione's son in William Shakespeare's *A Winter's Tale* (c. 1611), dies of shock at the loss of his mother. This reference appears to be to the way he tells a story to his mother in Act II Scene i.

147. Mildred Cable and Evangeline and Francesca French were prominent members of the China Inland Mission in the late Nineteenth and early Twentieth Centuries.

148. Samuel Johnson speaks of 'wells of English undefiled' in his Preface to his *Dictionary* (1755).

149. *Mao's Works* is here probably a reference to the *Selected Works of Chairman Mao* (published in English by Lawrence and Wishart, 1954ff.), since the *Collected Works of Chairman Mao* were not published until after Nan Green's death. Chairman of the People's Republic of China, Liu Shao Chi's *How to be a Good Communist* was published in 1951 (Peking: Foreign Language Press).

150. During the 1950s and early 1960s the Anti-Rightist campaigns, initiated by Chariman Mao Tse Tung, aimed to purge rightists from within the Communist Party of China. For a brief period

during 1956-57 the Hundred Flowers Campaign encouraged Chinese Communist Party members to become more heterodox in their thinking. It as soon followed by a crackdown on such heterodoxy.

151. Part of the Great Leap forward, the backyard steel campaign aimed to increase iron and steel production by encouraging people to set up small 'backyard' furnaces. It soon petered out, because the quality of the metal produced was simply too poor to be of use. Also during the 1950s, campaigns were introduced to reduce the numbers of rats and mice and sparrows, regarding them all as vermin. The campaign against sparrows, centered on Peking, became particularly infamous, since the method selected for killing them was to encourage people throughout the city simultaneously to bang on pots, pans and other implements to keep the birds flying, until they flopped, exhausted to the ground, where they could be killed. Although many sparrows were killed in this way, the campaign was soon stopped, because it was discovered that sparrows, as well as consuming grain and other foodstuffs, also usefully controlled insect numbers.

152. See Psalm 100: 'Make a joyful noise unto the Lord, all ye lands'.

153. 'A Dissertation on Roast Pig', by Charles Lamb (1775-1834), was an essay humorously arguing that human beings perform things circuitously at first, learning by chance, and then gradually refine what they do so that more direct methods can be adopted. See Lamb's *Elia: Essays which have appeared under that signature in the London Magazine* (London, 1825).

154. 'Step-by-step' was a common epigram used during the Chinese Cultural Revolution.

155. Antaeus, the son of Gaia and Poseidon in Greek mythology, was a frightful giant who compelled people to wrestle with him. As long as he remained in contact with the earth (and hence able to draw upon the strength of his mother, Gaia), he

was invincible. Hercules, learning of this, defeated him by lifting him completely off he ground.

156. This is possibly a reference to a phrase used in V. I. Lenin's *The Achievements and Difficulties of the Soviet Government*, March-April 1919.

157. See Mao Tse Tung, *Some Questions Concerning Methods of Leadership* (1 June 1943), which argues that all correct leadership is necessarily 'from the masses to the masses' (*Selected Writings*, Peking: Foreign Language Press, 1961, III: 117)

158. Kruschev's anti-Stalin speech at the 1956 Twentieth Congress of the Communist Party of the Soviet Union alienated Kruschev from Conservative elements in the USSR.

159. Laventy Pavlovich Beria (1899-1953), a counter-insurgency expert in Stalin's Soviet government, helped enforce Stalin's rule. He was executed on 23 December 1953 by Kruschev's regime.

160. Edmund Gosse (1849-1928), in *Father and Son: A Study of Two Temperaments* (London: William Heinemann, 1907), offered a sensitive portrayal of his Puritanical upbringing.

161. Sir Eric Teichman (1884-1941) was a British military leader who became a key member of the British Embassy in Peking, 1907-1937, and travelled extensively around China. His *Journey to Turkistan* (London: Hodder and Stoughton) was published in 1937. The opening pages of Nan Green's long letter home which follows is written as a parody of the upper class register that Nan Geen imagines the persona, 'Mrs Thompson Glover' would use; there is an underlying satire of such travellers and travelogues running throughout its paragraphs.

162. The coinage 'brightest jewel in Britain's Imperial Crown', or similar phrases referring to India, have been attributed to both Disraeli and Queen Victoria. Plausibly, Queen Victoria coined the term, in conversation with Disraeli in 1847 and then in a letter to Lord Canning, Governor General of India 1855-62 (a

period spanning the 1857 Indian Mutiny). Her letter of 2 August 1858 spoke of India as 'so bright a jewel of my Crown'.

163. Novosibirsk and Irkutsk are two important Siberian cities.

164. 'White Russians' is a term used to describe the military and political elements opposed to the rapid rise of the Bolsheviks after the October Revolution and during the subsequent Civil War. Lacking central co-ordination, the White Russians mustered resistance until 1921. 'White' has monarchist connotations in Russia, and the term also helped distinguish this loose coalition from the Red Army and (less significantly) from the Nationalist Green Army.

165. This is most probably a reference to Heavenly Lake (Tianchi Lake), near Urumqui in Sinkiang's Tianshan Mountains (now a major tourist attraction).

166. Kumiss is a Mongol beverage made from fermented mare's milk.

167. This is a reference to either *World News Illustrated* (commencing publication in 1937) or *World News*, 1954ff., a continuation of *World News and Views*, which began life in 1938.

168. The Great Leap Forward, spanning the years 1958-1960, aimed to effect China's rapid economic and technological development. It established People's Communes to help bring about these changes. Generally it was not a great success (the 'backyard steel' campaign providing one example of it shortcomings) and its failure weakened its main architect, Mao Tse-Tung's position.

169. Cecil Williams, born in Cornwall, moved to South Africa in 1928. A wealthy theatre director and impresario, he also became a prominent South African communist and anti-apartheid campaigner, most famous for his arrest alongside Nelson Mandela, when the latter as finally apprehended in August 1962. For some time, Williams had been assisting Mandela to travel illegally around the country, by disguising Mandela as his

chauffeur. Williams died in 1978.

170. Mao Tse-Tung used the phrase 'All Reactionaries are Paper Tigers' in August 1946 in a talk with Anna Louise Strong. See his *Selected Writings* (Peking: Foreign Language Press, 1961), IV: 100: 'All reactionaries are paper tigers. In appearance the paper tigers are terrifying, but in reality they are not so powerful'. The phrase was much used subsequently.

171. SACTU is the acronym for the South African Congress of Trade Unions, founded on 5 March 1955.

172. Phyllis Altman and Bram Fisher were both prominent anti-apartheid activists. Fisher (1908-1974), a South African Communist Party (SACP) member and Queen's Council, led Nelson Mandela's defence at his trial in 1964. Fisher was arrested in 1966 for violating the South African Suppression of Communism Act.

173. The Treason Trials stretched from 1956-1961, and stemmed from the rounding-up of members of the Congress Alliance – an alliance chiefly consisting of the African National Congress (founded in 1912 as the South African Native National Congress), the South African Indian Conference (founded in 1924) and SACTU. The Trials were a desperate gambit by the South African government to silence its opponents (principally by alleging that all those it arrested were Communists).

174. Chief Albert Luthuli was African National Congress (ANC) President from 1952-67.

175. Lillian Masediba Ngoyi (1898-1967), affectionately known as 'Ma Ngoyi', joined the ANC in 1950 and became President of its Women's League in 1951.

176. 'Mayibuye, Afrika' roughly translates as 'Long Live Africa'

177. Molly Fisher, anti-apartheid activist, married Bram Fisher in 1937. She died in 1963. Joe Slovo (1926-1995), born in Lithuania, became a prominent South African Communist Party member and one of the leaders of Umkhonto we Sizwe (the Military Wing of the ANC). In 1963 he went into exile on instructions

from the SACP and ANC. He spent his exile years in the UK, Angola, Mozambique and Zambia. Slovo was based in Mozambique until 1984, when he was elected general secretary of the SACP. He returned to South Africa in 1990 to participate in the early 'talks about talks' between the government and the ANC. At the SACP congress in South Africa in December 1991 Slovo was elected SACP chairperson. Slovo was a leading theoretician in both the SACP and the ANC. Ruth First (1925-68), anti-apartheid activist, was a Jewish immigrant to South Africa who married Joe Slovo in 1949. She was killed by a parcel bomb in 1982. Fatima Meer (b. 1928), author, was a passive resistor to apartheid from her youth and became a founder member of the anti-apartheid Federation of South African Women. Lionel (Rusty) Bernstein played a crucial role in the drafting of the 1954 Freedom Charter – the ANC's central policy statement. Bernstein joined the Communist Party in 1938 and married Hilda Watts (b. 1915), another courageous anti-apartheid campaigner, and, like Meer a founding member of the anti-apartheid Federation of South African Women. Helen Joseph (1905-1992), author, for forty years dedicated herself to opposing apartheid. Her commitment earned her the ANC's highest award, the Isitwalandwe/Seaparankoe Medal. She became yet another founder member of the anti-apartheid Federation of South African Women. This group played a key role in women's demonstration against the Pass Laws, such as the march to the Union Buildings, Pretoria, on 9 August 1956. The Pass Laws, the common term used to describe the paradoxically-named 'Natives (Abolition of Passes and Co-ordination of Documents) Act' of 1952, compelled blacks to carry identification with them at all times. This 'pass' included a photograph, details of place of origin, employment records and details of any encounters with the police. It was a criminal offence to be unable to produce a pass. No black person could leave a rural area for an urban one without a permit, and a permit to seek work had to be obtained within 72 hours of arriving in an urban area. Winnie Madikizela-Mandela (b. 1936) became involved in the ANC as a youth and met Nelson Mandela in 1957, marrying him in 1958. She was constantly imprisoned and banned for her anti-apartheid activities. She adopted a less conciliatory line than many in the ANC towards the Apartheid regime's architects after Apartheid collapsed and became embroiled in a series of controversies. However she retained her popularity for long time, being elected ANC Women's League president in 1993 and 1997.

178. Julius Lewin, anti-apartheid activist, author and lecturer on South African native law.

179. J.D. Bernal (1901-1971), prominent international scientist and Communist, wrote *World Without War* in 1958 (London: Routledge and Kegan Paul).

180. A.W. is probably Alick West, a Communist Party member who wrote for *The Daily Worker.* See his autobiography, *One Man in His Time: An Autobiography,* London: George, Allen and Unwin.

181. *Long Live Leninism* is the title of a pamphlet addressing the issue of 'how to conceive of the proletarian socialist revolution' (Peking: Foreign Language Press, 1960, p. 36).

182. Margaret Page was at that time Secretary to Rueben Falber and Peter Kerrigan in the office of the Communist Party in King Street, London.

183. Nan Green returned to the United Kingdom in 1960 to live in London, where she died in 1984. Martin Green's introduction to these memoirs briefly describes these years of her life.